PHILOSOPHY OF RELIGION
FOR TODAY

Simon and Christopher Danes

with Seeta Lakhani

Text copyright © 2009 Simon and Christopher Danes and Seeta Lakhani
This edition copyright © 2009 Simon and Christopher Danes and Seeta Lakhani

The authors assert the moral right to be identified as the authors of this work.

Published by **St Mark's Press**, Pavenham, Bedfordshire MK43 7PP
ISBN 978-1-907062-05-6

Typeset in Garamond
Printed by Stonebridges, Bedford

Illustrations and graphics

Cover by Tony Cantale graphics

Cartoons by Ruth Danes

Line drawings by Marion Danes

Photographs sourced from Shutterstock; other photographs by the authors.

Biblical and other quotations

Acknowledgements

The authors wish to express their thanks to all those who have assisted in any way with this book, especially Sarah Gaskin, Liora Wulf and all at Christian Aid; Jay Lakhani; Emma Danes; and those who have given permission for the publication of photographs, especially Fr Martin Harper, the rector of Brede with Udimore; Shelley Jebb of St Mary's Church, Rye; St Paul's Church, Bedford; The Reverend Alan Hulme, vicar of St Mary's Church, Ely; Michael J de Smith and Fr Howard Cocks, rector of Winchelsea; the Reverend Neville Gallagher, Church of St Peter and St Paul, Appledore.

Photocopying this book

www.stmarkspress.com

Philosophy of Religion for Today

FOR DAVID, JOHN and HANNAH (SD)

FOR LUCY and WILLIAM (CD)

FOR MY FATHER, JAY LAKHANI (SL)

Contents

Part One

Does God exist?

1
What is God?

If we produced a set of adjectives about God, what would we come up with?

Here are a few:

good

loving

immortal

all knowing

forgiving

all powerful

caring

compassionate

KIND

generous

personal

(a person, or like a person)

infinite

Many people, of course, would say that there is no God anyway, so this is all a waste of time. Others would say it is impossible to tell whether God exists or whether he doesn't.

However, part of what we're doing in this chapter is to look at **definitions.** Whether God exists, or whether he doesn't, we have to know what the word means: to define our terms, to know what we're talking about.

Suppose we said, 'God is a superhuman being who looks like a man, lives on Mount Olympus, and throws thunderbolts at people.' It's pretty obvious that something like that doesn't exist.

Also, the definition's faulty: it would be very hard to find someone nowadays who'd define 'God' like this. Certainly, none of the major religions would. So it's important to get our terms right.

What we're really saying, then, is something like:

> *If God exists, then God would be...*

and then we complete the sentence with lots of words like the ones given above.

Looking deeper

Let's start with a word used for God in many religions:

Father

What does it mean?

Does it mean:

1. God is biologically our father, producing the genetic material that fertilised our mothers' ova?

2. God is our Dad, who gets the 7.15 train to the office, wears a suit, reads the *Daily Express* and falls asleep in front of *Match of the Day*?

3. God is male? (Fathers are!)

4. God is *like* a human father, in certain ways?

1 and 2 are clearly not what 'God is Father' means. God isn't our Dad in the human sense (and if God exists, he isn't human anyway). 3 is interesting and worth coming back to; we'll do so later on.

The answer is 4: 'God is like a human father, in certain ways.'

But in what ways?

Calling God 'Father' would make some people shudder. If their dad was violent, abusive or frightening, they'd most likely carry around this 'baggage' with them: 'Father' is bound up with ideas of someone who hurts you or someone you're frightened of. ('If God's like *my* Dad, you can keep him!')

On the other hand, if your own father has been a good dad to you, calling God 'Father' is probably going to mean more to you.

So, how we interpret words used about God is going to be coloured by our *personal* experience.

And it's going to be coloured by our *cultural* experience too.

This is because a human father's role in different cultures and at different times in history is not always the same. In some cultures – in Victorian England, say – fatherhood was very much bound up with the idea of discipline, and that discipline was very harsh. So, if dads in our culture are the parents who deal out the discipline, we're more likely to interpret 'Father' as meaning God is a rather remote and harsh figure, who's not very pleased with us, and who's prepared to punish us to keep us in line.

Bad Dad 2

Bad Dad 1

The largest religion in the world is Christianity.

As a result, whether we're Christian or not, it's important to understand what Christianity teaches – after all, 1.6 billion or so people believe it! Moreover, religious people can sometimes be surprised by what their faith *actually* teaches, rather than what they *think* it teaches. There are plenty of Christians who have a 'Victorian Dad' view of God, which isn't at all what Christianity says God is like.

Christianity tries to follow the teaching of Jesus, so what kind of a Father did Jesus say God is?

The answer's found in one of his parables: it's usually called the parable of the prodigal son. Charles Dickens called this the best short story ever written. As you read it, think especially about the character of the father in the story. What sort of a person is he?

15.11 Jesus went on to say, 'There was once a man who had two sons. 12 The younger one said to him, "Father, give me my share of the property now." So the man divided his property between his two sons. 13 After a few days the younger son sold his part of the property and left home with the money. He went to a country far away, where he wasted his money in reckless living. 14 He spent everything he had. Then a severe famine spread over that country, and he was left without a thing. 15 So he went to work for one of the citizens of that country, who sent him out to his farm to take care of the pigs. 16 He wished he could fill himself with the bean pods the pigs ate, but no one gave him anything to eat. 17 At last he came to his senses and said, "All my father's hired workers have more than they can eat, and here I am about to starve! 18 I will get up and go to my father and say, Father, I have sinned against God and against you. 19 I am no longer fit to be called your son; treat me as one of your hired workers." 20 So he got up and started back to his father.

'He was still a long way from home when his father saw him; his heart was filled with pity, and he ran, threw his arms round his son, and kissed him. 21 "Father," the son said, "I have sinned against God and against you. I am no longer fit to be called your son." 22 But the father called his servants. "Hurry!" he said. "Bring the best robe and put it on him. Put a ring on his finger and shoes on his feet. 23 Then go and get the prize calf and kill it, and let us celebrate with a feast! 24 For this son of mine was dead, but now he is alive; he was lost, but now he has been found." And so the feasting began.

25 'In the meantime the elder son was out in the field. On his way back, when he came close to the house, he heard the music and dancing. 26 So he called one of the servants and asked him, "What's going on?" 27 "Your brother has come back home," the servant answered, "and your father has killed the prize calf, because he got him back safe and sound."

28 'The elder brother was so angry that he would not go into the house; so his father came out and begged him to come in.

29 But he answered his father, "Look, all these years I have worked for you like a slave, and I have never disobeyed your orders. What have you given me? Not even a goat for me to have a feast with my friends! 30 But this son of yours wasted all your property on prostitutes, and when he comes back home, you kill the prize calf for him!" 31 "My son," the father answered, "you are always here with me, and everything I have is yours. 32 But we had to celebrate and be happy, because your brother was dead, but now he is alive; he was lost, but now he has been found."'

Luke 15.11-32

As you've probably guessed, the character of the Father in the story represents God. Jesus is saying that's the sort of Father God is.

We can say, then:

> Most words used of God
> mean God is like this in *some* respects
> but is not like this in *all* respects.

(Assuming God exists!)

For example:

> In Christianity,
> God's personality *is* like the father's personality in the parable of the prodigal son
> but he's *not* like a Father in that he's not like a bad father, or a drunken father, or an abusive father.

1. Look again at the words used to describe God (in the oval on page 8).

Which 10 words do you consider to be the most important? Why?

Can you select what you consider to be the most important 5? Why did you select these?

2. In Jesus' parable of the prodigal son, the father's personality is the same as God's personality.

a) What sort of a father is Jesus saying God's like?
b) Some people might say the father in the story is actually over-generous.

Why might they say this?
Do you agree with them?
Does this add to the understanding of Jesus' view of God?

c) If God's like this, how might he expect human beings to behave?

2
God and words

In the last unit, we looked at what it means to say God is Father.

As we saw, Jesus taught his disciples to call God 'Father'. In fact, he went even further than that: he called God 'Dad' or 'Daddy' ('Abba' in his own language, Aramaic). The New Testament shows the early Christians did this too (Romans 8.15). If you can call someone 'Dad', it generally means you're on much closer or more loving terms with him than if you have to stick to the more formal 'Father'. (Are there other differences between 'Dad' / 'Daddy' and 'Father'? What do you think they are?)

The Lord's Prayer was taught by Jesus and it begins 'Our Father in heaven'. (Older translations have 'Our Father who art in heaven'.) In fact, a lot of New Testament scholars think it's likely that it originally began 'Abba' – 'Dad'. Some later Christians then changed it to 'Our Father in heaven' because they thought calling God 'Dad' wasn't respectful enough.

The parable of the prodigal son shows the sort of Dad God is like. (According to Christianity. This is all assuming God exists!)

There are other names or titles used for God. Some of the names used for God in the Bible include:

Father, Son and Holy Spirit
(we'll look at these terms in detail later on)

King
Lord
Master

In the Koran, the Muslim scriptures, the titles for God include:

The Eternal
The Absolute
The Most Gracious
The Most Merciful

The Lord and Cherisher of the Worlds
The Supremely Wise
The Sustainer
The Greatest

In the Sikh faith, God is called by the Sanskrit word

Sat
or
Satnam

which means

Truth.

When we looked at what it means to call God 'Father', we said that it meant God is like this in *some* ways (the positive ones, particularly), but not in *all* ways.

The same can be said of many other words used for God. For example, God is not 'Lord' in the sense of a member of the House of Lords: he doesn't come from an ancient family who were made lords by some long dead king; he doesn't drive a Bentley or have gin and tonic at 5.30 every afternoon. But the idea of 'Lord' does get across that God is in charge: he's not human beings' equal; he's greater than they are.

It's worth going through the words for God given on page 11 and thinking about these two questions:

- In what ways might God be thought to be like this?
- In what ways might God be said not to be like this?

You may notice that with some terms, like 'the Eternal', it's not quite so easy to come up with answers to the second question. 'Eternal' means God always has and always will exist. In a sense, it describes what God actually *is*, rather than what he's *like*.

We could say, for example, that God *is* eternal, but he's *like* a King or a Lord or Master.

So, some words used of God describe what he *is*. Other words used of God describe what he's *like*.

St Augustine

St Augustine was one of the great writers and teachers of the Christian Church. (His dates are 354-430 AD). There's a story told about him which goes like this.

St Augustine was walking along a beach, deep in thought about the latest book he was writing (which was about God, of course). He bumped into a small boy, who was playing by a rockpool. Every now and again, he would take a bucket, walk over to the sea, fill the bucket with seawater, walk back to the rockpool and pour the seawater into the pool.

This went on for quite some time. The saint, distracted from his thoughts, watched what the boy was doing.

After a while, St Augustine went over to the boy, tapped him on the shoulder, and said, 'What are you doing?'

'I'm trying to put the sea into this rockpool,' said the boy.

'But that's daft!' explained the saint. 'You can't put all the sea into a tiny little rock pool. It's huge. It just can't be done!'

'Well, you're trying to put God into a book,' said the boy.

Yes, it's probably just a story. But there's a point to it. It's said to have got St Augustine thinking hard. Was what he was doing – trying to pin God down into words in a book – pointless, like trying to pour the sea into a rock pool? Or was it actually worth trying?

If you think about the story, part of the idea behind it is that there *is* a sense in which a rock pool is like the sea. The main difference is that the sea is just much, much bigger (billions of times so, in fact). If you'd never seen the sea, you might ask what it's like. 'Well, it's like a pool, only bigger' the answer might be.

It's not a *wrong* answer. A pool does give you a (mental) picture of the sea. But it is a 'not enough' answer: an *inadequate* answer, but not a false answer.

Many theologians – people who think about and study God – would say much of religious language is rather like this. It's *inadequate*, but it's not *wrong*.

Take a statement like this. It's from the first letter of John, in the New Testament.

God is love.

(1 John 4.8)

What does that mean?

Well, we know what love is: the love of caring parents for their children, love between members of a family, or between friends. We know what it means to talk about a couple being in love. Most of us would agree that we all want love and we probably value it more highly than anything else. As we said, we know what love is.

And John says God is love.

When we talk about God – and this still assumes that there is one – we can only use words, because that's all we've got. And the best word John can find to describe God is 'love'.

Again, it's not a wrong word, but it is inadequate.

What John says means that God is not *less* than human love, he's much, much greater than it. 'Love' is the nearest word we've got for what God is. There's no single word for 'infinite love' and we wouldn't be able to imagine infinite love anyway: it's too big to grasp. But human love *is* like God's love. It's just that God's love is so much more: like the difference between a light bulb and the sun, or a rockpool and the sea.

The quantity of God's love is different. And the quality of God's love is different, too. There's much more of it, and it's much purer. Human beings are quite frail; human love can be changeable and, as we all know, it can be mixed up with things like jealousy, irritation and anger. People aren't easy to live with;

we don't always love people with the same intensity, and love can fade, too. God's love doesn't change in that way. It's always constant: always the same. The extraordinary claim made by Christianity about God is that God loves each one of us – and far, far more than our parents, our friends or our partners do.

So, a lot of the words we use about God are 'the nearest we can get'.

If God is said to be x (a human quality, or like a human in some way)

– God is like that, only much, much more.

This brings us on to another question. Let's use the example of God as Father, again. If we say God is our Father, or our Lord, it raises the question:

Who says God's like this, anyway?

There are two possible answers:
• Human beings try to work out what God is like, and they come up with the words **or**
• God tells us which words to use.

Let's consider the first idea: human beings who come up with the words. Suppose some thinkers in ancient times looked up at the sky, saw the stars, thought about how amazingly complex the universe

was, and wondered about questions like, 'Where does it all come from?' They might have come up with the answer that there must be a being who created everything.

But what would that being be like?

They might have thought: the being who created everything must be extraordinarily powerful; much more powerful than a human. He (or she, or it) must have had a reason for creating everything.

Did that mean the being – let's use the word 'God' for now – cared about what he / she / it had created? Did God love us? Or were we just like ants to God: tiny little creatures that aren't worth thinking about?

Some thinkers concluded that there must be a God, but God had no interest in us and therefore God was not worth bothering with, one way or the other. (This view is sometimes called deism.)

Other thinkers concluded that God was interested in us and cared about us. Maybe he even loved us. Maybe the way God cared about us was like the way good fathers care about their own children. So, a good word to use for this God might be: Father.

So, you end up with this situation:

I'm not saying!

We think he must be a bit like our Dads.

According to this idea, then, **it's human beings who try to work out what God is like, and then they come up with the words.**

On the other hand, many theologians – experts who study religion – would say:

God tells us which words to use

(at least some of the time).

So it's much more like this:

I am your Father!

Righto!

This is a bit silly, perhaps, but you get the idea. If this is right, God tells us that he's our Father – or is Father, Son and Holy Spirit, or anything else. So they're not things human beings have thought up, which might be right or might be wrong. They're correct; they're the way things are.

We can add that this idea also means:

- God may not tell us these things *individually*. He doesn't email or phone us and let us know what to call him. But he did reveal (show) people in the past that this is how he describes himself. In Christianity, the fact that Jesus calls God 'Father' (or 'Dad') shows that this is what God calls himself. Christianity teaches that Jesus was and is God, so what Jesus says is what God says.

- It's better to say that it's the *concept* and not the precise *word* that God reveals to people (tells people). Jesus didn't call God 'Father' because 'father' is an English word and there was no such language as English 2000 years ago! So, the word Jesus used, presumably in Aramaic, has been translated into English.

- Not *all* words used for God would have been revealed. If we said, 'God is nice', that might be true, but it's a human way of getting ideas across about God. The same might be said to be true of some words the biblical writers used for God. For example: 'The Lord is my Shepherd' (Psalm 23.1) or 'The Lord is my Rock (Psalm 18.2).

- If we say God 'reveals' or 'revealed' concepts about himself to people in the past, these concepts are put into language (words). This language can then be said to be **revealed language.**

The Old Testament image of God as a shepherd was taken up by Jesus, who called himself 'the good shepherd'.
Stained glass window from St Peter and St Paul's church, Appledore, Kent

Aren't these words about God a bit out of date?

Some theologians would say so. Take the idea that God is King.

Perhaps that idea made more sense in the ancient world, when lots of societies were ruled by kings.

Lots of them were tyrants: ruthless, greedy and cruel. It's not hard to see that God wasn't meant to be like *this* sort of king. The Old Testament history books, such as 1 and 2 Samuel and 1 and 2 Kings, contain lots of advice about what a *good* king should be like: he should be merciful, generous, compassionate, and remember that he's answerable to God for the way he runs the country. Many kings of Israel were deeply unpleasant, and the Old Testament says they got their come-uppance. (An example is in 1 Kings 16–22, which details how the villainous King Ahab met his doom when he took on the prophet Elijah.)

However, whether kings are good or bad, we're no longer ruled by them – at least, not in the Western world. We elect our leaders: we live in democracies. Bad rulers can be thrown out at an election; we don't have to hope God will bring about their downfall. So, it could be said that calling God 'King' used to be a meaningful idea, but it's much less so now.

Some people are much more concerned about the fact that so many terms used for God are male ones. God is Father, King, Lord – and the pronoun used for God in the Bible is 'he', not 'she', as though God's male. But shouldn't it be said that God is neither male nor female? If God is a spirit, then a spirit can't be either male or female. Isn't it the case, in fact, that traditional terms for talking about God are just sexist? Don't they come from ancient societies when men were in charge? If all rulers used to be men, it would have been natural for people to think God was male too. But this isn't so useful today.

It's sometimes suggested that we should replace the traditional words used about God with their female equivalents – at least some of the time. God or Goddess is Mother, Queen, Lady; and it's fine to use the pronoun 'she' instead of 'he'.

Or we could perhaps invent new words, which better describe God. S/he isn't 'Father' or 'Mother', but is 'FatherMother'.

What about saying 'God / Goddess is our ruler' instead of 'God is King'?

Certainly, religions like Hinduism have very little problem with thinking about God in female terms.

What do you think?

Behind some of this sort of thinking is that Christianity – and perhaps the other religions – has not always treated women as men's equals. It's then argued that thinking of God in male terms reinforces this bad treatment of women, because it suggests men are more like God than women are.

Some theologians would suggest some problems with the idea of replacing traditional language for God with 'politically correct' language:

- It's true that Christianity's record on treating women well has not always been great. However, it's actually a separate issue from the language used about God. You can believe in sexual equality *and* still use traditional language about God.

- It depends on whether you think all religious language is invented by human beings. If it is, you're much more free to change it. If a metaphor doesn't work, it's fine to use a different one that makes more sense to you. However, as we saw above, many theologians think some religious language is revealed. *If* God says he's like this or that, we can't say, 'Well, that's just

God's opinion!' He's going to be right. Jesus said God was our Father and Jesus used the pronoun 'he' for God. For Christians, Jesus was and is God. Most would say they're not at liberty to overturn what Jesus said and substitute something else.

- One well known Christian writer is C. S. Lewis. You may remember the Narnia books or have seen the films. Lewis also taught English at Oxford and Cambridge Universities and wrote a great deal about Christianity.

  Lewis said that God was not *male*, but God is *masculine*. In lots of languages, things are masculine or feminine but they're not male or female. Living things are male or female: that means they have male or female reproductive organs, so they're of the male sex or the female sex. God has no physical form: God is *incorporeal*. Therefore he cannot be of the male *sex*. Lewis said that male*ness* is a very pale reflection of *masculine*-ness or *masculinity*. God has the real thing: masculinity. Maleness is the pale reflection of masculinity, the nearest we can get

to it in our world. But, using our picture of St Augustine again, it's like the difference between the rockpool and the sea.

So, God is 'beyond' gender, 'beyond' sex. It's just that using male terms gets us a more accurate understanding of God than using female terms.

- We could say:

> *If God's neither male nor female, let's call God 'it'.*

But there's a problem with this, too. In English, human beings are very rarely called 'it' (although the word's sometimes, perhaps not very nicely, applied to babies). Human beings are 'he' or 'she': they're persons, not objects. God, too, is a person – and much more, rather than much less, a Person than we are. Calling God 'it' makes God less than a person. But God is actually much more than a person, not less!

- Mixing up male and female titles for God actually confuses the picture, rather than making it clearer.

  It's true that the Old Testament sometimes pictures God in female terms (e.g. Isaiah 49.15). But it has to be said it very rarely does so.

  Some say that God is both our Father and our Mother. Maybe that's OK. But some would go further still and argue we should call God 'FatherMother'. The problem with that is there's no such thing as a 'fathermother'. (Unless you're an earthworm, of course.) If you say, 'God is our Father' or 'God is our Mother', you get a clear picture – because we know what a father's like, and we know what a mother's like. But 'FatherMother' gives a much less clear picture. It may communicate something, but it doesn't communicate as clearly as saying 'God is Father'.

  It's a bit like saying you can't use the words 'brother' and 'sister'; you have to say 'sibling'. It makes things less clear, not more clear.

- It's true that the Bible's writers were people of their own time. If they lived in a patriarchal society – a society where men were in charge – they're going to think of any ruler or master in male terms. They're *culturally conditioned*. But then, so are we. If we swap 'Father' for 'Mother' or for 'FatherMother', we're just swapping one lot of cultural conditioning for another.

Most Christians would be unhappy with ditching language that has been used of God throughout the history of Christianity. They would be especially uncomfortable with saying that, when Jesus called God his Father, his Dad, he didn't really understand what he was saying and we can do better than he did.

Some of the following questions assume that God exists.

1. The first letter of John, in the New Testament, says 'God is love'.
a) In what ways would Christianity say God's love is like human love?
b) In what ways is it different?

2. 'God is...'
You're limited to ten words! Can you complete the statement? You need to select the ten words which would best help someone to understand what God is said to be like.

3. Someone who's religious might say:

'A light bulb helps us to understand what the sun is like. In a similar way, the words we use to describe God tells us what God is like.'

What does this mean?

4. 'God is male.' How might a Christian respond to this statement?

5. 'The terms people use for God are sexist and out of date.'
a) Why might someone say this?
b) Why might someone disagree?
c) What do you think, and why?

3
What is God like?
(1): The Christian View

Most of the world's religions say that there is one God. The technical term for this idea is **monotheism**: one-God-ism. People who believe in monotheism are called **monotheists.** (The view that there are many gods is called **polytheism** and the people who hold that view are **polytheists**.)

Christianity is a monotheistic religion. Christianity says there is one God, but Christians go on to say that **God exists in three ways at once:**

- God the Father
- God the Son
- God the Holy Spirit

The religious teaching (or **doctrine**) that God exists in three ways at once is called the doctrine of the **Trinity**. 'Trinity' means 'tri-unity': three-in-one.

As God has no physical form, he is sometimes represented in Christian art by a triangle. This image helps us to understand more about the Trinity

God the Father:
God is so great and powerful that he is beyond human understanding. Yet he loves people as a good father loves his children.

God the Son:
We would not know what God was like unless he showed us. God became a human being as Jesus Christ.

God the Holy Spirit:
God is everywhere. He is always with his people.

The three 'bits' of the Trinity – God the Father, God the Son, and God the Holy Spirit – are called the three **Persons** of the Trinity. But **'Persons' does not mean the same here as 'people' or 'individuals'.** (Otherwise, how many Gods would there be?) 'Person' means here 'way of appearing' or 'aspect'. Christians believe that God has three ways of appearing or three aspects. **God has three ways of being God.**

This is what Christianity means when it says that there are three Persons in one God.

- All three Persons of the Trinity have always existed, and always will exist. They are *eternal*.

- All three Persons of the Trinity are equal. Despite their names, the Father is not greater than the Son or the Holy Spirit. (How is the idea that all three persons are equal shown in the diagram of the triangle?)

- All three Persons are called 'he'. As we saw in the last chapter, calling God 'he' does not really mean he's male. But it *does* show that he has a personality. He is a person (as well as, in a different sense, being three Persons – it gets confusing!). He's not a thing, or an 'it'. The Holy Spirit is he, not it.

- **God the Son** became a human being as Jesus. Christians believe that Jesus was and is *both* a human being *and* God himself. Jesus is a human being in the same way as you are or I am: he wasn't a superman, or God walking around disguised as a human being (otherwise, you'd end up with God using a lump of flesh as a machine to travel in – hardly a human being). Jesus got tired, he got ill, he could be hungry or thirsty, he had friends – and so on.

- The Father and the Holy Spirit did not become a human being as Jesus; Jesus was God the Son, not God the Father or God the Holy Spirit. However, all three Persons of the Trinity work together – it was not as though the Father and the Holy Spirit did not know what the Son was up to!

- All three Persons of the Trinity are *fully* God, not one third of God. So, as Jesus was God the Son made human, Jesus is *fully* God, not one third of God.

- As we said above, we would not know what God was like unless he became a man as Jesus. Jesus shows us what God is like. The idea that God shows us what he is like, or that God tells us things, is called **revelation**: God **reveals** to human beings what sort of a God he is – or he reveals other things, such as how he wants human beings to behave.

Someone might ask, 'But how could God become a human being? They're too different.' (This is one reason why Muslims, who regard Jesus as a messenger of God, do not believe in the Incarnation.) How could someone who is all powerful, who can create an entire universe simply by thinking it into existence, who knows absolutely everything – how could someone like that 'fit into' a human being? It would be like trying to get a double decker bus into a matchbox!

Well, if God is going to become a human being, he is going to have to give some things up. A human being cannot be all-powerful, and does not know everything. To become human, God would have to give up some of the things that make him God – he'd have to give up some of his *attributes*. He would have to give up most of his power and most or all of his knowledge.

The doctrine that God gave things up in order to become human is called **kenosis**.

Jesus was not God disguised as a human being. Nor was he a sort of puppet, with God pulling the strings all the time. Jesus was fully human and fully God.

So why did God bother?

Christians say God is so great that he is far beyond human understanding. Our minds cannot comprehend something that is infinite and has enough power to create the universe. We just can't take it in.

But if God 'scaled himself down' to our size, we'd be able to understand him. We'd be able to get an accurate idea of him.

We may not be able to understand God, but we can understand a human being. So, God scales himself down. He becomes a human being. Christians believe he did this to show us what sort of a God he is – what he's like.

If someone asks, 'What's God like?', Christians would say they have the answer. God is 'like' Jesus. The sort of person Jesus was is the sort of person God is. Jesus was loving, generous, forgiving, understanding, kind; he was willing to welcome everyone into his friendship, no matter what they had done, or who they were. He paid no attention to the barriers human society put up of race, class or gender. The only people he condemned were those who thought they were perfect and didn't need help. A Christian writer called Dietrich Bonhoeffer called Jesus 'the man for others'.

Christians also believe that God became a human being to save us from our sins – what we have done wrong. Jesus' execution on the cross abolished death.

Describing God:
the technical vocabulary

There are a lot of technical words used to describe God. These are some of them.

This isn't assuming God exists. It's trying to pin down the concept. We're saying, 'if there is a God, then God would be..' so and so.

- **Omnipotence.** This means 'all powerful'. There is no limit to God's power – except that God can't do things which are logically impossible to do, like both exist and not exist at the same time. Also, God isn't *capricious*: that means he doesn't use his power for the sake of it, to do daft things because he feels like it. When God uses his power, he does so out of his goodness, so his purpose is always good. The adjective from 'omnipotence' is 'omnipotent', so it is said that 'God is omnipotent.'

- **Omniscience.** God knows everything. Human beings' knowledge is limited; God's isn't. (Some theologians have suggested God doesn't know the future, but most would disagree. This raises a question: if God knows the future, why doesn't he intervene to stop evil things from happening? This is not an easy question to answer. We'll return to it later in the book.) The adjective from 'omniscience' is 'omniscient', so it is said that 'God is omniscient'.

- **Omnipresence.** God is everywhere: he is **omnipresent**. He has no physical body, so he's not limited by time or space. There is no corner of the universe, and no point in time, in which God is not present. He is present in the most distant galaxies, and he is present within every human being. Lots of Christians would say that, when you pray, you're not just reaching out to someone who's 'out there'; you're getting in touch with someone who is also within you.

  In Christianity, Judaism and Islam, God creates or makes the universe – out of nothingness. He thinks it into existence. So, while he's *present in* every part of his creation, he's not *the same as* what he's created.

- **Benevolence** or **omnibenevolence.** 'Benevolence' means 'goodness'. 'Omnibenevolence' means 'infinite goodness' or 'total goodness.' In the New Testament, the first letter of John says, 'God is love'. The suras of the Koran open with the words, 'In the Name of God, the Compassionate, the Merciful.' (The adjective from the noun 'benevolence' is 'benevol*ent*'. The adjective from 'omnibenevolence' is 'omnibenevol*ent*'.)

- **Supremacy.** God is supreme: he's in charge. He created the universe and he tells people how he wants them to live their lives: to be generous and compassionate. In Christianity, the most important way he does this is through the life and teaching of Jesus Christ.

- **Transcendent.** (This is the adjective; the noun is 'transcendence'.) If you say God is transcendent, it means God is 'up there'. God's totally beyond human understanding. We can imagine something that's huge, but something that's infinite – well, our minds can't take it in. God's beyond human understanding. Without God's help, without his revelation, we'd have very little idea of what he's like.

  In Christian thought, it's sometimes said that God is Father is the aspect of God that is transcendent.

  Some people accept that there is a God but don't follow a religion. They'd say that God exists, but he's totally beyond our minds and we have no way of understanding him. So, he's not much more than a concept, really – something that explains where the universe came from, but something that's so utterly different from us that, to be honest, he's not worth bothering with.

  However, if you think back to the last unit and the story of St Augustine and the rockpool, you'll see that transcendence isn't the end of the story. There is a sense in which God is totally removed from human experience – but we can also get an accurate picture of him. In Christianity, Jesus himself is that picture.

  Moreover, Christianity and Judaism teach that human beings are made 'in the image of God' (Genesis 1.26-27). God is not utterly different from us – in the way, say, that a stick of chewing gum is utterly different from the planet Saturn. Human beings are not *un*like God: they're *like* him. They bear his image. The idea of the image of God doesn't mean people look like God; it refers to the non-physical aspects of people. God, like people, has a personality, he can think, he remembers, he creates, he loves people. So, once again, while our ideas of God may be *inadequate* – they're not the whole story, and they're a scaled down version of the reality – they're not *wrong*.

- **Knowable**. Religions generally say that God is knowable: we can know him, we can find out about him, we can try to live as he wants us to. Again, for Christians, the most important way to understand God is to learn about and grow closer to Jesus. Other faiths don't place so much importance on Jesus. Muslims would say we come to know God by studying the Koran and by living out its message. Sikhs would say we come to know God by studying the teachings of the Gurus.

  As we saw, some people say that God is transcendent, and they get no further than that. God is utterly different from human beings and has nothing in common with them. He's so much greater than we are that he recedes into the distance. Someone who takes that view would say that God is **unknowable.**

- **Immanent.** (The noun for this is 'immanence'.) This doesn't mean that God's about to get here at any moment: that's 'imm*I*nent', whereas this is 'imm*A*nent'! If God is immanent, it means he's not just 'up there', he's also 'down here': present in the universe, with us, among us. If God is our Father – still more if he's Dad – he's not an absentee father. He's really and genuinely here. Christianity usually says that the way in which God is among us is as God the Holy Spirit.

- **Personal.** God is a Person – or, at least, to call God a person is the closest we can get to it. God is *more than*, not less than, a person. At least, that's what Christianity, Islam and Judaism would say. Some Hindus would say that God is **impersonal** – not a person. The supreme reality can't be thought of in human terms, and to say God is a 'person' is to use human terms.

  If you said God is a force – just a power that brought the universe into being, but not something you could say is alive – then God would also be impersonal.

There's a lot of material here. This summary may help:

Omnipotence / Omnipotent	All powerful
Omniscience / Omniscient	All knowing
Omnipresence / Omnipresent	Everywhere
Benevolent / Benevolence	Good
Omnibenevolent / Omnibenevolence	All good, infinitely good
Supremacy / Supreme	God's in charge
Transcendent / Transcendence	God 'up there', beyond our experience
Knowable	We can come to know God, and to know about him
Unknowable	No we can't!
Immanent	God 'down here', among us and with us
Personal	God is a Person: God has a personality and is like a human person, only he's more than a human person
Impersonal	God is an it, not a he or a she. God is so far beyond our understanding that you can't really use terms like 'person' to describe it.

1. Explain the meaning of the following words:

- monotheism
- monotheist
- polytheism
- polytheist
- doctrine
- Trinity
- revelation

2. Put the heading: Christian Beliefs about the Trinity.

The statements below all have mistakes in them. Write them out, correcting the mistakes.

- There are three persons of the Trinity. 'Person' means 'individuals'.
- 'Trinity' means six-in-one.
- The doctrine of the Trinity means that God has six ways of being God.
- The Father is greater than the Son and the Holy Spirit and the Father existed before they did.
- God the Holy Spirit became a man as Jesus.
- All three persons of the Trinity are called 'it'.
- Jesus was not really human. He was God.
- Only God the Father is fully God. God the Son and God the Holy Spirit are not fully God.
- The sort of person Moses was is the sort of person God is.

3. For GCSE, you need to learn the technical vocabulary used about God (omnipotence, omniscience, and so on: the words listed on the left hand side of the table.

The easiest way to do this is to use what's called 'spot learning' techniques.

This means you write out the information you need to learn, say on a piece of A4 or A3 paper, and put it up somewhere at home where you'll see it. (The front of the fridge is a good place!) Every time you walk past it, you look at it, even if it's only for a few seconds. After a month or so, you'll find you've learnt it!

Learning things like this by doing it little and often is more effective than trying to sit down and cram it all into your brain in one hour. Hint: it's also a good way of memorising things you have to learn by heart, like vocabulary in languages, formulae in science, or quotations for RS or English!

(Another hint: it doesn't work if you leave it until the night before the exam! The sooner you put up the spot learning things, the better.)

So, make a small poster of the technical vocabulary by copying out the table we've given above.

The more memorable you can make it, the better. It will help if you do each row in a different colour. Try, too, to add little illustrations. For example, if you write the word 'unknowable' in the shape of a question mark, it will help you to learn it. With a bit of imagination, you should be able to come up with a picture that gets across the idea of 'all knowing', 'all powerful', and so on.

4
What is God like?
(2): The Hindu View

by Seeta Lakhani

One of the greatest misconceptions about Hinduism is that it is viewed as a polytheistic religion (meaning belief in many almighty gods), or that it is a henotheistic religion (promoting a hierarchy of gods). Both these claims are incorrect. The best way to classify Hinduism is to call it a **pluralistic** religion.

Pluralism is a uniquely Hindu idea. It suggests that every one of us relates to God in a different way. As we are all different, individually or as groups, the way we relate to God also has to be different. The concept and approach to God that we adopt has to reflect our inclinations, including our social and historical backgrounds. It cannot be otherwise.

To gain a better understanding of pluralism, let's ask ourselves:

> Why should God be thought of only as our Father in heaven?
> Why not as our Mother in heaven?

We can then go even further and ask:

> Why should God be thought of only as a personality, as male or female?
> Why shouldn't God be thought of as the *principle* that underlies everything?

Some of the brightest minds in modern times prefer this second approach. It does away with the idea of God as a personality. In their opinion, thinking of God as a personality introduces too many unanswered questions.

Pluralism opens up a plethora of perceptions and approaches to God in Hinduism. These approaches are classified into three broad groups:

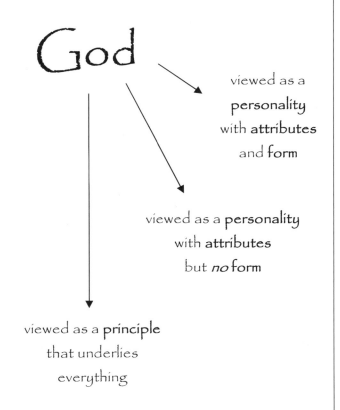

The three main approaches to God:

God

viewed as a **personality** with **attributes** and **form**

viewed as a **personality** with **attributes** but *no* **form**

viewed as a **principle** that underlies everything

Let's look at these three approaches in more detail.

1. God viewed as a personality, with attributes and form

The most popular Hindu approach is to see God as having attributes (*saguna*) and form (*sakara*).

If you think of God as having physical form, it allows you to develop a relationship with God, who you think of as a personality. This is the simplest way of relating to God.

This personified God can be regarded as kith or kin: as a father or mother, a brother or sister, or maybe a child or friend. There are a vast number of relationships to choose from in order to build up a relationship with God. This is not a limitation: it's a very practical way of relating to and approaching God.

Brahma

Vishnu

Man is not made in the image of God; God is made in the image of man

As we are human, it is easy to relate to God as a *super*human. So we portray God in our image. The depiction of God in human form has to incorporate superhuman attributes. This is traditionally done through the portrayal of a deity with many arms or heads.

Higher beings: devas are not God

The misunderstanding that Hinduism is polytheistic may have arisen from Hindu literature. This talks of 'higher beings', called *devas* and *devis* (meaning the 'shining ones', who live in other astral planes). These two words often get loosely translated as 'gods' and 'goddesses', which creates the misunderstanding that Hindus believe in many gods.

Infinite power must include the power to become finite

Christianity, Judaism and Islam think of God as having attributes such as being omnipotent (all powerful) and omniscient (all knowing), but they resist giving a form to God. Judaism and Islam say that the infinite God cannot become finite.

Hindus disagree: they say that having infinite power must include the power to become finite. They claim that the gracious God assumes a finite form for the devotee who loves him. The form he assumes is imposed by his devotee. This is why we find many images of gods and goddesses in the Hindu tradition. This is a celebration of pluralism; it shouldn't be confused with polytheism.

The same God fulfilling different roles

The same God is often considered to fulfil three different roles. This is called *trimurti*: three-in-one. God is depicted in the three roles of Brahma, Vishnu and Shiva.

Brahma is God playing the role of the **creator** of the universe.

Vishnu is God in the role of the **preserver** of the universe.

Shiva is God (sometimes) depicted in the role of the **destroyer** of the universe. The Shiva devotee, however, would strongly disagree with this. For them, Shiva is creator, preserver and destroyer.

God as feminine: Shakti

The idea of thinking of God as female is very popular with many Hindus. The Ultimate Reality as female is called **Shakti,** which means 'power'. It is believed that the energy driving the universe should be viewed as female. The essential nature of every physical object in the universe is energy, Shakti. Thus worshipping God as a female acknowledges that the cosmic power is viewed as feminine.

Some well known forms of God as Mother are **Parvati, Durga, Kali, Lakshmi** and **Saraswati.**

Vishnu and the avatars

Vishnu, in the role of the preserver of the universe, takes on human forms called the **avatars.** He descends to the world for the destruction of evil and the benefit of mankind. One scripture says that he descends to the earth ten times.

Some avatars are given greater prominence and are worshipped as God by many Hindus. Two of the most popular are **Rama** and **Krishna.**

Rama is considered to be the ideal man, *Purushotama.* He is the best example of how an ideal son, ideal father or ideal king should behave, and he is the hero of the epic, the *Ramayana.* He lived for principles and not for possession. It is difficult to find any other king, ancient or modern, who has lived up to such high moral ideas.

Rama's consort, **Sita,** is recognised as the personification of loyalty, grace and chastity, and is revered by Hindus as the ideal woman.

Krishna is regarded by his devotees as the perfect avatar. He is the author of the Hindu scripture, the *Bhagavad Gita.* He is shown with a peacock feather in his hair and carrying a flute. His consort is **Radha.** The love they share is not physical but the spiritual love that draws all souls to God.

2. God viewed as a personality, with attributes but *no* form

Some Hindus prefer to think of God as having attributes, like love, truth or power. However, just as in Christianity, Judaism and Islam, God is not given any form or shape (*nirakara*).

So how can Hindus think of God both as having form, and as having no form?

A recent Hindu prophet called Sri Ramakrishna (1826-1886) explained this by using the example of ice and water. Both ice and water are essentially the same, but one has form and the other is formless.

Shiva

Durga

Lakshmi

Saraswati

In the same way, Sri Ramakrishna said:

> God can be both with and without form. It is the love of the devotee that freezes the formless God into the form the devotee chooses. Many are the names of God and infinite the forms through which he may be approached.
>
> In whatever name and form you worship him, through that you will realise him.

3. God viewed as a *principle* that underlies everything

This is the third approach to God in Hinduism.

This approach thinks of God as formless, *nirakara*, as well as without attributes, *nirguna*.

This may appear very abstract and difficult, and yet this approach provides the best link between science and religion. It takes pluralism to the other extreme. It moves dramatically away from the idea of God as a personality, to the idea of God as a principle.

The ideas that God has a particular form, or that he has superhuman attributes like omniscience or omnipotence, are seen as human limitations imposed on the concept of God. As we are human, the only way we can relate to God is in human terms, and thus we give him various human forms and superhuman attributes like being 'all compassionate'. Some people recognise the limitations of such approaches and thus prefer to adopt this third approach.

The word 'God' is now replaced with the term 'Ultimate Reality' or 'Cosmic Reality': **Brahman.**

Brahman: God as a cosmic principle

This third approach to God in Hinduism requires us to think of him or her not as a personality (with attributes like love or power), but as a principle underlying absolutely everything. This principle forms the basis of everything we experience. Brahman is the Ultimate Reality *appearing* as everything. It manifests as all the galaxies, all the living and non-living things, and even as our mental and intellectual faculties. Everything is seen as an expression of this Ultimate Reality, Brahman. This approach is similar to the one used by scientists who are also trying to find a unity from which everything is manufactured. To pay tribute to this idea, Hindus define the universe as *shrishti,* meaning 'projection' of Brahman.

Note: Hindus do not say that the universe is God. That theory is called **pantheism.** Instead, they say that God or the Ultimate Reality appears or manifests as the universe. In this manifested universe, living beings are considered to be more special than non-living things. Brahman becomes more manifested in living beings. This gives rise to the second key concept in Hinduism: **Atman.**

Supreme dignity offered to mankind: Atman

Hindus say that we are all essentially God.

This is a dramatic statement. No religion has given such dignity to mankind. We are being equated to God!

Many people are frightened off by such ideas. They ask, 'We do not feel like God, we certainly do not behave like God, so how can we be God?'

Hindus say that the reason is because we have never tried to discover our true Self. We get attached to what *we think we are* rather than to what *we truly are.* We associate ourselves with our bodies and minds, and not with the essential thing that is looking out through our minds and bodies. That essential thing is God.

To illustrate this point, let's use a metaphor.

One God looking out through all these eyes.

Imagine going to the seaside on a sunny day. On the peak of every wave, we see the sparkle of the sun. It appears as if the sea has come alive with thousands of suns sparkling on the surface of the water.

In the same way, say Hindus, the same one God sparkles as *consciousness* in the eyes of every living thing. The conclusion of the Hindu philosophy is that 'It is God alone who manifests himself as the universe (defined as Brahman), and finds clearer expression as *consciousness* in all living things (defined at *Atman*).'

Our essential nature is God. The sole aim of religion is to discover this spiritual fact. This Hindu idea offers supreme dignity to mankind, and also offers the best reason why all living things should be respected and why we must help each other.

God, according to this belief, is not somewhere 'out there' in the heavens, but is really our own true Self. By beginning this journey of self-discovery, we end up by discovering God.

According to this finding, the highest worship of God is service to mankind and respect for all living things. It is the same God who percolates through nature and appears most transparently in all of us.

This is the Hindu version of Humanism: it is called **Spiritual Humanism.**

The relationship between Atman and Brahman

Brahman is defined as the Ultimate Reality (God) appearing as everything, including all living things. Atman is defined as the Ultimate Reality (God) appearing as our essential Self. Simple logic suggests that there cannot be two Ultimate Realities,

Rama and Sita

Krishna and Radha

27

otherwise we have a contradiction in terms. How could there be two Ultimates? So, we are forced to conclude that Atman is the same as Brahman.

Some Hindus dislike the idea of equating ourselves with God as it sounds arrogant, hence they modify the relationship. They say that Brahman (God) is like the fire and the individuals (Atman) are like the sparks of that same fire.

So which of the three Hindu approaches is best?

The answer is:

The approach that suits our temperament and needs is the best approach for us.

Many in the Hindu tradition prefer to think of God as a personality like Shiva or Vishnu, or the Mother Goddess, as it is easier to relate to them and build a loving relationship with them. Some Hindus prefer to think of God as their essential self (Atman), and some Hindus who are perhaps more scientifically orientated prefer to think of God as the essential nature of everything (Brahman).

The approach that suits us is the best for us. No one particular approach is considered to be better than any other approach. As we are all different, the way we approach God will necessarily be different. As Sri Ramakrishna states:

As many individual opinions, that many paths to God.

'My religion is best'

The idea of pluralism offers the best prescription to how people of different religions can co-exist with full dignity. Pluralism teaches that all religions are different pathways to the same God.

How to translate this teaching of pluralism into practice can best be illustrated through a story:

Two young boys were playing in the school ground. One boasted, 'My mum is the best in the world.' The other objected strongly and said that his mum was the best in the world. Both the boys loved their mothers and were not prepared to accept the other's statement. Soon they came to blows.

A wise man, passing by, enquired why they were fighting. Both the boys declared passionately that their mother was the best, and hence the other was wrong.

The wise man told the boys, 'Take my advice: feel free to declare passionately "My mum is best," but then add two little words at the end of the sentence. Say, "My mum is best... *for me.*" You will then find that there is no disagreement or cause for quarrel.' The two boys readily agreed and became friends.

The moral of the story is that it is fine to declare that our religion is best, but we must add the two little words at the end: our religion is best *for us.* This idea needs to be incorporated by all the major world religions, especially those who claim exclusivity. Exclusivity is the claim, made by some faiths, that theirs is the only true pathway to God, while all others are wrong.

This is bound to create a lot of strife and conflict in the name of religion. The resolution of this serious global issue lies in the pluralistic teaching of Hinduism. *All* religions are *true* and *valid* pathways to God. 'My mum is best *for me*' becomes 'Our religion is best *for us* – but not necessarily for the rest of mankind.'

1. There are three main approaches to God in Hinduism. To help you remember this, copy the diagram on p.23.

2. Look again at the section, **God viewed as a personality, with attributes and form.** This is one of the ways Hindus approach God.

  Write your own notes to explain this view. You need to include the following key words:

saguna
sakara
trimurti
Brahma
Vishnu
Shiva
Avatar
Rama
Kirshna

3. Now look at the section, **God viewed as a personality, with attributes but *no* form.**
Sri Ramakrishna (1826-1886) used an image of ice and water. What did he say and what does it mean?

4. We've said: 'This third approach to God in Hinduism requires us to think of him or her not as a personality (with attributes like love or power), but as a principle underlying absolutely everything.'

(See pages 26-27, in the section **God viewed as a *principle,* that underlies everything**.)

  Read the section again, carefully, at least once more.

  Work in pairs. Assume your partner knows nothing about the idea. You've got to explain it to her or him! Both of you need to try this. It would help, too, to discuss (politely!) how well you think the other person's done.

  You've now got to write up what you've said, so you have your own record. You might prefer to do this as a mind map.

5. Explain the relationship between Brahman and Atman.

6. 'God appears as everything, as all living things.' What is your view of this idea? Give your reasons and show that you have considered more than one viewpoint. Explain why someone might disagree with you, and why in turn you disagree with them.

Talking points

'There are many paths to God.'
'No one religion should think of itself as having all the answers. My religion is best *for me*, but not for everyone.'
'God is beyond personality.'

'Religion is just superstitious rubbish. You might as well believe in fairies at the bottom of the garden as believe in God.'

The problem with this view is that it doesn't really leave much room for debate. It's not really a good starting point for a discussion. The speaker seems to have gone for the nuclear option. He or she may have good reasons for saying what they do – but it's certainly strong stuff!

And it looks likely that they're not aware of something:

There are, in fact, very strong arguments for saying that there is a God.

These are not silly arguments which no-one takes seriously. In fact, they've convinced some of the most intelligent people that God does exist. But they're not *conclusive*. This means they don't absolutely prove 100% that God exists.

(In fact, there may be good reasons why God – if he exists – wouldn't allow people to be able to prove he was there. We'll come back to this later.)

Many highly intelligent people who've studied the arguments say they're *specious*, which means they look good but they're actually wrong.

So, as there are good *arguments* for saying there is a God, it's unfair to say belief in God is just

superstition. (This is what the fairies at the bottom of the garden thing is saying.)

Also, there are no good arguments, which would convince intelligent people, for saying there are fairies at the bottom of the garden!

Isn't it just a matter of opinion?

Someone might say:

> I don't believe in God. You do. I respect your belief but I don't agree with you. For you, there's a God. For me, there isn't. Let's just agree to disagree.

Isn't this really the situation? Isn't it all just a matter of opinion?

The speaker's certainly being generous. Most of us would regard it as a good thing to respect other people's opinions.

The problem is, it's more difficult than that.

Here's why:

If God exists, it is a fact that he exists.

If God does not exist, it is a fact that he does not exist.

He's either there, or he isn't!

- So, if I choose to believe in God, but *in fact* there isn't a God, my belief won't make him exist.

- And if I choose not to believe in God, but *in fact* he's really there, my disbelief won't stop him existing.

Suppose there's a big spider in the corner of your classroom. One of you has noticed it. Another one of you hasn't. One of you believes the spider is there; the other one doesn't. Does that affect whether the spider's there or not?

Arguments in favour of the existence of God

Philosophers of religion say there are two types of arguments in favour of God's existence:

1. Arguments from **reason**: things we can work out for ourselves.
2. Arguments from **revelation**. Revelation means God telling us things, so this would mean **we know God exists because he tells us he does.**

This unit concentrates on one of the arguments from reason (our first kind of argument). This argument is given two technical names; it's called:

the first cause

or

the cosmological argument

Basically, the first cause or cosmological argument goes like this:

We know the universe exists. The universe couldn't have created itself. Something must have caused it. That something is God.

Let's examine this in a bit more detail.

We know that everything that exists is caused by something else. Otherwise, it wouldn't be there.

→ I'm caused by my parents,

→ my parents were caused by my grandparents,

→ my grandparents were caused by my great-grandparents,

→ my great-grandparents were caused by my great-great-grandparents,

→ my great-great-grandparents were caused by…

And so it goes back, for millions and millions of years:

→ back to the earliest human beings, who evolved from other creatures;

→ back to the origins of life itself, when the chemicals in the primeval soup on the young planet came together to produce the first life forms;

→ back to the formation of the Earth and the solar system from a swirling cloud of matter;

→ back to the beginning of the universe and the big bang, and –

And what? Do we stop there, and say that's the beginning? Atheism says we do. There was the big bang, and that's how everything started.

But it doesn't answer the question: **what caused the big bang?**

Atheism has to say it caused itself. It just happened. Something came out of nothing.

Theists, people who believe in God, would say

this doesn't work. It's like saying this:

Suppose you could have a big cardboard box and empty it. Not just of the junk that's in it, but empty it of absolutely everything: no air, no matter of any sort, no dimensions, no time. (I know this is impossible, but go along with it for now!)

If you stuck that box on a shelf, a box full of nothingness, it's very, very unlikely you'd be able to come back the next morning and say, 'Goodness me: a universe appears to have popped out of it!'

But that's what atheism means you have to believe.

OK. But if everything is caused by something, the atheist might say, what caused God?

Get out of that one!

It's a fair question, in fact.

Behind it is the concept of **self-existence**. This means something can create itself. It's not made by anything else.

The atheist is saying that God can't exist, because he'd be self-existent. And self-existence is impossible.

What this misses is that the atheist actually *does* believe in self-existence. The universe created itself. So the universe is self-existent.

So, you can't say God can't be self-existent because self-existence is nonsense. You already believe in self-existence. It's just that you believe the universe, rather than God, is self-existent.

The evidence seems to be that the universe had a beginning, about 14 billion years ago. So, either it made itself, or God made the universe.

And either the universe is self-existent, or God is.

Some would say:

It makes more sense to say that God is self-existent because God is eternal. This means more than 'he always has existed and always will exist.' Eternity is 'bigger than' time. God 'sees' and perhaps experiences all times at once. God does not exist in time; time exists in God. The relationship between eternity and time is like the relationship between a cube and a square (or a straight line!). Something that is eternal must also be self-existent. God never had a beginning and will never

end. But the universe had a beginning. Self-existence makes more sense when it's applied to God than it does when it's applied to the universe.

And the idea of God explains not just what started the universe, but **why** it's here at all.

What do you think?

The book of Genesis

Lots of people would be surprised by some of this. They might say, 'Hang on: aren't Christians meant to believe in the Bible? What about the stories in the book of Genesis? They say God made the world in seven days, and the first humans were called Adam and Eve. Don't Christians have to believe all that?'

Actually, Christians don't have to believe that what the Book of Genesis says is a record of what actually happened. Some do, but they're in a minority. Most Christians don't have a problem with what science tells us about the origin of the universe. For example, the Roman Catholic Church is the largest of all the Christian denominations, and most Christians are Roman Catholics. The Catholic Church's teaching is that there is no problem with accepting the findings of science about the origins of the universe. Most educated Christians, from all Churches, would agree with this.

On this view, the stories in Genesis are just that: stories. The technical word for them is *myths*: stories which aren't historically true, but which contain religious truths – in this case, that God made the universe, and that the universe was made for the benefit of the beings who live in it. God created the universe because he's creative, and because he is a God of love. He created human beings (and maybe sentient life of other planets) for the same sort of reason as human beings themselves decide they're going to have children. They *could* decide to keep their love for themselves, but they decide to share that love with other beings, with their children. On this view, science tells us *how*, but it doesn't tell us *why*. The answer to 'why?' is found in religion, not in science.

We'll explore the relationship between religion and science, and the accounts of creation in the book of Genesis, later in this book.

Thomas Aquinas

Thomas Aquinas (c.1225 – 1274), also known as St Thomas Aquinas, was an Italian Christian writer and philosopher. He was a Roman Catholic priest and a monk, of the Dominican order.

Thomas Aquinas wrote an immense book called the *Summa Theologica*. This includes five arguments for the existence of God, which are now known as the **Five Ways.** One of these is the Argument of the First Cause, which is also the argument we have outlined in this chapter: you cannot keep going back and back for ever, saying x was caused by y, y was caused by z, z was caused by a, a was caused by b... You eventually have to stop and say that one thing must have caused everything else – and that one thing is God.

Aquinas didn't invent the argument, but he's the most well known philosopher who explained it.

Thomas Aquinas, history says, was so fat that a U-shaped piece of wood had to be cut out of the monastery's dining table so that the saint could accommodate his tummy.

1. People say we know God exists because he must have created the universe. You need to explain this idea in your own words. Try out your explanation on another member of the class. Does it make sense to them? You may need to redraft it!

Make a note of the fact that this is known as the first cause or the cosmological argument.

2. Write a paragraph to explain who Thomas Aquinas was and what he said.

Talking points:

'The universe could not have created itself. God must have done it.'

'Science on its own is all you need to explain where the universe came from. You do not need God. Science has all the answers.'

'God only exists in people's minds. For people who believe in God, God is true for them. For people who don't believe in God, he doesn't exist. That's all there is to it.'

6
The argument from design

To start with, here are three (rather bizarre) situations to think about. You might like to discuss what you make of them, in groups.

Situation One

Every week, you buy your National Lottery ticket. The chances against winning are 14,000,000 to 1.
   And you win.
   Next week, you win the jackpot again.
   And the next week, you win the jackpot.
   And the next.
   And the next.
   This is a bit surprising and you begin to think someone must have fixed it in your favour. So you phone up the Lottery company. They assure you it's not a fix; it's still random and you're just very, very lucky.
   You find this hard to believe. Surely it must be a fix?

Situation Two

You're an alien explorer from the planet Zog.
   You and a fellow explorer land on the seashore on part of the planet Earth, which is a completely new planet to you. You're walking along the beach, wondering what the strange wet stuff is and why there's so much of it. You come across an object and you show it to your fellow explorer, who's called Xut.
   The object is a yellowish disc of metal, about 2 cm in diameter, and about 3 mm thick. There are tiny grooves cut all the way around the rim. On one side of the disc is a strange pattern; on

the other side is what appears to be an artistic representation of the profile of the head of one of the Earth creatures. There are markings on the disc, which you assume to be letters.
   The object baffles both of you and you wonder what it could be for.
   You say to Xut that the object must have been designed and made – presumably by the Earth creatures. It must have a purpose, even though you're unsure what it is.
   Xut disagrees. She says it is a purely random phenomenon. She draws your attention to the wet stuff, which she says has worn the many stones on the beach into smooth, rounded shapes. There is no purpose behind these stones; they just happened. This object is another example of something randomly produced by the wet stuff. It may look more complex but that is an illusion. It was not designed or made by any creature or being. It just happened.

34

Situation Three

For no very good reason, you take a load of high explosive into a scrap metal yard. When no-one is about, you blow everything to smithereens – it seemed like a good idea at the time. Everything is blown to bits and falls to the ground.

The bits and pieces just happen to fall to the ground in the shape of a combine harvester.

This is totally random. But it is such a good combine harvester that you drive it away and become a virtuous and productive citizen, happily cutting corn for the rest of your days. And never again do you play with high explosives.

There is a point to all this. You've probably guessed that it's to do with the idea of how you can argue in favour of God's existence.

- In the first example, it would be so unlikely to win the jackpot every week – at 14 million to 1 each time – that you'd be quite right to think it was a fix. It is massively more likely to be a fix than to say it just happened.

- In the second one, you're right and Xut is wrong. What she says is possible but very, very, very unlikely. It is much more likely that the object was designed and made than that it 'just happened'.

- The third situation is just about possible but so unlikely as to be ridiculous. The odds against something coherent – like a combine harvester – coming out of a random event – like a bomb in a scrap yard – are so tiny as to be very, very nearly impossible.

These are all connected to **the argument from design**, which is also called **the teleological argument.** The argument from design says God must exist because the universe is far too complex just to have happened by chance. It looks as though it is designed, as though it has a purpose. Therefore, it must have a designer. That designer is God.

Atheism says the universe 'just happened'. Theists (people who believe in God) might point out:

- If it just happened, why is it so complex? Why isn't it just random? If a human being could design something as complex, intricate and brilliant as the human brain, he'd win every Nobel prize going for the next thousand years. Could something as amazing and extraordinary have just come about by chance? Doesn't it look as though it's been designed? And that's just one example. There are billions of phenomena in the universe, from galaxies to fleas. And they're so complex. And they work. Is it more likely that they just happened to turn out like that, purely by chance, or that there's some mind behind them, who designed the whole thing?

- Maybe a universe without God just might happen, but would we expect nothingness to produce such a fantastic result? Perhaps it could throw up a few particles – but all the billions that there are? And why did they come together in the way they did, looking as though there's a purpose in nature rather than a lack of purpose? Surely someone must be running the show.

For many theists, the fact that the universe is coherent, that it makes sense, that it's so staggeringly clever, suggests very strongly that it's been designed. Therefore there must be a designer. And the designer is God.

Maybe it's crazy to believe in God. But isn't it crazier to believe there isn't a God? Austin Farrer, a New Testament scholar, once said, 'It seems to me incredibly unlikely that we should exist.' But we do. Surely the most 'natural' state of things would be nothing at all: no God, no universe, nothing whatsoever. But: we're here, against all the odds. The odds against an atheistic universe, a totally mindless and meaningless thing, eventually producing human beings are billions upon billions to one. But if God exists, it cuts down the odds massively, because the universe has design and purpose, and therefore it's going to produce us – because that's why God made it.

The atheist might reply, 'Yes, the universe is very unlikely, but it's just here. It happened. It just turned out that the universe that was produced is orderly. It could have been very different.' The theist answer is – well, look back to the first situation at the beginning of the chapter.

Most theologians would say that the argument from design, taken with the other arguments, provides strong evidence that God really does exist.

Did Paley nail the argument from design?

For experts in the philosophy of religion, one of the best known defenders of the cosmological argument is **William Paley** (1743-1805). He was a teacher at the University of Cambridge but he saw his real work as trying to serve God and his fellow human beings as a parish priest in the Church of England.

In 1802, just three years before his death, he published *Natural Theology; or, Evidences of the Existence and Attributes of the Deity.* ('The Deity' means God and theology is the study of God; it literally means 'God talk'.) The book's more simply known just as *Natural Theology*.

Natural Theology puts forward what's come to be known as the watchmaker theory. We've printed what Paley actually wrote. As it's not in the easiest English, there's a translation below it!

In crossing a heath, suppose I pitched my foot against a stone, and were asked how the stone came to be there; I might possibly answer, that, for anything I knew to the contrary, it had lain there forever: nor would it perhaps be very easy to show the absurdity of this answer. But suppose I had found a watch upon the ground, and it should be inquired how the watch happened to be in that place; I should hardly think of the answer I had before given, that for anything I knew, the watch might have always been there... There must have existed, at some time, and at some place or other, an artificer or artificers, who formed [the watch] for the purpose which we find it actually to answer; who comprehended its construction, and designed its use... Every indication of contrivance, every manifestation of design, which existed in the watch, exists in the works of nature; with the difference, on the side of nature, of being greater or more, and that in a degree which exceeds all computation.

Natural Theology

Suppose, when I crossed a heath, I kicked a stone, and was asked how the stone got there. I might answer that, as far as I knew, it had been there for ever. It might not be very easy to show that this answer was daft.

But suppose I'd found a watch on the ground, and someone asked how the watch got there.

I'd be unlikely to think of the answer I'd given before: that, as far as I knew, the watch might have always been there.

At some time or other, there must have been a skilled craftsman or craftsmen who made the watch for a purpose [i.e. to tell the time]. This craftsman would have understood how to make it, and would have designed it too. The watch shows it's been made and designed. In just the same way, the natural world shows it's been made and designed too – and much more than the watch does. Infinitely more, in fact!

You may have noticed that we've pinched Paley's argument for the story of the two aliens arguing over the pound coin!

William Paley also said that living things were too complex to have happened by chance. They had to have been designed. God had designed 'even the most humble and insignificant organisms' and all of their most intricate features, like the antennae of an earwig. If God took so much care over earwigs, he must care even more for human beings!

So Paley argued the natural world shows God exists. He went further. The natural world, he said, shows that the God who made the universe is the Christian God: he loves what he has made because he took such care over designing it.

Paley knew that one objection to there being a God was that there was suffering. But his defence was that there was much more pleasure than pain in life. The good outweighs the bad. (We explore this issue later in this book.)

Much earlier than Paley, **Thomas Aquinas** (see p.33) had also dealt with the argument from design.

The fifth of Aquinas' **five ways** (see p.33 again) is the teleological argument. It's slightly different, in that it's about *purpose* rather than *design*, but the way the argument works out is very similar.

Aquinas said:

→ Inanimate things, things that aren't alive, still act for a purpose. They nearly always act in the same way. [Can you think of some examples?]

→ This means they can't do so by chance, or it would be totally random.

→ Inanimate things can't act for a purpose unless someone makes them behave with a purpose. An arrow doesn't shoot itself. There has to be an archer.

→ Therefore, there must be some intelligent being who makes natural things behave with a purpose.

→ That being is God.

(In fact, the reason why it's called the *teleological* argument is more to do with Aquinas' version of the argument than Paley's. 'Telos' is Greek for 'end' or 'purpose'.)

The French philosopher **René Descartes** (1596–1650) also accepted the teleological argument.

(Descartes is actually more associated with the ontological argument – which is horribly complicated and which we don't have to cover for GCSE!)

Descartes said the **purpose** and the **order** in the natural world meant we had to assume there was an all powerful (omnipotent) being behind it all.

(Notice Descartes thinks about **purpose**, as Aquinas did, and **order**, as Paley would go on to do. What Descartes says about the teleological argument, if you like, combines both Aquinas and Paley – though remember Descartes died long before Paley was born!)

The great scientist and mathematician
Sir Isaac Newton (1643-1727)
wrote:

In the absence of any other proof, the thumb alone would convince me of God's existence.

What do you think he meant?

Does the argument from design actually work?

Lots of people think it doesn't.

So, if the argument from design is wrong, that means God doesn't exist. Right?

Not necessarily. There'd still be other arguments for saying there is a God. All it would mean is that *this* argument doesn't work – but the others might.

Atheists would say the argument from design doesn't work. (Atheists are people who say there is no God.)

Lots of scientists today agree with Newton: the argument for design shows that God exists. Other scientists, however, are atheists. **Richard Dawkins** is a famous biologist at New College, Oxford. His view is that evolution on its own is enough to explain how species came to be as they are today. He certainly wouldn't accept Paley's idea that the wings and antennae of an earwig show God's care in designing it. Earwigs' antennae and wings are that way because that's how they evolved!

Dawkins also claims that the universe was not designed. Instead, it 'mimics' design. In other words, it looks *as though* it was designed – but it wasn't.

On the other hand, how could you tell the difference between:

something that *mimics* design

and

something that *was* designed?

Wouldn't they both look the same?

For some other criticisms of the argument from design, look again at situation two on page 34.

1. Write an explanation of the argument from design (the teleological argument) for someone who's never heard of it.
It's not easy!
Draft your work and then redraft it until you're happy with it.

Can you now try to get it down to one paragraph?!

2. William Paley talked about finding a watch on the ground. What did he say and what does it mean?

3.a) What did *either* Descartes *or* Aquinas say about the argument from design?
b) Make a note of Newton's quotation about the thumb!

4. 'The argument from design is a stronger argument than the cosmological argument.' Do you agree?

Talking points

'The argument from design is a good one. It's very good evidence for saying God exists.'
'It's far more likely that the universe was designed than that it just happened.'
'The universe was created by the big bang. Billions of years later, life evolved. Science has all the answers. You do not need God.'

Random

Random?

7

Religious experience

Have you ever been alone – but felt as though you weren't?

You probably have, if you think about it – though it's more likely to have been an unpleasant rather than a pleasant experience.

Have you ever read a ghost story, or watched a programme about hauntings on TV, and then been too worried to turn the light off when you've gone to bed? Or have you ever been in a place which, for no reason you can put your finger on, has given you the shivers?

Experiences of being 'spooked' like this are very common, particularly for little children. We'd probably put this sort of thing down to imagination. And we'd be right to do so, too. Small children's parents tend to be careful about what they're allowed to watch or read, and for good reason. Imagination can be very powerful. (Much as I like reading ghost stories, even nowadays I'm careful to avoid the scarier ones because I know I'll pay for it later!)

There's another sort of experience of feeling not alone, but this time it's a positive experience. And the person who seems to be there is still invisible, but isn't evil; quite the opposite, in fact.

This sort of experience, the positive kind, is much rarer. Some people never have an experience like this. Others have only one or two of them in their lifetimes. They're claimed by people who have had them to be tremendously powerful.

What follows is an account of an experience of this sort. This isn't fictional. John Williamson, the person who wrote it, says it really happened. He's someone the authors, Simon and Chris Danes, know very well.

'When I was about 30, my wife and I were on holiday in Ireland. This was in the 1990s. We'd hired a car and were touring through Kerry. As I'm quite interested in church history, I like exploring churches (though I can understand why other people don't share this interest!).

'We parked the car by a little church in the countryside and went in. I was mildly disappointed because I wanted to see whether there were some surviving features from before the Reformation, but there weren't, and it wasn't a particularly beautiful church either. I had a quick look round and then stood briefly in front of the altar to say a prayer.

'And then I knew, very powerfully, that we weren't alone.

'There was somebody else there. I didn't see anything, I didn't hear anything, I just knew. It's very difficult to describe. When you fall in love, or when you see your child being born, it's such an overwhelming experience that words can only paint a very inadequate picture. You want to say, "Yes, it was like that, it was just much, much more than that." What happened in that church was totally real, perhaps the most real experience I've ever had.

'What was it like? Well, it was more than a vague feeling of wellbeing. This wasn't a *feeling* I was encountering; it was a person. And I knew immediately who it was, too, because I experienced what sort of a person he was, what his personality was. I knew it was God – and, more specifically, I knew it was Jesus. It wasn't an illusion: he was, if anything, more real than anything else in that building, including me, and – it's very hard to describe. There weren't any words, and there wasn't any specific message, except a feeling of reassurance. There was a sense of – well, vastness, hugeness. The person I was in the presence of was gigantic, but, strangely enough, the experience wasn't frightening. In fact, as I said, it was reassuring.

'What surprised me – well, the whole thing was surprising – was that the person I was meeting was rather different from the God I believed in up until then. I believed that God was good, but I couldn't get rid of the suspicion that he was cross with me much of the time, that he disapproved of me. This person wasn't like that. I knew I was loved – loved even more than I love my wife or my children. And I knew I was accepted for who I was. I guess I could say that, when I met him, God was much nicer than I expected him to be.

'The experience lasted for about a minute and faded fairly rapidly. I hadn't been drinking, I've never taken drugs, there's no history of mental illness in my family. If you were to ask me if I think there is a God, my answer would be I know there is.'

What's your reaction to this?

There are some possibilities to explain this 'experience':

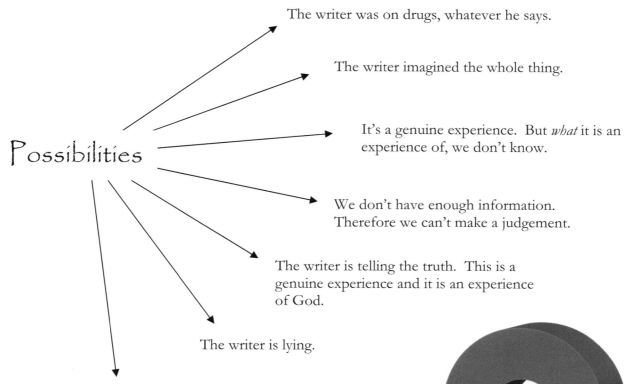

Possibilities

The writer was on drugs, whatever he says.

The writer imagined the whole thing.

It's a genuine experience. But *what* it is an experience of, we don't know.

We don't have enough information. Therefore we can't make a judgement.

The writer is telling the truth. This is a genuine experience and it is an experience of God.

The writer is lying.

The authors are lying by including this in the book. They made it up. (We're not and we didn't, but how do you know we're telling the truth? You've never met us. How do you know we're not liars?)

- Think about the problem or problems of each of these explanations.
- Which explanation do you think is most likely to be correct?

And a couple more questions:

- Suppose someone you knew and trusted said she'd had a similar experience. Would you be more likely to believe her than someone you hadn't met? Why?
- Just suppose John Williamson's experience happened to you. How might you react to it?

A number of experts in the philosophy of religion have collected together accounts from thousands of different people, who've had similar experiences. They might happen to an individual once or twice in a lifetime, and they don't always happen to religious people. This type of experience is sometimes called an **experience of the numinous** – or, more simply, **religious experience.**

John Williamson's account is a pretty 'clear' or unambiguous experience of the numinous. What's said to have been encountered isn't vague at all. Experiences of the numinous aren't necessarily felt as encounters with a person or a god: they can be much 'vaguer', less well defined. People have spoken of encounters with a feeling of vastness, or otherness, holiness – or a feeling of being overwhelmed. John's account says he knew he was encountering God, and more particularly, he was encountering Jesus Christ.

It could be said, 'How did he know it was Jesus? He'd never met him before, had he?!' This is a good point. However, we may know *about* things without having *experienced* them. Suppose you've never been in love. That doesn't (usually!) mean you have no idea of what it means. Even if we've never been in love ourselves, we've seen enough films or TV programmes to have a good idea of what it's like. So, when we fall in love, we're very unlikely to say, 'What is this strange yet powerful thing I'm feeling?'! We'd recognise immediately something we'd previously only known *about*.

Philosophers of religion often say this is the same with many experiences of the numinous. *If the account from John is genuine (and he says it is), then it would be correct for him to say he recognised the person he encountered. He knew who and what Jesus was said to be like, and he recognised him when he met him. Interesting, too, that he claims the Jesus he met was more loving than the mental picture he'd previously had of him.

(What do you think?)

As we have said, some experiences of the numinous aren't quite so clear or unambiguous. They're still powerful, but they're vaguer, less specific.

And they're not easy to put into words, either. Really intense human experiences aren't. It's not easy to describe things like falling in love, or what it feels like to see your baby being born. (Incidentally, have you ever wondered why we say 'falling' and 'in' love?)

One way people have tried to convey intense experiences to other people is through poetry.

There's a famous example in the poems of William Wordsworth (1770-1850). This in an extract from *Tintern Abbey*, or, to give it its full title, *Composed a Few Miles above Tintern Abbey, On Revisiting the Banks of the Wye During a Tour, July 13, 1798*. Wordsworth went back to Tintern Abbey, which he had often been to when he was younger, when he was 28. It's a stunningly beautiful area (the photo below is of the Wye valley). Wordsworth describes what we would call experiences of the numinous, which come to him when he's contemplating the beauty of the world. Here's the extract, with some notes to help explain it. Read it slowly, several times, and think about what he's saying.

For I have learned
To look on nature...
And I have felt
A presence that disturbs me with the joy
Of elevated thoughts; a sense sublime
Of something far more deeply interfused,
Whose dwelling is the light of setting suns,
And the round ocean and the living air,
And the blue sky, and in the mind of man;
A motion and a spirit, that impels
All thinking things, all objects of all thought,
And rolls through all things. Therefore am I still
A lover of the meadows and the woods,
And mountains; and of all that we behold
From this green earth; of all the mighty world
Of eye, and ear, – both what they half create,
And what perceive; well pleased to recognise
In nature and the language of the sense,
The anchor of my purest thoughts, the nurse,
The guide, the guardian of my heart, and soul
Of all my moral being.

There are lots of things to notice here:
- Wordsworth feels his thoughts are lifted up, elevated – and this is utterly joyful, but it also disturbs.
- The 'presence' is 'sublime': wonderful, beautiful, beyond words.
- The presence's dwelling is in nature: in sunsets, the ocean, the air, the sky – and in the human mind. It 'rolls through all things'.
- In nature and through his senses, he recognises 'the nurse, the guide, the guardian of my heart, and soul of all my moral being.' The presence is described in these last few lines through four images:
  - nurse
  - guide
  - guardian
  - soul

What does each image convey?

Wordsworth was a Christian and would have seen this presence as the presence of God. God is present in nature and within human beings. Philosophers of religion would say – much less beautifully than Wordsworth! – that this is a description of God's omnipresence (everywhere-ness). Some commentators might say it goes even further than that. Wordsworth's God is pantheist. That means he's not just everywhere, he *is* everything. Everything is God.

So, Wordsworth gives us a description of this more 'vague' or 'non specific' type of religious experience. It is much less concrete or specific than the account we've given by John Williamson. But it's real to the poet, and creates a yearning, a longing, within him. There's far more to the beauty of nature than meets the eye: there's someone beyond it, underneath it, and within it – though Wordsworth doesn't describe the Presence as Christ – or even as God.

(Maybe the use of the word 'vague' is a bad one. What do you think? Is Wordsworth's experience vague?)

The less specific type of experience of the numinous is said not to be confined to religious people. There are examples of agnostics having experiences like this. Religious people would probably see them as experiences of God. Agnostics might describe them as a sense of being overwhelmed by the beauty of the universe, or an intense feeling of oneness with everything that exists. ('Agnostic' comes from the Greek for 'I don't know'. Agnostics are people who don't know whether God exists or not. The word can also mean people who say it is *impossible* to know whether God exists or not.)

Some atheists would accept this type of experience of the numinous but would be very uncomfortable with accounts like John Williamson's. This is because they don't fit in with their world view. They have two options, then:
- to change their conclusions about God and change their minds, or:
- to dismiss the evidence and find other explanations for it.

For theists (people who believe in God, remember), experiences of the numinous are less of a problem. After all, if God exists, God is:
- omnipresent (everywhere), so it would be easy for him to reveal his presence if he wanted to;
- loving, so he might have a good reason to show his presence to individuals: to give them comfort, to help them realise he loves them, to get them to think about where their lives are going...

On the other hand, maybe theists are too credulous: too ready to believe stuff like this. Perhaps they'd be prone to exaggerate, or to read things into an experience that aren't really there.

(Do you think we're being fair to atheists – and to theists, come to that – here? It's important not to generalise. Not all atheists think the same thing. Not all theists agree with each other, either.)

Can God win?

Actually, there's a sense in which God can't win, one way or another, when it comes to religious experience.

Let's suppose God exists and that he wants to let people experience him. He gives them the experiences, to let them know he's real and that he loves them. But he can't push too hard, because he also wants people to have free will. This means that, when God gives people religious experiences, they have to be free to question it – or to reject it. Otherwise, they'd have no choice but to believe in him. And that would go against their free will and God doesn't want that.

Lots of people who have had religious experiences find them totally compelling – so powerful that their lives are changed.
- For some people who've had them, religious experiences are very strong evidence, even proof, that God exists.

- For others who've had them, they're *good* evidence, but not quite proof.
- And for others still who've had them, the experiences seem very dubious or questionable.

If God exists, it's understandable that he's going to want to hold back in religious experiences. He doesn't want to overwhelm people and he doesn't want to override their free will.

And he's also got the problem that, certainly in this country, he's dealing with people in a secular (non religious) society. People are often very cynical. We are bombarded by secular messages. Most of the media assumes religion is nonsense. TV programmes sneer at it, nasty jokes are made about it, and the media frequently implies that no-one with half a brain could possibly believe in God. Opinion poll evidence shows that people under 20 are far less likely to believe in God than people over 40.

It's very hard to insulate yourself from this, whether you're a religious person or not. And it does mean that people who have religious experiences are going to question them. Five hundred years ago, when almost everyone in this country believed in God and assumed Christianity was true, religious experiences would have been accepted much more easily. You almost wonder what God would have to do to convince people he was there, if experiences of the numinous won't convince them!

This is rather like a story in Mark's Gospel, where the Pharisees, who don't believe in Jesus and assume he's an imposter, ask him for a sign from heaven: for proof, in other words. But the evidence is already there for them to see; the problem is they don't want to. Jesus won't play their games. The problem is their prejudice: they've made up their minds and don't want to be confused by the evidence (see Mark 8.11-13).

1. Explain what is meant by a religious experience / experience of the numinous. You're limited to five statements!

2. What is meant by
a) pantheist,
b) an agnostic?

3. Think about the following statements.
- 'Religious experiences are strong evidence for the existence of God.'
- 'Religious experiences are just delusions.'
- 'Religious experiences are the strongest argument in favour of God's existence.'
What do you think of these views and why? (You might want to discuss this before you write your answer.)

Talking point:

If God exists...
Could he prove to people that he exists,
and at the same time
give them the freedom not to believe in him?

8
Revelation

Suppose you're in a pitch black room.

You stand by the doorway and don't move. There's actually someone else in the room, but he's wearing black from head to foot, his face is covered, and he's totally silent and still. You'd have no way of knowing there was someone else there.

But then he starts talking to you and you realise he's there. And the more you listen to him, the more you come to understand what he's like, what sort of a person he is.

Philosophers of religion say one type of argument in favour of God's existence is the **arguments from reason:** things we can work out for ourselves. So far, we've mainly been dealing with them.

But there are also **arguments from revelation:** God tells us things. So we know God is there because he shows us he is. 'Revelation' means 'uncovering' or 'bringing to light'. God, it is said, reveals himself to us.

Even if the arguments from reason don't really work – and many would say they don't – it's said *we can still say that God exists because he reveals himself to us.*

So far, then, we've been mainly covering arguments like this:

Whereas revelation is like this:

These chapters cover the following areas:
- **General revelation:** the idea that the creator can be known through what he creates. This is similar to saying we know about an artist through his art: what she paints, draws or sculpts tells us something about what sort of a person she is.
- **Revelation in history:** there were specific times in the past when God acted, usually through human beings. These occasions in the past are especially important to religious people today. God revealed himself to, or through, particular human beings. Sometimes, one revelation in history is considered to be more important than any other: it's the supreme revelation. For Muslims, the supreme revelation was when God gave the Koran to the Prophet Muhammad. For Christians, the supreme revelation happened between about 4 BC and 30 AD, in the life, death and resurrection of Jesus Christ.
- What we can call **revelation in religion**: God can be known and experienced through the teaching and practices of religion. We're going to cover religious teachers and religious example under this heading, as well as worship and prayer.

We'll also look at visions, dreams and enlightenment.
- And we'll consider the problems with the idea of revelation:
    - problems caused for religious people, and
    - whether supposed 'revelation' is trustworthy anyway.

General revelation

The idea here is that **you can tell God exists by looking at the universe itself.** There are things about the universe which show us that someone created it, and perhaps some of the characteristics of the person who created it.

It has to be said that this idea doesn't convince everybody. However, people who believe in general revelation would say that it shows *everyone* – or everyone who's prepared to think about it – that there is a God. This sort of revelation, it is said, can only go so far. It can show us that God exists, and maybe some of his characteristics. But it can't show us things like the Trinity, or that God became man as Jesus Christ. Those things have to be revealed by God in other ways; we can't work them out through looking at the universe.

So, then, the idea is: **by looking at the universe, you can tell there's a God and some things about what he's like.**

Actually, many of the arguments from reason can be classified as 'general revelation'. We've already covered the cosmological argument and the argument from design. They could be seen as arguments from reason, as we've called them before. Or it could be said they're actually part of general revelation. It's as though these clues to God's existence don't just happen to be there. Rather, God *deliberately* writes these clues into the creation. It's as though he said, 'I'm going to create the universe, but I'm also going to put into it some clues that I'm here. If people use the minds I've given them, they'll work out for themselves that I exist.'

What else?

Nature's beautiful. We've all had the experience of being wowed by a sunset or a stunning view or something like that. I'm not a good enough writer to put this sort of thing into words, so maybe it'd be best if you think of your own experiences. When was the last time you were wowed by nature? What about other times? How did you feel?

Some people would argue that the beauty of nature, or the goodness of human beings, tells us something about God. We have a conscience and a sense of the difference between good and evil. It is said this points to someone who really knows what good and evil are, and who passes this awareness on to us. (We'll explore this idea later on.)

The fact that the universe exists at all is said to reveal God's omnipotence: he has the power to create it. And the fact that we exist shows God's wisdom and love: he made the universe so that intelligent beings like us could emerge. The physical conditions of the solar system have to be just right to support life on earth. And they are. So that shows us God loves us.

(Convinced? How strong do these arguments seem to you?)

We've tried to look at some arguments like this by the following (made up) discussion between two students, Sam and Alex. (You'll notice 'Sam' and 'Alex' can be both boys' and girls' names!) We come in in the middle of their conversation.

SAM: Look, Alex, it's pretty simple. It's obvious God exists. There was an amazing sunset last night. It was so good, I went outside to watch it and had to miss the end of *Eastenders*. The whole sky went peach colour, then pink, then purple. Just amazing. Best show on earth. Didn't you see it?

ALEX: Sure. It was great. What are you getting at?

SAM: Well, if there wasn't a God, things like sunsets would be pretty dull, wouldn't they? If the universe is just random, why aren't sunsets really boring?

ALEX: What, just grey and then black, you mean?

SAM: Yeah. But there's all this colour. It's beautiful. It's stunning. God must have put it there so we can enjoy it. He wants us to have experiences of beauty. And it's got to mean that he loves beauty too, because he puts it everywhere. He's a brilliant artist. We could never paint as well as he can!

ALEX: It doesn't work, Sam. OK, the sunset's beautiful. I agree with you. But that's only because *you* think it's beautiful, or I think it is. It's just a natural thing. The sky seems to change colour because of the angle the sun's rays are hitting it or something – I don't understand the science. But it only looks nice because *we* like it. It isn't really beautiful. The sunset doesn't think, 'Oh look at me, aren't I lovely?' And there are probably lots of people who think it's boring.

SAM: Yeah, but that's only because they're being silly.

ALEX: OK, maybe, but an earthworm or a cat isn't going to be wowed by it, are they? You can't say that because we think things are beautiful, then there must be a Mr Super Beautiful who works it all out. It's all just random. We only think things are beautiful because that's how they appear to us. It's all –

what's the word? – subjective. It's like some people like Shakespeare but lots of people think he's boring. Ideas like 'that's pretty' or 'that's beautiful' only exist in our heads. Nothing's really beautiful or ugly. It's only how things appear to us.

SAM: But so many things in the world are absolutely beautiful. Doesn't that show God must be good – that he must be generous to give us so many things to enjoy?

ALEX: Well, if you're going to say that, you might as well say God's evil.

SAM: Pardon?

ALEX: Come on, Sam, think about it. What about wasps? What about sharks? They're not beautiful, are they? My Mum says there was some nature programme on the other night. You know David Attenborough? Well, he was saying that he met a little boy in Africa who had a worm burrowing through his eyeball. That was how it fed.* If you're going to say beauty shows that God loves beauty, then what about disgusting things like that? You could just as well argue that it shows God's evil.

SAM: Yeah. That's a problem. I don't know the answer to it and I wish I did. I just think there's too much goodness around for it not to have

* This example is genuine. David Attenborough says he doesn't believe in God because a benevolent God would never create things like this.

47

come from somewhere. I think an evil God just wouldn't create beauty. The world would be really horrible – you know, all food would taste like it was rotten, everything would stink, we'd always be in pain and people would all be evil too. But if the Bible's right, people are made in the image of God. So, if someone's really good, or kind, or loving, he or she's going to show us God's like that too.

ALEX: Yes, but there are also people like Hitler.

SAM: But someone like him decided to make evil decisions. He didn't have to. He could have chosen goodness. What about Martin Luther King or someone like that? He's got to be one of the greatest human beings. And everything he did, he said, was inspired by the idea of God. He believed God wanted him to do those things. If we're made in the image of God, then we're going to show what God's like much more than the nasty things in nature. Martin Luther King's a really good example of someone who's on the way to showing what God's like.

ALEX: Well, he was a great person, but he got shot, didn't he? There may be great human beings like him, but there are also bad human beings like the man who shot him. You can't just pick one example out like that. What you're doing is ignoring all the bad bits in the world, the bits that don't fit in with your argument.

SAM: But what about when you look up at the stars at night? Isn't it amazing? The universe's vastness, and here we are, part of it, on our little planet. We're part of that vast system God created and he really loves us very much.

ALEX: But if I look up at the stars, it just convinces me we're alone. The universe is cold, and it's mostly empty. We're tiny and we don't mean very much. It doesn't affect the universe whether we live or die. It'll still be there. If God created the universe for us, wouldn't he have made it, well, smaller?

What do you think?

Summing up, then:
- General revelation means that we can work things out about the creator by looking at what he creates.
- General revelation can be taken to include some of the classic arguments for God's existence, like the cosmological argument and the argument from design.
- It has its limits. It can't convey things like the role of Jesus or the existence of the Trinity.
- Lots of people find it unconvincing. For atheists, it can sound very much like wishful thinking. Some Protestant theologians think human minds are so messed up by sin that people just can't work out for themselves that God exists. He has to tell us specifically, and he does so through the Bible.

1. a) What does 'revelation' mean?
   b) What is meant by 'general revelation'?
   c) Give some examples of general revelation.

2. 'General revelation is totally unconvincing.' What do you think?

Talking points:

If God exists, then he's going to tell people he does.

If God exists, then general revelation must be true.

9
Revelation in Jesus and in the Bible

You might be able to work out that there is a being called Simon Danes. There is evidence for this. The book you're holding must have been written by someone, and the cover says there are three authors. One of them is Simon Danes.

The thing is, you've never met me. You *might* be able to work some things out about me from the book, which seems to suggest I'm interested in religion and can read and write. This presumably means that I'm a human being, rather than, say, a wombat.

(But even those things might not be true. Simon Danes could be a false name for Zeke Zzz, or might be completely fictitious because Christopher Danes and Seeta Lakhani thought it would be funny to invent an imaginary character.)

But if I do exist, and I am not a wombat, and I am interested in religion, you still don't get much of an idea of me as a person. (Someone might say at this point, 'But his book shows he's really boring.') I might be six foot eight tall, have played cricket for my county, be 84 years old, and like *Captain Scarlet*. I might be married and have children, or I might be single. You just don't know.

Unless you meet me and I tell you.

We could argue, then, that we know God exists because of general revelation. That tells us (if the arguments work!) that there is a God, but not much more about him.

We're going to need something much more specific if we're going to learn about what God's like. In other words: **he's going to have to tell us.**

There are various ways God could do this. He *could* communicate directly with each individual, as though he were phoning them up. But he couldn't do that if he wanted them to have free will, because they wouldn't be free to choose not to believe in him.

He could communicate through 'appearing' in some way to some individuals and asking them to pass his message on.

Christianity teaches that God did indeed communicate with individuals and they passed on his message. (Or at least what they thought was his message; perhaps they got it wrong at times.) However, there was a better way to communicate with people about himself.

Right: Jesus healing the sick. Stained glass window, St Thomas' Church, Winchelsea, Sussex.

Statues

Imagine a statue of a person. It's the size of the entire earth. You're standing at its base (by the toes!). How easy would it be to work out what it was a statue of? How much of the statue would you be able to see, to take in?

Now imagine an exact copy of the same statue but scaled down to be six foot tall.

Which statue would you be able to see and understand properly?

Christianity teaches that God did not just communicate with human beings in the past. God *became* a human being: the human being called Jesus of Nazareth (c.4 BC – 30 AD).

We can't understand what God is like in himself. He is beyond our understanding. But if he scales himself down, we can understand him. Christianity teaches that Jesus is God. He also acts as an image of God, a reflection, if you like. By looking at Jesus, you're looking at God. The sort of person Jesus was is the sort of person God is. God's personality is the same as the personality of Jesus.

(This is what the statue analogy means. It comes from an early Christian

writer called Origen (c.185-254).)

There's more detail on Christian beliefs about Jesus in chapter 3. It is worth going back and reading that chapter again.

Can we trust the evidence?

There are four complete books which detail the life and teaching of Jesus. They're the four Gospels (which means 'good news') and they can be found in the New Testament in the Bible. They're called by the names of their authors – or, at least, the people who the very early Christians thought were their authors: Matthew, Mark, Luke and John. To a large extent, they cover the same ground and tell the same story. However, each has a different emphasis and each includes material which isn't found in the other Gospels.

But how do we know they're not all made up?

This is a good question and it's not an easy one to answer. At least, it's not an easy question to answer briefly.

If you study history, you'll know that history's full of questions. Suppose we ask, 'What caused the Second World War?' The best answers are going to come from historians, from the experts. You can find out what the experts think by reading their books or articles, by searching the Internet, or by watching TV programmes in which they present their views. (And history teachers in schools know their stuff, too, so it's worth listening to them!)

You may also discover that they don't all give the same answers. Some historians would say the main cause of the Second World War was Hitler's desire to expand Germany's 'living space' into other parts of Europe. Others would say it was actually all the Allies' fault: if we hadn't tried to ruin Germany after the First World War, Hitler would not have come to power.

Experts disagree, then. It can be very confusing for us mere mortals, who want clear answers – but life's not generally as simple as that.

There are also experts in Biblical studies. Biblical studies is partly about history, partly about the careful study of documents. The major universities have departments where the Bible continues to be examined by experts, some of them Christians, some of them not. Thus there are informed opinions about the Bible; we don't have to rely on uninformed opinion.

OK. The experts almost all agree:

- The Gospels can be dated pretty accurately:
  - Mark was the first Gospel (or the first one that's survived, anyway). His book was written around 64 AD.
  - His Gospel was used as a major source – but not the only source – by Matthew and Luke. They both wrote between about 70 and 80 AD.
  - John was the last of the Gospels to be written, in about 90 AD.
- Jesus existed. (Actually, all serious scholars accept this.) He was crucified around 30 AD. We can't be certain of the precise year. There's a bit more than 30 years before Mark was writing. 30 years gives plenty of time for things to be

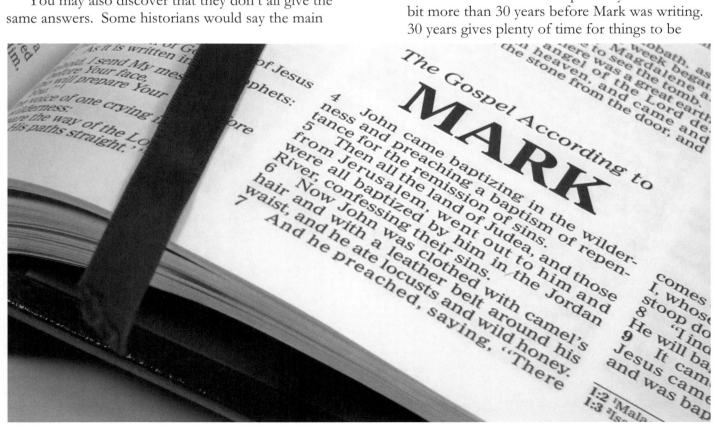

invented about Jesus (though this is making a big assumption: that the early Christians *wanted* to invent things). However, it also means that people who knew Jesus personally were still alive when Mark was writing. There's good evidence that Mark had access to Peter, Jesus' chief disciple – but the evidence isn't conclusive. There would still have been eyewitnesses around when Matthew and Luke were writing, even if they were getting on a bit. Some might have survived into John's time too.

- The early Christians did not always get it right when they said the authors were Matthew, Mark, Luke and John. Very briefly:

  - Luke, in fact, probably did write his Gospel. Luke travelled with Paul, the early Christian missionary, who wrote many of the letters we now have in the New Testament. Luke was not a disciple of Jesus but he did know people who were, including Peter.

  - Mark may well have written his Gospel. Mark, too, was a companion of Paul and he was also called John Mark. Again, he was not an eyewitness of Jesus but he knew people who were.

  - It is very unlikely that John, the disciple of Jesus, wrote John's Gospel. We do not know who the author really was.

  - Matthew, the disciple of Jesus, did not write Matthew's Gospel. Again, who the author really was is unknown.

- The Gospel writers used various written and oral sources when they were writing. Oral sources are not necessarily unreliable. We have to remember that people in those days were much better than we are at learning things off by heart. They had to be, because this was the cheapest way of recording information; paper was actually horribly expensive.

(There are about a thousand 'ifs' and 'buts' left out of this! We just haven't the space to cover everything, though you might want to read up more on these topics. Wikipedia is a good place to look.)

Almost all the experts would agree with the points above (though some would passionately disagree!). However, if you asked them the question, 'Do the Gospels give us an accurate picture of Jesus?' you'd get very different answers:

- Many would say yes, they do. While some of the material may not go back to Jesus himself, the overall picture of Jesus is accurate. Even where there are historical errors, they still tell us the sort of thing Jesus did or said. (Let's take a parallel situation. Suppose I found a source that claimed Martin Luther King said, 'The black man and the white man are not born enemies. They are born brothers.' Actually, this isn't something he said – but it is the *sort of thing* he said.)

- Many experts would say the Gospels contain genuine incidents from Jesus' life, and things he genuinely said. However, much of the material is inaccurate.

- Some scholars, though perhaps not so many now, would see the Gospels as basically unhistorical. There was a Jesus of Nazareth, a Jew who was crucified, but everything else about him has been made up by the early Christians. These Christians were – huge assumption coming up here! – not interested in history, and were quite happy to invent stories to get their message across.

If the experts disagree, how does that help us?

A couple of points here. One is that this is a long and complex debate and we just haven't got the space to cover everything. The more we know, the easier it is to come to a conclusion – and it is worth reading up on these topics.

The second point is that scholars and experts, like the rest of us, can sometimes let their own views influence what they say. It's very hard to be unbiased. So, a Christian expert is perhaps more likely to say the Gospels are accurate than is a non-Christian expert.

For what it's worth, my own view is that the Gospels are not totally accurate in everything they say. I don't think it's always possible to be certain that this or that incident definitely happened. Or that we can always be certain that every word we're reading was genuinely said by Jesus. Some things, like the crucifixion, are certainly historical. However, I do think that the overall picture of Jesus in the Gospels is trustworthy. If you read them as a whole, rather than just read bits of them, it seems to me that the personality of Jesus comes across; we get a genuine understanding of what he was like. Eyewitnesses *were* still around when the Gospels were being written – or at least when the first three Gospels were written. Saying the early Christians didn't care about history is, I think, ridiculous. It's an assumption, and it's made by some writers because they need it to make their theories work.

(But then, I could be wrong!)

The authority of the Bible

The writers of the Gospels did not know they were writing part of the Bible. It was only later that their separate books came to be incorporated into the Bible itself.

Christianity claims that the supreme revelation of God is in Jesus Christ. As a result, the Gospels are the most important part of the Bible, because they record Jesus' life and teaching.

Obviously, the Bible's important for Christians. It's not just read at home; it's read as part of worship, in church. Most Christians are Roman Catholic. In the Roman Catholic Church, and in the Anglican Church (which includes the Church of England, the Church of Ireland and the Church of Wales), readings from the Bible form a substantial part of the opening of their main service. This service has various names, but the Eucharist is one that would be accepted by both Churches. When the reading from the Bible is over, the reader usually says, 'This is the word of the Lord.'

The word of the Lord. In some sense, then, Christians believe that the words in the Bible are the message of God himself. God reveals himself through the Bible, especially through the Gospels.

Does this mean that Christians believe every word in the Bible to be the word of God? Every single paragraph is a vital part of God's revelation to human beings?

Some do believe this. They would argue that every single thing in the Bible is literally true, that it really happened. The Bible is infallible: it cannot err. It may have been written by human beings, but God the Holy Spirit prevented the writers from making even the smallest human error. Christians who hold this view are called **fundamentalists.** We touch on fundamentalist views in this book in the chapters on the creation stories and science, and on miracles.

Most Christians are not fundamentalists because there are too many difficulties with the fundamentalist viewpoint. There are scientific problems with it, and there are historical problems too. Most Christians would agree with these sorts of ideas:

- God genuinely reveals himself in and through the Bible.

- But this revelation isn't uniform. Some parts of the Bible tell us more about God than others do. For example, there are some fairly bloodcurdling passages in the Old Testament, where God tells the Israelites to exterminate their enemies, including the children, and that anyone who disobeys this instruction must be executed. Passages like this are very hard to fit in with Jesus' teaching of a God of love and compassion! They tell us more about the people of the time than they do about God. When we read the Bible, we have to think about Jesus' commands to love God and to love our neighbours as ourselves (Mark 12.28-31). We have to interpret what we read so that it fits in with what Jesus said. If it doesn't fit in, it may be interesting as part of the record of people's ideas about God, but it has no authority for us. We don't have to do what it says.

- The New Testament is more important than the Old Testament. The Gospels are the most important part of the New Testament.
- The experts are worth listening to. Scholarship can help us to understand the Bible. At the end of the day, the point of such scholarship is to help people to understand God's revelation.

Christians who think in these ways may be called **conservative.** This doesn't have anything to do with politics! It means they want to conserve, to keep hold of, the important truths of the Bible.

A minority of Christians would go further than conservatives and argue that the Bible is historically of very little value. This sort of view is called **liberalism.** Some liberals would go as far to say that Jesus was not God, that he did not rise from the dead, and that we know very little about him because the early Christians made it all up. (Some thinkers, though not all, would argue that this sort of position has gone so far that it's stopped being Christianity. It raises a question: how much of a faith can you stop believing in, and still be a member of that faith?

What do you think?)

Other liberals are actually rather closer to conservatives in their thinking. It's just that they're prepared to allow for more historical errors in the Bible than most conservatives are.

To sum up this section, then:

- Christianity says that, in some sense, God reveals himself through the Bible.
- They disagree on how much he does this in every section of the Bible.
- **Fundamentalists** believe that every word in the Bible is absolutely true.
- **Conservatives** do not go this far. They accept some of the Bible may tell us more about the people of the time than they do about God. There may be factual mistakes in the Bible. But the New Testament and the Gospels are essentially trustworthy.
- Some liberals would agree with this last point, though they'd say there's actually quite a lot more unreliable material than that. Other liberals would go further still and say the Bible is of very little historical value.

How much you pick up of a transmission is going to depend on the quality of your receiver. It could be said that the quality of the transmission of God's revelation was always good. The problem was with the quality of the receiver. Some of the earliest transmissions didn't get received properly. The reception could be poor because people couldn't always step out of their cultures. If they lived in brutal times, they had set views and these stopped the message being received properly.

What is the Bible?

We've said that Christianity teaches that God reveals himself in the Bible – but it's important to know what the Bible is.

The Bible is not one book but a collection of many different books.

True, they have been collected together and published as one long volume, but there are over 60 individual books. (Even the exact number varies, as we shall see.) They were written by more than a hundred different writers, over a period of around a thousand years.

The Bible consists of the Jewish scriptures, which Christians call the Old Testament, and the later, Christian scriptures: the New Testament.

The Old Testament

The books of the Old Testament were written in Hebrew between about 900 and 160 BC. (A few short sections are in Aramaic.)

After that date, a Greek translation of the Old Testament was made, which is called the *Septuagint*.

There were also some other Jewish books, written in Greek, and written later than the Hebrew books. These Greek texts were added into the Septuagint.

So, there are two versions of the Old Testament:

* the Hebrew version, which the original;
* the Septuagint.

When Christianity began, the Christians looked through the Old Testament for passages which they believed predicted things about Jesus. They believed that the history of God's love to human beings did *not* begin with Jesus; it had been going on long before he was born. So, they kept the record of God's earlier work as recorded in the Old Testament.

Most of the early Christians spoke Greek, so they used the Septuagint. Their Old Testament was, then, a Greek translation of the Hebrew Bible plus the extra books.

The Jews later decided (and this was after Jesus' time) that only the Hebrew books were part of the Bible. They stopped using the Septuagint.

The Roman Catholic Church, which actually makes up the majority of Christians today, keeps to the earliest Christian practice. It has all the books of the Septuagint included in its Old Testament.

Most other Christians keep to the Jewish practice. Their Old Testament is shorter than the Roman Catholic Old Testament. This is because it consists of just the Hebrew books. (The extra Greek books are sometimes added to their Bibles as an appendix to the Old Testament. This appendix is called the *Apocrypha*.)

The New Testament

The New Testament consists of:

* the four Gospels;
* the Acts of the Apostles, a book by Luke about the work of the early Church and its leaders;
* letters from early Christian leaders, especially Paul;
* the Book of Revelation (also called the Apocalypse), a series of visions which a man called John claimed to have been given by God.

The Old Testament is important for Christians, but the New Testament is even more important. This is because it either *tells Jesus' story* or *applies his teaching to Christian life*.

The New Testament was finished by AD 100. Almost all the books were written when there were still people alive who knew Jesus personally.

---

1. Here are some assumptions that people often make:
* 'The Gospels were not written within living memory of Jesus.'
* 'Jesus did not exist.'
* 'The Gospels were written by eyewitnesses of Jesus.'
* 'Oral sources are always unreliable.'

Explain why these assumptions are incorrect.

(Note: we don't have to believe in Christianity to say these assumptions are wrong. Any good historian would argue against these assumptions, regardless of whether he or she was a Christian or not.)

2. 'The Gospels give us an accurate picture of what Jesus was actually like.'

Why might someone argue:
a) in favour of this?
b) against this?

In your answer, you need to include the following key words: **fundamentalists, conservatives, liberalism.**

Talking points

'You're only going to believe in revelation if you believe in God in the first place. If you're an atheist, so called revelation isn't going to convince you.'

'If God exists, then the best way to reveal himself to us would be to become a human being.'

'If Jesus was God, God would want to make sure the records about Jesus were accurate. The Gospels have got to be trustworthy.'

'Religion's claims have to be able to stand up to hard questions and analysis. If they can't, the religion's worthless.'

10

Can people encounter God through practising a faith? (1)

Religious people would say the answer is yes.

This is not going to convince atheists. They would argue that any such encounters would be imaginary. Religious people think there is a God, and then pretend to themselves that they are in touch with him by worshipping him. It's a circular argument. They assume God exists, and because they assume this, they assume they are meeting him by worshipping him. And because they assume they are meeting him by worshipping him, they assume God exists.

The reply of a theist – someone who believes in God – might go like this.

Atheists, the theist might say, are trying to make conclusions about something they have no experience of. They just don't get it, and they can't be expected to. If you've never been in love, say, you can't write off the experience of being in love. You just don't know enough about it; you don't know what it's like. It's something you can only appreciate properly if you've been in that state yourself. So you can't make conclusions about worship if you've never actually done it. An atheist might attend a service or an occasion of religious worship. But they're not actually worshipping because you can't worship unless you believe in God. (Or, perhaps, unless you accept that there might be a God.) After all, you can't make a phone call if you don't think there's anyone there to answer your call.

Many people would say you do encounter God by worshipping him, and that worship is essential to faith. It's not that God is a big headed megalomaniac who demands that people tell him how wonderful he is the whole time. It's more that human beings will always respond to things that they find beautiful or amazing. You want to carry on looking at a sunset. You want to talk about a new piece of music that's impressed you – and you'd talk to the singer if you could. 'We love, because he loved us first,' says the first letter of John in the New Testament (1 John 4.19).

Almost all the religions teach that prayer and worship are essential parts of faith. Going to church, to the mosque, synagogue or temple regularly are said to build up a person's faith and strengthen the relationship with God. It's a bit like a friendship: the more time you spend with a friend, the better you get to know them. And if you never speak to a friend – if you never meet, phone, text, email or whatever – the friendship's in real danger of getting

weaker or dying off altogether (at least, it is on your side).

The reason going to church regularly – or mosque, synagogue or temple – is said to matter is that it reminds people what's important. It helps them to re-centre themselves, to refocus on what really matters. Couples will still say 'I love you' to each other, even if they've been together for many years. Using another analogy, if you don't recharge your mobile regularly, the batteries run down. (And then you might eventually decide you can get rid of your mobile altogether!)

So, what might religious people *feel* when they worship? Are they going to get what we've called a religious experience? Does worship give you some sort of a 'holy buzz'?

There are plenty of religious people who say it does. This might be in a spectacular way. Many Christians, particularly from the Protestant communities, might say they feel filled with the Holy Spirit when they worship. Worship lifts you up, makes you happy, feel fully alive. There are reports of miracles or speaking in tongues from Churches of almost all denominations.

Or it could be in a much more quiet way. Less a spectacular firework display, more a silence and stillness. (There's a story in the Jewish Bible about this. When the prophet Elijah experienced God, he saw a hurricane, an earthquake and then a fire. But God wasn't in any of those; he was in the silence. (1 Kings 19.9-15))

Having said all this, it's probably a big mistake to expect to get 'feelings' out of worship, to expect it to be wonderful and powerful. Is emotion necessary for worship? Does it matter if it's not there?

To explore this point, here's an extract from *The Screwtape Letters* by C. S. Lewis. Screwtape, an old and experienced devil, writes regularly to his blundering nephew Wormwood, who's been allocated a human 'patient'. Wormwood's job is to guide his patient into hell. (The idea in the book is that, just as every human has a guardian angel, they also have their very own devil who's there to try to ruin them.) Screwtape's letters advise Wormwood how to twist each development in his patient's life, so that the Devil ('Our Father below') can eventually claim his soul.

Here's the letter Screwtape writes when – well, see for yourself. We've explained some of the more complex vocabulary.

My dear Wormwood,

I note with grave displeasure that your patient has become a Christian. Do not indulge the hope that you will escape the usual penalties; indeed, in your better moments, I trust you would hardly even wish to do so. In the meantime we must make the best of the situation. There is no need to despair; hundreds of these adult converts have been reclaimed after a brief sojourn in the Enemy's camp and are now with us. All the *habits* of the patient, both mental and bodily, are still in our favour.

One of our great allies at present is the Church itself. Do not misunderstand me. I do not mean the Church as we see her spread out through all time and space and rooted in eternity, terrible as an army with banners. That, I confess, is a spectacle which makes even our boldest tempters uneasy. But fortunately it is quite invisible to these humans. All your patient sees is the half-finished, sham Gothic structure on the new building estate. When he goes inside, he sees the local grocer with rather an oily expression on his face bustling up to offer him one shiny little book containing a liturgy which neither of them understands, and one shabby little book containing corrupt texts of a number of religious lyrics, mostly bad, and in very small print. When he gets to his pew and looks round him he sees just that selection of his neighbours whom he has hitherto avoided. You want to lean pretty heavily on those neighbours. Make his mind flit to and fro between an expression like 'the body of Christ' and the actual faces in the next pew. It matters very little, of course, what kind of people that next pew really contains. You may know one of them to be a great warrior on the Enemy's side. No matter. Your patient, thanks to Our Father below, is a fool. Provided that any of those neighbours sing out of tune, or have boots that squeak, or double chins, or odd clothes, the patient will quite easily believe that their religion must therefore be somehow ridiculous. At his present stage, you see, he has an idea of 'Christians' in his mind which he supposes to be spiritual but which, in fact, is largely pictorial. His mind is full of togas and sandals and armour and bare legs and the mere fact that the other people in church wear modern clothes is a real – though of course an unconscious – difficulty to him. Never let it come to the surface; never let him ask what he expected them to look like. Keep everything hazy in his mind now, and you will have all eternity wherein to amuse yourself by producing in him the peculiar kind of clarity which Hell affords.

Work hard, then, on the disappointment or anticlimax which is certainly coming to the patient during his first few weeks as a churchman. The Enemy allows this disappointment to occur on the threshold of every human endeavour. It occurs when the boy who has been enchanted in the nursery by *Stories from the Odyssey* buckles down to really learning Greek. It occurs when lovers have got married and begin the real task of learning to live together. In every department of life it marks the transition from dreaming aspiration to laborious doing. The Enemy takes this risk because He has a curious fantasy of making all these disgusting little human vermin into what He calls His 'free' lovers and servants – 'sons' is the word He uses, with His inveterate love of degrading the whole spiritual world by unnatural liaisons with the two-legged animals. Desiring their freedom, He therefore refuses to carry them, by their mere affections and habits, to any of the goals which He sets before them: He leaves them to 'do it on their own'. And there lies our opportunity. But also, remember, there lies our danger. If once they get through this initial dryness successfully, they become much less dependent on emotion and therefore much harder to tempt.

I have been writing hitherto on the assumption that the people in the next pew afford no *rational* ground for disappointment. Of course if they do – if the patient knows that the woman with the absurd hat is a fanatical bridge-player or the man with squeaky boots a miser and an extortioner – then your task is so much the easier. All you then have to do is to keep out of his mind the question 'If I, being what I am, can consider that I am in some sense a Christian, why should the different vices of those people in the next pew prove that their religion is mere hypocrisy and convention?' You may ask whether it is possible to keep such an obvious thought from occurring even to a human mind. It is, Wormwood, it is! Handle him properly and it simply won't come into his head. He has not been anything like long enough with the Enemy to have any real humility yet. What he says, even on his knees, about his own sinfulness is all parrot talk. At bottom, he still believes he has run up a very favourable credit-balance in the Enemy's ledger by allowing himself to be converted, and thinks that he is showing great humility and condescension in going to church with these 'smug', commonplace neighbours at all. Keep him in that state of mind as long as you can.

Your affectionate uncle
SCREWTAPE

sojourn: stay

liturgy: here, the words of a service

the body of Christ: an expression used in the New Testament for the Church, the people of God

aspiration: hope

1. Why might religious people say that worship is important?

2. 'People might say they encounter God when they worship him. They don't. It's all imagination.' Do you agree? Explain your answer. You also need to explain why someone else might disagree with you, and what you think of their views.

Talking point: 'If you encounter God when you worship him, you'd have to *feel* that you've encountered him, too.' What do you think?

Further reading:

The whole of *The Screwtape Letters* is very funny and well worth reading. Whether you're religious or not, it's full of some very perceptive insights into what human beings are like. (And most people find they recognise a lot of themselves in what Screwtape says about humans!)

11
Can people encounter God through practising a faith? (2)

If God exists, then he can be encountered through worship. This is the claim of religions.

A major aspect of worship is prayer. We need to look at this more closely.

Prayer

Why bother?

If God exists, then God is omniscient: he knows everything. So why bother praying at all?

One answer is that prayer doesn't help God. It helps the people who are doing the praying.

Christians believe that Jesus himself was a human being. Even Jesus, who was closer to God than anyone who's ever lived, prayed (see, for example, Mark 6.45-46). If he needed to pray, Christians would say other human beings need to pray too.

We could say that prayer and other forms of worship *keep alive someone's relationship with God*. We've already said that if you've got a good friend, but never talk to them or contact them, the friendship on your side will wither and die. In the same way, people need to keep their relationship with God polished up.

Praying can be said to get things in life into perspective. Prayer reminds people what really matters. Perhaps praying at the beginning of the day helps people to think less about themselves, and more about other people.

Praying doesn't work

Dear God: please send the following immediately, or I won't believe in you any more: a DVD player, good exam results, and a house by the seaside. And also make me very popular, funny and rich. Yours sincerely...

Lots of people think that praying is rather like writing to Father Christmas. You submit your requests and then sit back until they arrive. If they don't turn up, then that shows there is no God.

A reply to this is that it is too narrow a view. Tiny children may pray like that but adults need a deeper understanding.

Small children are, though, taught to say sorry, please and thank you. This isn't a bad description of what praying could be. The only bit that's missing is praise. An acronym (memory jogger) which takes up this idea is *ACTS:*

A   Adoration (praise)

C   Confession (sorry – apologizing to God for what someone's done wrong)

T   Thanksgiving (thank you)

S   Supplication (please – praying *for* things or people)

When people think 'praying doesn't work', they're only thinking of one type of prayer: supplication. Adoration, confession and thanksgiving don't require an 'answer' to the same extent. They're ends in

disadvantaged people in their community and they hadn't got a penny. Their own community couldn't raise enough on its own. A week later, someone contacted them to offer a regular payment every month. They saw that as answered prayer.

Another example is of a church praying for someone in their community who had cancer, and who was dying. There was no miracle. The cancer took its course. Yet the man faced death bravely and quietly: he accepted what was happening, and died in peace. This was seen as prayer being answered, but being answered in an unexpected way.

themselves. There might be an answer to these sorts of prayers, though. It could be said that confession can bring the experience of feeling forgiven: you no longer need to feel guilty about the past and the slate's wiped clean. (There may, though, be some 'follow up' to be done. 'I'm sorry I was horrible to so-and-so' may bring the answer, perhaps in the form of a feeling, 'You need to apologise and make it up to them.' And the even less comfortable: 'You need to try hard not to do that again.')

Perhaps the 'thank you' has an answer too. Counting your blessings helps people be more content with what they have. 'You life is not the same as the number of things you own,' Jesus said (Luke 12.15). We live in a society which proclaims the message that the more stuff you've got, the happier you'll be. We may know it's nonsense, but it's hard not to live as though it's true. And perhaps it helps people move their attention from 'I'm really fed up because I haven't got...' to 'I've got what I need; what do other people need and can I help?'

This isn't always the case. There are sometimes genuine needs in our own lives and in other people's. And religious people will pray about them.

Does God answer prayers like these?

If he does, it's not in the form of a direct message or direct words. People have certainly reported that they've prayed for x, and then it's happened. Some friends of mine – they're from a different religious background to me – were in the situation where their church needed money. They were helping some very

Professor Richard Swinburne, who's a philosopher of religion at Oxford University, suggested God will help, but on the mental rather than the physical level. Rather like the example above, he will give people the strength to endure their suffering. Someone I know was facing enormous problems in her own life: she was being very badly bullied at work and it had been going on for a long time. It had got so bad that it was an enormous difficulty to drag herself into work every morning because she knew when she got there that the bullying would start straight away.

So she prayed for courage.

It didn't turn her into Superwoman. She wasn't able to say, 'I am superb! Now I shall snap my fingers in the faces of my tormentors!' But she believed that God did help her through that difficult period in her life. Putting it into words, she said it was as though the answer to her prayer was, 'I will help you with this, but I'm afraid it's not going to be easy. You're going to have to do a lot of the work on your own. But I'm there to support you.'

And there are times when people can be effectively saying: 'Here's a problem, God. Deal with it!' If I pray for someone at school who's lonely and who nobody likes very much, the answer may well be, 'Well, what are you going to do about it?'

Supplication can become silly. If I'm ill and refuse to go to the doctor because I expect God to perform a miracle, that doesn't show my great faith. It shows I'm an idiot.

With much of this, an atheist could say, 'But it was just a coincidence' or 'If you pray for courage and you feel courageous, it just shows you accessed something within you. It's got nothing to do with God.'

Not easy to answer.

Some might say that God can't win. If he does answer prayers, people are just going to say it's a coincidence. If he doesn't appear to answer them, people will say he's not there.

And why didn't God hear the prayer of the Jews in the gas chambers of the Third Reich? Why doesn't he answer the prayers of parents whose children are dying of diseases that God created?

The answer of most religious people would probably be: I don't know.

(This area is part of 'the problem of evil', which is examined later.)

Jesus' teaching on prayer

To round off this section, here are some things Jesus taught about prayer. As we said, the popular idea of prayer is about asking for things and expecting to get them. It's interesting to consider what Jesus was teaching, which is rather different.

When you stand and pray, forgive anything you may have against anyone, so that your Father in heaven will forgive the wrongs you have done. (Mark 11.25)

When you pray, do not be like the hypocrites! They love to stand up and pray in the houses of worship and on the street corners, so that everyone will see them... But when you pray, go to your room, close the door, and pray to your Father, who is unseen. And your Father, who sees what you do in private, will reward you.

When you pray, do not use a lot of meaningless words, as the pagans do, who think their gods will hear them because their prayers are long. Your Father already knows what you need before you ask him.
(Matthew 6.5-8)

When you pray, say:
Father,
hallowed be your name,
your kingdom come.
Give us each day our daily bread.
Forgive us our sins,
for we also forgive everyone who sins against us.
And lead us not into temptation.' (Luke 11.2-4)

Other encounters with God?

It's alleged that God can be encountered in other ways. Let's examine these.

Through people. These might be people like Jesus and the saints, who are considered to be especially in touch with God. Or it might be through people who are alive today.

There are charismatic people in every faith, who can be very influential in their own communities. Obvious examples could be Martin Luther King or the Pope. They could be less well known. Some communities on a local level could have a priest or minister who seems particularly saintly.

Through music and art. Language – talking – isn't the only way human beings have of expressing meaning. Most religions and religious traditions make use of art or music in their worship. These can be much more effective at conveying meaning than words can. Lots of music and art isn't very good, it has to be said. But the best is genuinely beautiful. Beauty is said to reflect the supreme Beauty of God himself.

Through set practices. Practising a religion brings God into the immediate. This could be in set forms of worship. But it could be through rituals and practices that are a constant reminder of the presence of God. A Jew who touches the mezuzah on the doorpost every time he or she leaves the house is reminded of God's presence. Keeping the food laws, the rules regarding which foods may be eaten and which may not, is a reminder of God's presence at least three times every day. Both Judaism and Islam observe strict food laws.

Fasting – going without food – is another practice found in many faiths. Roman Catholics are meant to fast on Ash Wednesday (the first day of Lent, a 40 day period to reflect on one's sins) and Good Friday, the day Jesus died. They are meant to abstain from meat and alcohol as a sign of sorrow for what they have done (penitence). In the UK, there are also family fast days, when families eat simply and the money that would otherwise be spent on food is given to the poor.

In Islam, Muslims fast during the month of Ramadan. Muslims will not eat, drink or smoke between dawn and sunset. It is again a sign of penitence, and teaches modesty, patience and spirituality. Ramadan was the month in which the Koran was given to the Prophet Muhammad.

Not all Muslims have to fast during Ramadam. Elderly or ill people, or pregnant or breastfeeding women do not have to fast.

Ramadan ends with Eid ul-Fitr, the Festival of the Breaking of the Fast. People are encouraged to wear their best clothes, to attend the mosque, and to visit the graves of the dead. It is a time to thank God, to visit relatives and share meals to celebrate the Festival.

Through reading the scriptures. Religious people believe that God reveals himself through the scriptures of their faith. Therefore, they have an obligation to get to know their scriptures, as well as they can. This may be through worship: Sikhs, for example, usually hear the Guru Granth Sahib being read in the Gurudwara, rather than read copies at home. Muslims and Christians will hear the Koran or the Bible when they worship communally, but usually also have their own copies, which they will read in their own homes.

1. 'Praying doesn't work. Even if you get what you ask for, it's just a coincidence.' Do you agree? Give reasons for your answer, showing that you have thought about more than one point of view.

2. Look at the section 'Other encounters with God?' Construct a spider diagram or a mind map to show the ways people are claimed to have other encounters with God.

Talking points

'God always answers prayers but sometimes the answer's no.'
'If God answers prayers, then he's unfair. Why would God only do favours for his friends, and only his friends who pester him?'
'If God exists, he doesn't need our prayers.'
'Practising a religion is like self-hypnosis. The more you do something that's a waste of time, the more you convince yourself it's worth doing.'

If you need to know more about worship in different religions, do some research and present your findings to the group. Some suggestions:
- Use your school library and / or the Internet. (Wikipedia has some good articles but remember to put them in your own words – and to have a dictionary handy!)
- Research two different faiths.
- Look for information on the following key words:
  - prayer
  - scriptures
  - religious teachers (examples: Jesus, Moses, Muhammad, the Sikh Gurus)
  - kosher, halal, fasting
  - religious art
  - religious music (and you may want to download some recordings. See if you can find Mozart's *Ave Verum* or Vivaldi's *Gloria* – good places to start!)
- Work in groups, so you're not all covering the same material.
- Use powerpoint to present your material.

Pictures on these pages:
Page 62, clockwise from top: statue of Pope John Paul II; ivory statue of Ganesh, a Hindu way of thinking of God; a mezuzah; thirteenth century mosaic of Christ from Sancta Sophia, Istanbul (Constantinople).
This page: the Koran.

12
Mysticism (1)

What are your ten favourite films?
What about your ten favourite pieces of music (any sort of music)?

This may seem an odd way to start the chapter. Bear with it: all will become clear!

Working out your top tens may not be the best thing to do in a lesson (unless your teacher is in a very good mood!). However, it's worth thinking about for a minute or two. What do you come up with? Suppose you had to select three or four and then describe them in detail to someone else. How would you do it?

You'd probably find it would take a lot of time to describe them properly, and then when you'd done it, you might well feel you hadn't really done them justice. In fact, the best way to get across what they're like would be get the other person to watch them or listen to them – to experience them for themselves. They'd only really be able to appreciate them by experiencing them.

What about if you'd just said:

'It is a pattern of changing light on a screen' or 'It is a lot of different noises, put together' and then left it at that?

Well, they're true descriptions but they don't exactly get us very far. And they certainly don't convey any real understanding of what the films or music are like.

Writing about mysticism is actually rather like that. We've said several times in this book that describing ideas about God or describing what a religious experience is like isn't easy. Words can only give a very limited picture. (Think about Augustine and the rock pool in chapter 2.)

This is even more true of mysticism. Because of what it is – or what it's claimed to be – mysticism is something that you can hardly put into words at all – because it's beyond language and beyond words. This isn't meant to be precious; mysticism is (allegedly) a human experience which is totally different from, and way beyond, all normal human experiences – and that includes language itself. You can only understand what mysticism is by actually doing it, by experiencing it for yourself – and most of us have never had a mystical experience.

I haven't, either. Nevertheless, in this chapter, we're going to try to understand what mysticism is. However hard I try, though, I'm not going to be able to explain it properly. We're not going to be able to get much beyond the level of 'it's a pattern of

changing light on a screen' or 'it's a lot of different sounds, put together'.

Here goes.

To make all this easier to read, let's assume that there is a God. Otherwise there'll have to be 'ifs' and 'buts' every sentence and it'll make the chapter less clear – and far too long.

Mysticism is (and think about the words carefully):

An intense,
   first hand,
      direct,
         and transforming
            experience of
               the presence of
            God.

It's:

an immediate
   experience of
      and encounter with
   God
      or Jesus Christ.

Mysticism, then, is a type of revelation. The revelation here is direct to the individual (the 'mystic') rather than to a group. It tends to be experienced by people who are already religious, rather than to people who don't believe. Mystical experiences leave no room for doubt – at least to the mystic herself or himself. They know what they've experienced.

Mysticism isn't something found only in Christianity; it's found in all the world's religions. Accounts of mystical experiences from different faiths are similar. However, non Christian mystics would say their encounter is with God, rather than with Jesus. (Or it's an experience of ultimate reality, Nirvana, for Buddhists – which is rather different from God.)

Only a small percentage of people from each faith could be described as mystics. (Usually!) The names of the groups include:

- Kabbalah, in Judaism
- Sufism, in Islam
- Vedanta and Kashmir Shaivism in Hinduism.

Sometimes, mysticism arouses suspicion in other members of a faith. It's regarded as a bit 'dodgy'. It *can* be thought of like this, for example, in Judaism and Islam. In Christianity, Protestantism can be dubious about mysticism, though that's a generalisation. Roman Catholic, Orthodox and Anglican Christianity tend to accept mysticism as part of the richness of the Christian faith.

What's it like?

And another question: how do you get a mystical experience?

The answer to the second question is: not very easily! If someone's a couch potato and expects to be able to run a marathon tomorrow, it's going to be a bit of a challenge. As far as mysticism's concerned, most of us are in the couch potato class.

However, a couch potato can run a marathon, if she or he's prepared to put in the training and to work hard at it. All couch potatoes are potential marathon runners. Most mystics would say all believers are potential mystics.

Most Christians would agree with the Roman

Catholic view of mysticism: it's a potential for all Christians. Also, it doesn't mean mystics are 'better' or 'grade A*' Christians and the rest are second rate. Anyone can be as good a Christian as the greatest mystic is. We saw two chapters ago what Lewis – and Screwtape! – said about religious feelings. They're wonderful if you get them but you don't have to have them, or expect them. God's with you whether you can feel that he is or not.

Moreover, it would be quite wrong for Christian mystics to feel they're better than other Christians. Jesus was once asked which were the two greatest commandments in the Torah. He replied that they were to love God, and to love your neighbour as yourself (Mark 12.28-34). Mysticism could be said to be a way of loving God. But Jesus would not allow people to be content with loving God and then neglect their fellow human beings. They had to love other people, their neighbours, too. You can't be a mystic and then ignore other people and their needs. Anyway, if mysticism's really about encountering God, and if God is love, mystics are going to have a deep appreciation of what God wants them to do.

Mystical experiences have the following characteristics:

- They're more like states of feeling than things we can understand by using our minds. As a result, they're very difficult to get across in words.
- They're states of
  knowledge
    insight
      awareness
        and revelation of God.
- They're 'beyond' time and space
- It is said that you can attain mystical experiences by following a path, which is laid down by a spiritual master. Techniques include:
  prayer
    meditation
      chanting
        concentrating on music
          controlled breathing
  – and other activities designed to heighten spiritual awareness. Michael Ramsey called it 'getting quiet'. (Ramsey was Archbishop of Canterbury from 1961 to 1974.)
- They can seem to last for a very long time, though in fact they usually last for a few minutes or even a few seconds. It's very rare for an experience to last longer than an hour.

- The mystic feels swept up and held by God (or Nirvana). There may be a feeling of being separated from the body, or of a trance. There may be visions or voices.
- They're moments or sudden, deep understanding of God.
- Some mystics can still feel the difference between 'me' and God. This is often the case for Christian mystics. In Christianity, there's a distinction, a difference, between the human soul or self, and God himself. There's a deep appreciation of God's love for human beings: God's love for the soul, and the soul's love for God. And this love is far greater than human love can ever be – even at its most powerful.
- However, other Christian mystics express their experiences as though they're aware that they're one with God. There's a union with God. (Some would interpret this as a poetic way of expressing the love between the self and God. Rather like a human couple in love can sometimes feel as though they're actually one person, not two.)
- The experience of being one with God is a feature of Hindu mysticism. The soul (atman) is an aspect of God (Brahman). (See chapter 4.) The Hindu mystic realises that the difference between the human self and God is an illusion, and it is stripped away.
- Mystics generally say that they realise the language we use about God is totally inadequate. God is beyond words. (Augustine and the rock pool again.) Some would say we have to use words to describe God, but they don't get us very far. The encounter with God is so intense that it cannot be put into words. It *transcends* them.
- Sufis, Islamic mystics, say that God is the universal love that is present everywhere in creation, and that he can be experienced directly.

1. Make a note of the definition of mysticism on page 64. (This is the section that's set out in larger type, beginning 'An intense, first hand...' You also need the bit beginning, 'an immediate...')

2. Look again at the section 'What's it like?' On a piece of A3 paper (or A2 if you can get it), construct a spider diagram or a mind map. Write 'What is mysticism?' in the centre. On the branches of the diagram, put the information contained in the bullet points in the chapter. You may wish to use one bullet point for each branch.

3. 'Only mystics can genuinely know God.' Do you agree? Give reasons for your answer. You need also to explain someone else's viewpoint, and what you think are the weaknesses of their viewpoint.

Dreams and visions

Both dreams and visions can be characteristics of mysticism. There are records of people encountering God in both. How reliable these records are is another question. However, let's examine an example of a dream and of a vision from the Bible.

The **dream** comes from the book of Genesis and it's about Jacob, one of the forefathers of the Jews or patriarchs. Here it is:

> Jacob set out for Beersheba and went on his way towards Harran. He came to a certain place and stopped there for the night, because the sun had set; and, taking one of the stones there, he made it a pillow for his head and lay down to sleep. He dreamt that he saw a ladder, which rested on the ground with its top reaching to heaven, and angels of God were going up and down upon it. The LORD was standing beside him and said, 'I am the LORD, the God of your father Abraham and the God of Isaac. This land on which you are lying I will give to you and to your descendants. They shall be countless as the dust upon the earth, and you shall spread far and wide, to north and south, to east and west. All the families of the earth shall pray to be blessed as you and your descendants are blessed. I will be with you, and I will protect you wherever you go and will bring you back to this land; for I will not leave you until I have done all that I have promised.' Jacob woke from his sleep and said, 'Truly, the LORD is in this place, and I did not know it.' Then he was afraid and said, 'How fearsome is this place! This is no other than the house of God, this is the gate of heaven.' Jacob rose early in the morning, took the stone on which he had laid his head, set it up as a sacred pillar and poured oil on the top of it. He named that place Beth-el; but the earlier name of the city was Luz.
>
> (Genesis 28.10-19.
> 'Beth-el' means 'House of God'.)

Whether this is a historically true account – it was, after all, written centuries after Jacob's time – is a question, but not the major question for us at the moment. If you examine it as a story, there are certain features:

- The ladder, and the angels ascending and descending on it, between earth and heaven. This could be taken as imagery. If it is, then it's the story's attempt to put Jacob's dream experience into words. There's a link between earth and heaven. God is present in our world of experience (he's immanent), just as he is present in heaven (he's transcendent). 'Angels' in the Old Testament are not always meant to be beings separate from God. They can be manifestations of him – *circumlocutions* is the word Biblical scholars use.

- Jacob has an experience of God. God is 'standing beside him'. (The Hebrew can mean he's standing beside the ladder, which is less clear.)

- The experience has a profound effect on Jacob: he reacts with 'fear' to his encounter with God and to God's promises for the Jewish nation. The place where he has the encounter is holy, sacred. So he changes its name to the House of God.

This account, then, could be taken to be a story which tries to put into words a mystical experience, given in a dream.

The example of a **vision** comes from the New Testament. It's from the Acts of the Apostles, the second volume of Luke's Gospel, which was probably written around 70-80 AD (though it may be earlier). The writer was almost certainly a companion of Paul, and Paul took people like Luke with him on his travels. Paul wasn't one of Jesus' original disciples, though he knew at least some of them. However, he claims to have had an experience of meeting the risen Jesus, which changed his life.

Paul describes his vision when he appears before Porcius Festus and Herod Agrippa II. Festus was a successor of Pontius Pilate as governor of Judea; Agrippa was a puppet king of the Romans who governed another part of Israel. Here's what Paul says in Luke's account in Acts:

'I myself once thought it my duty to work actively against the name of Jesus of Nazareth; and I did so in Jerusalem. It was I who imprisoned many of God's people by authority obtained from the chief priests; and when they were condemned to death, my vote was cast against them. In all the synagogues I tried by repeated punishment to make them renounce their faith; indeed my fury rose to such a pitch that I extended my persecution to foreign cities.

'On one such occasion I was travelling to Damascus with authority and commission from the chief priests; and as I was on my way, Your Majesty, in the middle of the day I saw a light from the sky, more brilliant than the sun, shining all around me and my travelling companions. We all fell to the ground, and then I heard a voice saying to me in the Jewish language, "Saul, Saul*, why do you persecute me? It is hard for you, this kicking against the goad." I said, "Tell me, Lord, who you are"; and the Lord replied, "I am Jesus, whom you are persecuting. But now, rise to your feet and stand upright. I have appeared to you for a purpose: to appoint you my servant and witness, to testify both to what you have seen and to what you shall yet see of me. I will rescue you from this people and from the Gentiles to whom I am sending you. I send you to open their eyes and

Paul's conversion. Stained glass from St Thomas' church, Winchelsea, East Sussex

turn them from darkness to light, from the dominion of Satan to God, so that, by trust in me, they may obtain forgiveness of sins, and a place with those whom God has made his own."

'And so, King Agrippa, I did not disobey the heavenly vision...'

(Acts 26.9-19)

* Saul was Paul's Jewish name

It's interesting that Paul says – or Luke says Paul says – this was a vision. We may once again have an attempt to put into words something that can't really be put into words at all. The brightness that was brighter than the sun may not be meant as a literal description. It may be an image – and a very effective one at that. Mystics often claim that their experiences of God make everyday things seem pale by comparison. Paul's encounter with God, with Jesus, is like seeing the sun, only far greater.

(Paul wrote a number of the letters that now make up part of the New Testament. Interesting that when he gives us his own account, the first hand account, he goes into no detail at all. He simply says of the risen Jesus, 'In the end, he appeared even to me' (1 Corinthians 15.8). This may again provide evidence that the Acts version is trying to record in words something that was beyond words. In his own writing, Paul makes no attempt to describe his experience.)

Luke's account goes on to say that Festus couldn't take any more and shouted out, 'Paul, you are raving'. Like a lot of people, Festus tries to dismiss religious experiences as madness.

Festus goes on to say, 'Too much study is driving you mad.' You may sympathise with this view.

Dreams and visions, then, can be part of mysticism.

Enlightenment

'Enlightenment' can just be a synonym for 'mysticism' or 'mystical experience'. In the study of religion, though, it's more usually associated with Buddhism and with the enlightenment of the Buddha.

'Buddha' means 'the enlightened one': someone who has achieved enlightenment. It can be applied to anyone who has achieved this. However, *the* Buddha was a prince in North East India called **Siddharta Gautama.** He lived around 400 BC.

When he was a young man, his father, King Suddhodana decided it would be best if he never knew about human suffering. So he spent most of his time in palaces. He had everything he could possibly want.

Except that he hadn't. Siddharta grew restless. There must surely be more to life than wealth, than having your material needs satisfied. So, when he was 29, he decided to go and meet the people he was to rule. What he saw profoundly disturbed him.

He had never seen an elderly person before, so when on his travels he met an elderly man, he was totally shocked. Channa, his charioteer, told him old age was something that happened to everyone. Siddharta simply didn't know that. His compassion was aroused and he was further moved when he saw, for the first time, someone suffering from disease, and then a dead body which had been left to rot.

Was there a way to overcome suffering like this? Siddharta was determined to try. He and five companions tried various spiritual paths which were recommended by the religious teachers. He became an ascetic: someone who tries to discipline his spirit or himself by weakening his body.

In fact, Siddharta ended up almost starving to death. He realised this simply wasn't going to work. He started eating again. And he sat under a pipal tree – now called the Bodhi tree – saying he wasn't going to get up again until he had discovered the Truth. His companions were disgusted with him, thinking he had given up, and they left him.

Under the Bodhi tree, Siddharta achieved enlightenment. He realised the Truth: the realities of existence, which were quite different from what the religious teachers taught. Siddharta had achieved enlightenment; he had become the Buddha.

The Truth was not easy to understand. However, the Buddha explained it as follows:

There are **four noble truths.** They were 'noble' truths because they were realities, not theories.
- Life is suffering (dukkha).
- The origin of dukkha is desire: the desire or craving to cling on to earthly things. Buddha said, 'This is the noble truth of the origin of

- right effort – constantly making the effort to follow the right path
- right mindfulness – being constantly aware of the body, feelings, and what is going on around you, so that you can avoid temptation to fall back into desire and dukkha
- right concentration – meditation, spiritual discipline.

- **Anicca:** everything passes away. Nothing is permanent. We have to accept that nothing in this world will last for ever.

- **Anatta:** anicca includes human beings. The whole idea that there is a 'self' is an illusion.

Although some forms of Buddhism believe in deities, the Buddha himself seems to have regarded the gods as irrelevant – if they existed at all. Buddhism can be called an atheistic religion. Some people say you can't have an atheistic religion; it'd be like saying you can have silent music. They'd classify Buddhism as a philosophy rather than a religion. But here's the point:

The supreme reality in Buddhism is not God. It is **Nirvana.**

(We have to be careful here, because a lot of this is very simplified.)

Nirvana is the state when suffering and craving is extinguished. It is beyond words and cannot be explained. It can be experienced in this life through meditation. It's also the destiny of the individual – who's an illusion in any case – when he or she has escaped the cycle of birth and rebirth. It's the perfect state of happiness, though it's beyond happiness. There's no craving, anger, suffering, obsessions; instead, there's perfect calm and peace.

The word 'nirvana' actually means 'blowing out' in Pali: in other words, it's the state in which the fires of greed, hatred and illusion have been blown out.

The Buddha said of Nirvana:

'It is profound, hard to see, hard to realise, tranquil.'

'There is that dimension where there is neither earth, nor water, nor fire, nor wind.'

'It is not infinite space; it is not infinite consciousness; it is not nothingness; it is not this world; it is not the next world.'

'A flame that has been blown out by a strong wind goes to rest. It cannot be defined. The sage who is freed from name and from body and who goes to rest – he cannot be defined.'

suffering: it is this craving which leads to renewed existence, accompanied by delight and lust, seeking delight here and there, that is, craving for sensual pleasures, craving for existence itself.' Buddhism accepts reincarnation. Like Hinduism, Buddhism teaches that reincarnation is far from the highest good, and that one should seek to be freed from it.

- Dukkha will cease when desire is extinguished.
- To extinguish dukkha, the **eight fold path** must be followed.

The eightfold path means:
- right understanding – seeing things as they really are
- right intention – getting rid of anything in your life you know to be immoral
- right speech – not lying, not gossiping, not upsetting others
- right action – living a morally good life
- right livelihood – avoiding lifestyles which harm others

Dreams

1. Tell the story of Jacob's ladder (Genesis 28.10-19) in your own words.

2. If this is an account of a mystical experience, what are the ideas the story contains?

Visions

3. According to the Acts of the Apostles, Paul described his vision of the risen Christ (Acts 26.9-19).
a) In Acts, how did Paul describe this vision?
b) Paul says he experienced a brightness brighter than the sun. What might this be trying to say?
c) What does Paul say about the experience himself, in 1 Corinthians?
d) Why do you think Paul's own account doesn't go into details, as the Acts account does?

Enlightenment

4. What does the word 'enlightenment' mean? (This is enlightenment in general, not the enlightenment of the Buddha.)

5. Who was Siddharta Gautama and why and how did he try to find an answer to human suffering?

6. What happened to Siddharta Gautama under the Bodhi tree?

7. What are:
a) the four noble truths and the eightfold path?
b) anicca and anatta?
Try to devise diagrams or illustrations for your answers. They will also make them easier to learn!

8. What is Nirvana?
(This is actually an impossible question because Nirvana cannot be defined. Try, though!)

Talking points

'Dreams and visions can all be explained away. Dreams are just dreams. Visions can be signs of mental illness. They have nothing to do with God.'
  'Why shouldn't God use dreams and visions to reveal himself to people?'
  'If mysticism worked, you'd expect all mystics to experience the same thing. They don't. Therefore mysticism must be nonsense.'
  'We don't know enough about mysticism to be able to come to conclusions about it.'

Between 1975 and 1980, Peter Sutcliffe murdered 13 women. The murders were particularly savage and revolting. Sutcliffe attacked a number of other women, who survived. His youngest murder victim was 16.
  Sutcliffe was unhelpfully dubbed 'The Yorkshire Ripper' by the tabloids, showing their usual good taste in glorifying criminals.
  Many, though not all, of his victims were prostitutes.
  Sutcliffe is still alive and serving a sentence of life imprisonment in Broadmoor.
  Sutcliffe claimed he had been directly instructed by God to kill prostitutes. God had revealed this directly to him.

  Whether Sutcliffe believed in this revelation or not, religious people would say this could not have been a genuine revelation.
  Why not?

14
The argument from morality

Everyone would agree that there are some things which are just evil. It doesn't matter whether people are Christians, members of another faith, agnostics or atheists. They'd all say that there are some things that are totally wrong, totally immoral.

We all have our own views on what actions are simply evil. Can you come up with a list of them, which anyone you showed it to – anyone in the world – would agree with?

(This may be a point to turn the book over and take a break for discussion.)

You might have found that it isn't a terribly long list, if it's possible to make a list at all. There may be exceptions. There may be some people who do not think murder, rape, or torturing people for fun are wrong actions. However, almost everybody would be revolted by views such as this, and would say people who think that way are either being stupid or are sick. Perhaps, therefore, we could say that 'there are some actions which everybody in their right mind would regard as evil.'

There may be exceptions with some actions. This may be because of our definitions. For example, people in their right mind regard murder as evil. But murder is not committed every time one human being is killed by another. Many people would argue that killing someone in a war, execution, euthanasia or abortion are not murder. If you take the example of stealing, we'd probably agree that right thinking people believe stealing to be wrong – *but* sometimes stealing may be justified. If you or your family is starving, few of us would say that stealing food is morally wrong.

It's argued, then:

All right thinking people regard some actions, such as murder, as evil.

This is true, regardless of people's upbringing, and regardless of whether they're religious or not.

Do you think this is right?

If it is right, it begs a very short question:

Why?

Immanuel Kant (1724 – 1804)

Kant was a philosopher who argued that the existence of morality meant that God must also exist. He argued:

- All human beings believe it is their duty to seek the highest good.
- The highest good is a state in which the highest virtue (goodness) is joined to the highest happiness.
- A duty can only be a duty if you can actually carry it out. If my grandfather is dead, I have no duty to feed him. 'Ought' includes 'can': 'I *ought* to be kind' must also mean 'I *can* be kind.'
- If it's our *duty* to seek the highest good, we must be *able* to seek the highest good.
- But we may not be able to attain the highest good in this life. There may not be time.
- So, there must be an afterlife. This will give us the time we need to fulfil our duty.
- As there is an afterlife, there must also be God. Otherwise, an afterlife would be impossible.

What do you think?

There are actually lots of problems with Kant's view.

- Kant says we all believe our duty is to seek the highest good. But do we all believe that?

Perhaps some of us would be content with a 'second best' good.

- Suppose it is right to say we all seek the highest good. But it's a jump then to say exactly what the highest good is. Why say it's the highest virtue + the highest happiness? Couldn't it be something else?
- Let's suppose Kant's right here, though. We *do* all feel a duty to seek the highest good. The highest good *is* the highest virtue joined to the highest happiness.

But does it follow that we can actually get to that highest good?

Think about this. (It's a criticism made by Professor J. C. A. Gaskin.)

My great desire is to have a perfect garden. A garden that's absolutely beautiful. To achieve this, I'll have overcome everything that nature can throw at me: greenfly, slugs, snails, frost, floods, rabbits digging up the lawn and so on. I have a genuine desire for this garden – but that doesn't mean I'm ever actually going to get one (and I probably won't!).

Let's move aside from Kant and think about this:

If there's such a thing as morality, that must mean there's a God as well

But it depends where you think morality comes from.

Let's take an example.

'Murder is wrong.'

An atheist philosopher might say this:

'Murder is wrong, but that has nothing to do with God. There are good human reasons for having that rule. If murder was OK, society would fall apart. Human progress and human civilisation would be impossible. If it's OK to murder, then I can't say it's wrong for you to murder me, and I could well end up dead. I wouldn't like people to think of me as a murderer. It wouldn't be good for my self image to think of myself as a murderer. So murder's wrong.'

Theists would actually agree with all of this – except for the bit about its having nothing to do with God. But they'd say there's something missing.

That something is: 'Thou shalt not kill' or 'You shall not commit murder' – from the Ten Commandments. God has told us that murder is wrong.

This gives us a guarantee that morality is *real*. It's a *rule*, not just a nice idea. The problem with the atheist view is that it only gets us so far. It's not absolutely true. It's not part of the way things are. It's not a law written into the universe, which always applies – just as the law of gravity always applies.

The atheist view of why 'murder is wrong' is actually saying it's an *expedient*. This means it's nothing more than a matter of convenience. It's a useful idea, it's a way of behaving that makes human society possible. But it's also a *choice*. We *choose* not to commit murder, but we *could* decide on a different set of rules if they worked.

We know murder is always wrong because God tells us. God cannot lie and he cannot have a false belief because he knows everything. *We* don't decide what's right or wrong. There's a higher power, who never makes mistakes, who always knows what's right. And he says that murder is wrong.

This brings us to:

Another version of the argument from morality

This says:
- All right thinking people regard some actions, such as murder, as evil.
- This is true, regardless of people's upbringing, and regardless of whether they're religious or not.
- So, there must be **a Moral Law**, which really exists. People agree that there is such a thing as right and wrong, when they talk about morality. Even if they disagree about different issues, they do agree that there's such a thing as goodness, and such a thing as evil.
- As there is a Moral Law, it can't come from human beings – because people disagree when they make moral judgements.
- The moral ideal must exist in a greater, non human mind.
- And that mind is the mind of God.

But this doesn't really work, either. It's a big assumption to say that there is a moral law. Atheist philosophers would say there are good human reasons for behaving in a moral way. These reasons are the origin of morality, and morality's then been projected onto a non-existent God.

Does conscience prove that God exists?

Every human being has a conscience. It's an instinct, a reflex that tells us that we must not do something – or that we must do it. It makes demands on us, and it's always unsafe to disobey those demands.

So where does it come from?

It's sometimes claimed that the voice of

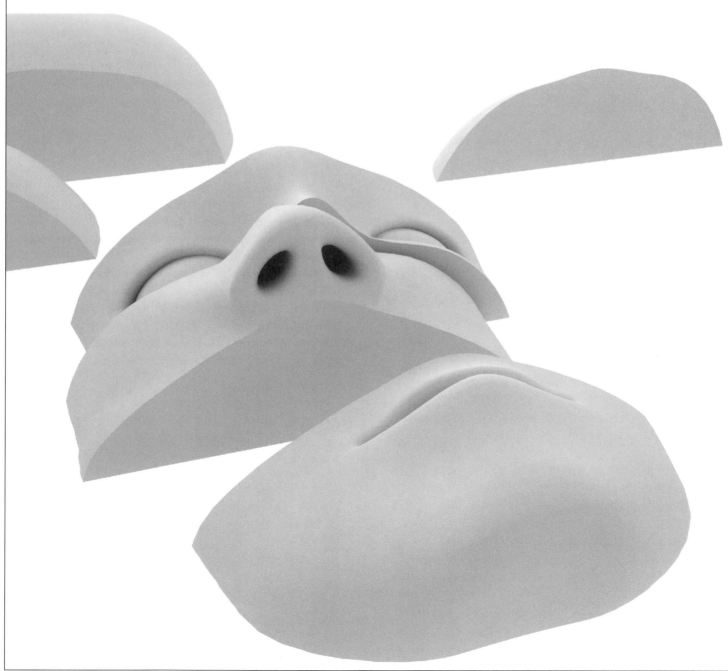

conscience is the voice of God. It's like a personal revelation to each one of us.

The argument goes like this.

If we really want to think about a moral problem, we're going to look at evidence, consider different viewpoints, and see which conclusion best fits the arguments. This takes a lot of time. (If you're studying moral issues as well as philosophy of religion, you may have spent a long time studying complex moral problems like euthanasia and abortion.)

However, conscience isn't really to do with thinking things through. We know immediately what we have to do – or not do. If we're persuaded to take part in bullying someone, we *know* automatically that we shouldn't do it. We don't think through the arguments, we just know.

So it's a reflex, as we said. If I stand too near the edge of a cliff, I know I should step back – unless I'm being silly. I don't calculate the acceleration that gravity would cause upon my falling body, the speed of impact with the ground, the air resistance or anything like that. I know I've got to step back. If I see a hungry tiger charging towards me, I don't stand there and muse, 'Here, approaching at considerable speed, is a carnivore of the species *felix biggushungrius*. How fascinating. I opine that its slavering jaws indicate it desires to feed. There is no other source of nourishment in the vicinity other than myself. On balance, I had better retire to a place of safety.' If I went through all that, I'd end up as lunch.

If conscience is an instinct, if it has nothing to do with thinking things through, then it makes sense to say it comes from God. Therefore God must exist.

Actually, many would say this argument doesn't work either.

Conscience, they say, *is* about thinking things through. It's just that we're not aware of the thinking process. It's so fast that the conclusion jumps out at us. Or we've already thought things through, the mind skips to the conclusion, and flashes it up before us in neon letters.

If this is right, conscience may well not have much to do with God, one way or the other. (Though some would say conscience can be helped by God, even if it's not a hotline to him.)

For another view, let's turn to look at what Sigmund Freud said.

Sigmund Freud (1856-1939)

Freud was the founder of psychoanalysis, a theory of how the mind worked – and how people could be helped through therapy. He was an atheist and believed religion was a form of neurosis or mental disorder. He made some interesting claims about the origins of religion. Sadly, we don't have time to cover them in this book, though you might want to read up what he said for yourselves.

Freud did, though, have a view of what the

conscience was, and he rejected any idea that it had anything to do with God.

Freud said that a lot of our 'programming' as human beings was laid down when we were very little. We accepted our parents' views about everything and we knew we'd be punished if we did things they disapproved of. Those judgements, and the fear of punishment, became part of us. We were too young to be aware that this process was going on.

Our minds set up a super-ego (an 'above I'): a part of our minds which carries on acting as a parent. Conscience is an aspect of our super-ego. We obey it because, without knowing it, we're trying to please mummy or daddy by doing what they want. And we're frightened that if we don't, mummy or daddy will punish us. That's why conscience is such a strong force in human beings. It's as though part of us is still a toddler, still loving mummy and daddy but still afraid of their disapproval.

What do you think?

1. Complete the following sentences. They explain Kant's version of the argument from morality.
1) All human beings seek...
2) The highest good is...
3) A duty is only a duty when you can actually...
4) So, it must therefore be possible to seek...
5) But we cannot get to the highest good in...
6) So there must be an...
7) And therefore there must be a...

2. Why doesn't Kant's argument work? (Think about Professor Gaskin and his garden on page 73!)

3. If there is such a thing as a **moral law**, why would that show that God exists?

4.a) How would you explain what the conscience is?
b) What did Freud say the conscience was?
c) 'Conscience is the voice of God.' Do you agree? Give reasons for your answer, showing that you have considered more than one point of view.

Talking points:

'Atheists' reasons for behaving morally are basically selfish.'
'If there's no God, there's no morality. You can do exactly as you like if you can get away with it.'
'If God did not exist, it would be necessary to invent him.' What do you think this means?

Part Two

Miracles

15
Miracles (1): What is a miracle?

This may seem a daft question at first. Everybody knows what the word 'miracle' means. You could say:

> 'A miracle is anything that happens that you weren't expecting'
> *('It's a miracle I managed to get a seat on the bus.')*

Or you could say:

> 'Miracles are accounts of things that didn't happen, which gullible people believe in, like feeding 5000 people with five loaves and two fish.'

Or perhaps:

> 'It's a miracle that human beings exist at all.'

These definitions are all rather different. In this book, we're really looking at the *religious* idea of miracles. Stories of holy people doing extraordinary things are found in most religions. If they happened – or if *some* of them happened, anyway – they're strong evidence that God exists.

If they happened. How on earth would you know? Isn't it the case that, say, Christians are going to *assume* Jesus did perform miracles, and atheists are going to assume they're all made up? Isn't it all just a matter of opinion?

This is a fair point and we need to examine it. Before we do, though, we need to try to define the word 'miracle' a bit more precisely. Let's start by examining one of the miracles performed by Jesus.

The miracles of Jesus

This story comes from Luke's Gospel, which was written around 70 – 80 AD.

In the course of his [Jesus'] journey to Jerusalem he was travelling through the borderlands of Samaria and Galilee. As he was entering a village he was met by ten men with leprosy. They stood some way off and called out to him, 'Jesus, Master, take pity on us.' When he saw them he said, 'Go and show yourself to the priests'; and while they were on their way, they were made clean. One of them, finding himself cured, turned back praising God aloud. He threw himself down at Jesus' feet and thanked him. And he was a Samaritan. At this Jesus said, 'Were not all ten cleansed? The other nine, where are they? Could none be found to come back and give praise to God except this foreigner?' And he said to the man, 'Stand up and go on your way; your faith has cured you.'

(Luke 17.11-19)

This seems a pretty straightforward story. In fact, it's more complex than seems. Have a look at the following points: they help explain the background, which the original readers would have known.

- Jesus is travelling south to Jerusalem. The region he grew up in was Galilee. South of Galilee is Samaria; the easiest way to reach Jerusalem was to travel through Samaria. The people who lived there were called Samaritans (hence the parable of the good Samaritan, which you may know). But Samaritans weren't Jews. They were of mixed race; centuries before, Assyrian settlers had intermarried with the Jews in the region. And although the Samaritans worshipped the same God as the Jews, they didn't believe exactly the same things about him. As a result, they were generally hated by the Jews – and they returned the compliment. Jews had as little to do with them as possible. (Remember Jesus and his disciples were Jews, too.)

- Leprosy: not necessarily what we call 'leprosy' today. The Jews were so terrified of this disease that they classed lots of other conditions as 'leprosy', just to be on the safe side. Lepers were not allowed to mix with ordinary people and lived in separate areas. This is reflected in the story by the fact that the men are standing 'some way off'.

- The Torah, the Jewish Law, accepted that some people might appear to recover from 'leprosy'. If so, they had to be examined by a priest, to confirm that the cure was genuine. That's why Jesus tells them to go and see the priests.

Bearing these points in mind, read the story again.

It's all actually a bit low key, strangely enough. So are lots of other accounts of Jesus' miracles. Yet when we hear the word 'miracle', we tend to assume it's got to be something really spectacular, like stopping a tidal wave in its tracks, making it snow in the middle of the summer – something like that. It's true that the 'wow!' factor is emphasised more in other miracles of Jesus; feeding five thousand people with a few scraps of bread and fish is pretty impressive, after all. But the 'wow' factor's not very important here.

So what's the story trying to say?

- What it isn't really trying to say is, 'Do you know what? Jesus could do miracles! They were really amazing!' Luke just takes it for granted that Jesus could. The focus is on something else. (The 'miracle' bit is dealt with in less than a sentence: 'while on their way, they were made clean.' No drumroll, no 'here it comes, brace yourselves!';

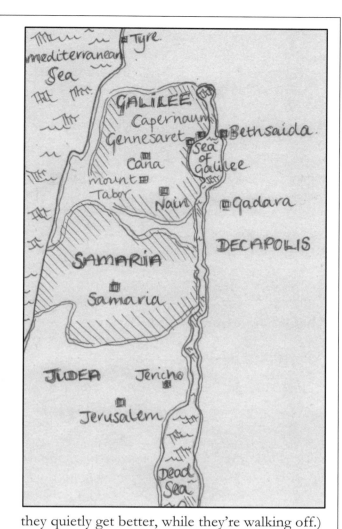

they quietly get better, while they're walking off.)

- Notice the men ask Jesus to have *pity* on them. The life they lived was harsh. Even if people felt sorry for them, they were still condemned to live a pretty miserable existence. They knew Jesus was said to be a miracle worker, but also to be compassionate and generous. So, the miracle shows Jesus' love and compassion for other people. The miracles of Jesus are acts of kindness. They're not done for show; in fact, when people ask for miracles just for the sake of it – to make him prove who he says he is, for example – he refuses to do them (see Mark 8.11-12). It's not just about 'wow'; it's saying that Jesus' followers should love other people, as he did.

- The only one who remembers to say thank you isn't a Jew; he's a Samaritan. Presumably, Luke thinks the rest are so excited about becoming well again that they just forget. When Jesus says that the 'foreigner' has thanked God, there's no 'edge' to the word. 'Foreigner' in English can suggest a slight sneer; this isn't the case in Greek, the language Luke was writing in. The Jews hated Samaritans; racism was a problem in the first century, just as it is today. Jesus opposes racism and treats everyone with the same compassion. His kingdom is open to everybody, regardless of their race – or any other barrier put up by human beings.

- It's the man's *faith* that has cured him. In this story, Luke is emphasising the need for faith. In fact, Mark's Gospel goes so far as to say that Jesus can't work miracles unless people have faith in him (Mark 6.5).

So, in the New Testament, miracles are much more than just amazing things to make people boggle. The healing of the ten lepers is also about the ideas of:

- compassion
- anti-racism
- faith

This brings us back to the question:

What is a miracle?

Here are three possible definitions:

1. **A miracle is** an extraordinary event in which God is at work.
2. **A miracle is** an event in which the laws of nature are broken.
3. The Christian philosopher St Thomas Aquinas (c. 1224 or 1225 – 1274) said: '**A miracle is**

something beyond the order of created nature. Therefore since God alone is not a created being, he also is the only one who can work miracles by his own power.'

While the New Testament writers such as Luke might have agreed with these definitions, they're not the whole story. There's too much emphasis in the definitions on the 'wow' factor. The word usually translated as 'miracle' in the Gospels of Matthew, Mark and Luke is the Greek word 'dunamis'. This actually means 'an act of power'. (It's also the root of the English word 'dynamic'.) The miracles show the *power* of Jesus, which is the power of God. They're not magic; Jesus does not mutter spells or perform any mumbo-jumbo to make extraordinary things happen. The miracles happen because of who he is. In the Old Testament, people who are said to have performed miracles usually ask God to do them (see, for example, 1 Kings 17.17-24). Jesus never asks God to perform the miracle for him: it's Jesus himself who does it.

As a result, John's Gospel uses the word 'semeion' – 'sign' – for a miracle. The miracles of Jesus are signs: things that show something else.

They're not just important, amazing events: they carry a deeper truth, such as showing who Jesus really is. For example, John's Gospel has the story of Jesus raising his friend Lazarus from the dead (John 11.1-44). John makes it clear that this miracle is a sign of who Jesus is: in the story, Jesus says:

I am the resurrection and the life. Those who believe in me, even though they die, will live, and everyone who lives and believes in me will never die.
(John 11.25-26)

To sum up, then:

- There are different ways of defining the term 'miracle'. We have given three definitions.

- We considered in detail one of the miracles of Jesus. With Jesus' miracles, the 'wow' factor is not the most important factor. They are trying to get across other ideas too – and ideas more important than just the 'wow' factor.

- Matthew, Mark and Luke use the word 'dunamis' for 'miracle'. 'Dunamis' means 'act of power'. The miracles of Jesus are acts of Jesus' power. It is *because of who he is* that he can perform miracles.

- John's Gospel uses the word 'semeion' or 'sign' for a miracle. Miracles carry a deeper truth, such as showing who Jesus really is.

Of course, what we haven't discussed is whether miracles can happen, or whether they're just made up. We'll look at this question in the next unit.

1. Look at the beginning of the section 'What is a miracle?' Give the three definitions of a miracle.

2.a) What word do Matthew, Mark and Luke use for 'miracle' and what does it mean?
b) What word does John use for 'miracle' and what does it mean?
You need to go into detail in your answers.
c) Compare your answers to a) and b) with what you wrote for question 1. Which do you think is the best definition of the word 'miracle'? Why?

3. We examined closely one example of a miracle story: the healing of the ten lepers in Luke's Gospel.
 a) Briefly tell the story in your own words.
b) What ideas is the story trying to get across?

c) 'Luke's more interested in these ideas than he is in the "wow" factor of the miracle.' Do you agree? Why?

4. 'You can believe in the message of the story of the healing of the ten lepers, without having to believe it really happened.' What do you think this means?
Do you agree with it, and why?

Make sure you know the definitions of the word 'miracle': you're going to need them for the exam. Spot learning techniques can help you learn the definitions.
For how to do spot learning, see page 22.

16
Miracles (2): Are miracles possible?

Well, those are some possible answers to the question. However, it's not as simple as just saying yes, no or maybe. What's *behind* the yes, no or maybe?

There are good arguments for saying that miracles are possible.

This may come as a bit of a surprise. Lots of people just assume the whole idea of miracles is daft and leave it at that.

There are good arguments for saying that miracles are impossible. (And for saying they're possible but they just don't happen.)

These arguments need to be thought through carefully. Once they've been thought through and discussed, our 'yes', 'no' or 'maybe' will be more than 'just an opinion': 'yes', 'no' or 'maybe' will be an **informed** opinion: an opinion based on careful thought.

Some opinions *aren't* based on careful thought. Opinions like these are very common and we all have them, about various subjects. If we're honest, they're often knee-jerk reactions. Opinions like this are called **uninformed opinions**. Some uninformed opinions are what's called **circular arguments**. A circular argument basically says, 'I think this because I do.' Put it another way:

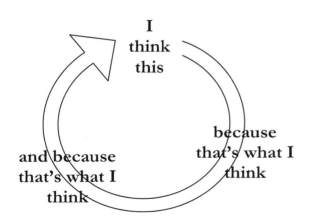

You'll see that there isn't a lot of difference between 'I think this' and 'because that's what I think'. It's saying 'I think this because I do.'

Circular arguments are pretty flimsy!

So, uninformed opinions can also be circular arguments.

They can be based on weak reasons, too. Things like 'It's true because my dad says so,' or 'it's true because that's what I've always thought' or 'it's true because that's what I was brought up to believe.'

(The *conclusion* that something's true may be correct. But we can't be confident that a conclusion is true, unless we know the arguments have been looked at carefully – unless we know it's an *informed* opinion rather than an *un*informed one.)

Let's consider, then, the idea of miracles.

If we start from the position that miracles are absolutely impossible, nothing much (except a miracle!) is going to make us change our minds. But is the starting point an informed opinion or an uninformed opinion? Have we given the evidence and the arguments a fair hearing?

One way of answering the question 'Are miracles possible?' is to look at some of the most famous accounts: the miracles of Jesus. (We considered one in the last unit.)

We'll then go on to consider whether the resurrection of Jesus really happened or not. In Christianity, the resurrection is the most important of all the miracles because without it, Christianity falls apart.

Before we get going, though, here are a few things to think about:

> Jesus didn't really exist anyway. So he couldn't have done any miracles.

- Lots of people would say Jesus did not exist. It's interesting to ask why. Is it an informed or an uninformed opinion? How good is the evidence for saying it?

  If we want to know what happened in the past, a good person to ask is a historian. We usually respect expert opinion.

  In fact, no serious historian would have any doubts: they all would say that Jesus was a human being who really existed. The evidence is too strong to deny. Movements as big as

Christianity don't pop into existence from nowhere, for no good reason; someone has to start them off. And Jesus is mentioned in other documents, other ancient historical writings, outside the New Testament. He's mentioned by the Roman writers Tacitus and Pliny, and by the Jewish historian Josephus.

If Jesus really existed, that's at least a *basis* for saying he could have performed the miracles.

- Almost all Christians believe Jesus performed miracles. The Bible is studied by experts all over the world, full time; experts who teach in the world's great universities. Many such experts have no problem with the idea of miracles. So, being clever doesn't rule out believing in such things. The media often loudly proclaims that religion is only an option for dim people and that anyone with half a brain must be an atheist. Not true – and an uninformed rather than an informed opinion!

Experts can believe in miracles. This doesn't make them correct in their beliefs. But it might make us more cautious about dismissing miracles out of hand.

Let's consider the idea that:

Jesus' 'miracles' were real events but were not miracles.

This idea was very popular in Victorian times. Some writers argued that there were other explanations for the miracles of Jesus. The sort of thing they said were that Jesus' miracles were:

- faked
- or they were normal events that were misunderstood
- or that they were coincidences.

So, for example, when the Gospels say that Jesus walked on water, he had actually faked it, maybe by laying stepping stones under the Sea of Galilee (Mark 6.45-52). When he raised a twelve year old girl from the dead, she wasn't dead at all: she was just asleep (Mark 5.21-24 and 35-43). Some of Jesus' healing miracles were cons: he and the person pretending to be ill had cooked it up between them and they were just playacting. When Jesus stopped a storm that was threatening to sink the boat he was in, it was just a coincidence that the storm stopped when Jesus told it to (Mark 4.35-41). When he fed 5000 people with five loaves and two fish, what really happened was that people just shared their packed lunches, or Jesus and the disciples had a secret stash of bread and fish, which they doled out (Mark 6.30-44).

Jesus calms a storm. Stained glass window, St Thomas' church, Winchelsea, Sussex

We can call these explanations for miracles **naturalistic explanations.**

They all sound pretty believable – at a first look, anyway. When you look deeper, there are major problems with naturalistic explanations. You have to ask: are they really *likely?*

A big problem is that there is no evidence for naturalistic explanations. Things *may* have happened like that, but there just isn't any evidence that they did. All we have are the account of Jesus' miracles in the Gospels, plus theories. That's it.

Naturalistic explanations of miracles rest on a big assumption: that Jesus was a fraud and a liar. He *might* have been. But, again, there is no evidence. It is just an assumption – and an assumption unsupported by any evidence.

Biblical scholars have been analysing the New Testament for over a hundred years. The Gospels have been analysed by experts more than any other books ever written.

So, opinion about the Bible can be *expert* opinion. Normally, we'd listen to what experts say.

Not all biblical scholars agree with each other, though. (If you put a bunch of experts on any subject in a room, you'll get lots of different opinions.) However, **almost no Biblical scholars nowadays accept naturalistic explanations of miracles.** Why? It boils down to two main points:

1. It is very, very unlikely that Jesus was a fraud and a liar. Not all biblical scholars believe in miracles. However, all the evidence is that Jesus was a good man – whatever else he was. There is no evidence whatsoever that he was a con artist.

Jesus raises Jairus' daughter from the dead (Mark 5.21 – 24, 35 -43).
Stained glass from St George's church, Brede, Sussex.

2. There were lots of accounts of miracles in the ancient world. They were not confined to the characters we meet in the Bible. Heroes from Greek, Roman and other cultures were believed to be miracle workers. Scholars have studied these different miracles stories from the ancient world. In many ways, especially in the way they're told, they're very similar to Jesus' miracles.

    This doesn't mean all miracles stories – of Jesus or from other cultures – are true. What it does mean, though, is that people in the ancient world were used to stories about people performing miracles. And miracles stories were a *literary* genre: a category of *written* material. (Literary genres today would include novels, newspapers, non-fiction books, emails and so on.)

    If they were a literary genre, then they're things that were *written*. Stories. No doubt a lot of them are untrue. But the point is: they're pieces of writing. They're not necessarily based on events. They are stories, and stories can be made up (though they aren't always).

As a result, some New Testament scholars today would say this:

either

The miracles of Jesus are stories which are made up, and which are not based on real events at all

or

They really happened.

The naturalistic explanation is not an option: it's just too unlikely. Either they happened, or they're invented.

It's true that lots of New Testament scholars think the miracles of Jesus are invented stories. A very important New Testament scholar was **Rudolf Bultmann** (1884-1976).

Bultmann still influences biblical scholarship today. He claimed that the miracles of Jesus were invented, to make Jesus appear as powerful and great as the other so-called wonder workers of the ancient world.

    But it has to be said that Bultmann's view is just a theory. Not all New Testament scholars accept that Jesus never did any miracles. **William Barclay** (1907-1978), a brilliant Scottish New Testament scholar, believed Jesus did indeed perform miracles. After all, a big proportion of the life story of Jesus in the Gospels deals with miracles. If you take them away, what's left? (Especially if you take away the greatest miracle: Jesus' resurrection. Without that, Christianity falls apart.)

The experts disagree, then. Few of them, if any, would accept that *all* the miracles of Jesus are historical. For example, we've already mentioned the feeding of the 5000 (Mark 6.30-44). But Jesus is also said to have fed a crowd of 4000 people with just a few loaves and fish (Mark 8.1-10). These stories are so similar that they are almost certainly two different versions of the same story. (Look them up. What do you think?)

And experts, like everyone else, can sometimes start with their conclusion and then look for evidence for it. If an expert assumes miracles are impossible, she or he is perhaps not very likely to be convinced otherwise. And if an expert assumes miracles are possible, it may not be easy to shift them in that view. Ideally, of course, people should keep an open mind, look up the evidence, and then make up their minds. And be prepared to change their minds if new and better evidence comes along. However, it's easier to say 'keep an open mind' than actually to do it! (How open minded do you think people in general really are?)

For these questions, you need first to read up some of the miracles of Jesus. (If you don't have a Bible, it's easily available online.) Have a look at:

The healing of ten lepers: Luke 17.11-19 (this is printed on page 78)
The healing of a paralytic: Luke 5.17-26
Jesus raises Lazarus from the dead: John 11.1-44
The feeding of the 5000: Mark 6.30-44
Jesus (and Peter!) walking on the water: Matthew 14.22-33

1. The miracle stories reveal some of the *characteristics* of God. They show us what sort of a God the writers believed in.
Here's a list of some of these characteristics.
Match them to the miracles of Jesus you've read.

Qualities of God that the miracles reveal:

God is compassionate / loving
God is powerful
God is generous
God is forgiving
God cares about people's physical needs
God does not discriminate
God gives people life after death
God wants people to believe in him

2.a) Think about the miracle stories you've read. We could say some of them sound more likely than others. Why might this be said? Do you agree with it?
b) Why might people argue that *none* of the miracles of Jesus ever happened?
c) How strong do you think their arguments are?

Talking point:

'If there's a God, he can't really win. Even if he performs miracles, people don't necessarily believe them. There's nothing about a miracle that forces you to believe – you can always find other explanations for them. Even if you saw a miracle, you'd only believe in it if you were open minded.' What do you think?

17
Miracles (3): the Resurrection of Jesus

The resurrection of Jesus is the most important of the miracles in the New Testament. Christianity teaches, and has always taught, that the death of Jesus was not the end. Jesus was crucified on Good Friday; he was executed along with two petty criminals. By the evening, he was dead and his body had been buried. His followers, his disciples, went into hiding, in fear for their own lives. (In fact, this was only the male disciples. Jesus' women followers were not so cowardly.)

And yet, on Sunday morning, reports began to circulate that Jesus had been seen. His disciples encountered him, come back from the dead. He appeared to his followers several times over a period of around forty days. Then the appearances ended.

This is an extract from John's Gospel's account of what happened:

Early on the first day of the week, while it was still dark, Mary Magdalene came to the tomb and saw that the stone had been removed from the tomb. So she ran and went to Simon Peter and the other disciple, the one whom Jesus loved, and said to them, 'They have taken the Lord out of the tomb, and we do not know where they have laid him.' Then Peter and the other disciple set out and went towards the tomb. The two were running together, but the other disciple outran Peter and reached the tomb first. He bent down to look in and saw the linen wrappings lying there, but he did not go in. Then Simon Peter came, following him, and went into the tomb. He saw the linen wrappings lying there, and the cloth that had been on Jesus' head, not lying with the linen wrappings but rolled up in a place by itself. Then the other disciple, who reached the tomb first, also went in, and he saw and believed; for as yet they did not understand the scripture, that he must rise from the dead. Then the disciples returned to their homes.

But Mary stood weeping outside the tomb. As she wept, she bent over to look into the tomb; and she saw two angels in white, sitting where the body of Jesus had been lying, one at the head and the other at the feet. They said to her, 'Woman, why are you weeping?' She said to them, 'They have taken away my Lord, and I do not know where they have laid him.' When she had said this, she turned round and saw Jesus standing there, but she did not know that it was Jesus. Jesus said to her, 'Woman, why are you weeping? For whom are you looking?' Supposing him to be the gardener, she said to him, 'Sir, if you have carried him away, tell me where you have laid him, and I will take him away.' Jesus said to her, 'Mary!' She turned and said to him in Hebrew, 'Rabbouni!' (which means Teacher). Jesus said to her, 'Do not hold on to me, because I have not yet ascended to the Father. But go to my brothers and say to them, "I am ascending to my Father and your Father, to my God and your God."' Mary Magdalene went and announced to the disciples, 'I have seen the Lord'; and she told them that he had said these things to her.

When it was evening on that day, the first day of the week, and the doors of the house where the disciples had met were locked for fear of the Jews, Jesus came and stood among them and said, 'Peace be with you.' After he said this, he showed them his hands and his side. Then the disciples rejoiced when they saw the Lord. Jesus said to them again, 'Peace be with you. As the Father has sent me, so I send you.' When he had said this, he breathed on them and said to them, 'Receive the Holy Spirit. If you forgive the sins of any, they are forgiven them; if you retain the sins of any, they are retained.'

But Thomas (who was called the Twin), one of the twelve, was not with them when Jesus came. So the other disciples told him, 'We have seen the Lord.' But he said to them, 'Unless I see the mark of the nails in his hands, and put my finger in the mark of the nails and my hand in his side, I will not believe.'

A week later his disciples were again in the house, and Thomas was with them. Although the doors were shut, Jesus came and stood among them and said, 'Peace be with you.' Then he said to Thomas, 'Put your finger here and see my hands. Reach out your hand and put it in my side. Do not doubt but believe.' Thomas answered him, 'My Lord and my God!' Jesus said to him, 'Have you believed because you have seen me? Blessed are those who have not seen and yet have come to believe.'

(John 20.1-29)

The whole of Christianity stands or falls on the idea that Jesus really rose from the dead. If that never happened, then Christianity is untrue and Jesus may be a nice man who taught some attractive things about morality, but that's it. (And Jesus would have been wrong in almost everything he said about every other topic, too.) If it happened, it shows that God does exist. People cannot raise themselves from the dead. Many people have become convinced that God exists because they have examined the arguments for and against the resurrection of Jesus and have concluded that he genuinely rose from death.

This is a **historical argument for the existence of God.** Instead of thinking about philosophical questions, it looks at history: at an event which, if it can be shown to have happened, must prove that there is a God. And not just *a* God: the God that exists is the God that Jesus preached about. But:

Did it happen? Did Jesus rise from the dead?

We have to be careful what we mean here. Some of the *accounts* of the resurrection of Jesus may contain some features which are not historical: they didn't happen. We're not asking whether every detail the Gospels describe is correct. The question is just: did Jesus rise from the dead, or not?

When Christians talk about Jesus 'rising from the dead', they're not talking about resuscitating a corpse. Jesus did not have his heart re-started. Nor was he a zombie. The resurrection is something to do with God, and, as is so often the case when people talk about God, they have to use picture language. So, the risen Jesus is said to have been raised to a new type of life. He would never die again; he was

immortal. He had a 'spiritual body'. He was clearly the same person, because his disciples recognised him. (John's Gospel, quoted above, says the risen Jesus proved this point to Thomas by showing

him the marks in his hands and side.) Yet his body was also different in certain ways. He could appear in a room when the doors were locked, and his followers didn't always recognise him at first (this was Mary Magdalene's reaction in our extract from John). We do not know exactly what the Gospel writers think the risen Jesus looked like. But then, they don't tell us what Jesus looked like before his resurrection, either.

But did it happen?

No serious scholar now doubts that the earliest Christians genuinely *believed* it did. Professor E. P. Sanders, a leading liberal New Testament scholar, is certain that the disciples genuinely *believed* they had experiences of the risen Jesus. (To be fair to Professor Sanders, he goes on to say that he does not know what the disciples *actually* experienced.)

'Did Jesus really rise from the dead?' is partly a question about whether something happened in history. If it's true, it's something that really happened. If it's true, there should be good grounds historically for saying that it took place.

If you're studying history, you'll know how to look at sources, and weigh up different interpretations of evidence. These are the skills we need here.

Normally, if a historical source said a dead man walked, we'd just dismiss it as ridiculous. In the case of Jesus, though, it's so important to Christianity that it's worth investigating carefully.

Maybe miracles can happen; maybe they can't. Different people have different ideas. If we start from the position that there is no God, and the resurrection of Jesus is impossible, then there's no point in debating it. It's a good idea, though, to shelve such reactions for a while as we examine the evidence. Is the evidence strong enough, if we keep an open mind, to show that Jesus rose from the dead?

If Jesus did *not* rise from the dead, then what *did* happen?

Various theories have been put forward. We examine them here. Not all of them are new, and they all re-surface from time to time.

Theory 1.
Jesus survived his crucifixion, and faked his own resurrection.

This sounds quite reasonable, until you start to think about it. It assumes that the Roman squad who executed Jesus were unrealistically stupid, and couldn't tell the difference between a dead man and someone who was unconscious. (Wouldn't they have checked his pulse?) John's Gospel says the Romans made quite sure that Jesus was dead: they

Christ in majesty. Stained glass, St Thomas' church, Winchelsea

thrust a lance into his body, presumably aiming for the heart (John 19.31-35). Although it's *just about* possible that someone *just might* survive that, the question has to be asked: *is it likely?*

It also makes Jesus a fraud and a liar. He *might* have been, but there is no evidence. It goes against what we know of the sort of man he was. Even very liberal New Testament scholars would hesitate at saying Jesus was a fraud. Again, the question is: is it likely?

Even if Jesus *could* have survived, what sort of shape would he have been in? We know what appalling mutilation crucifixion caused to the human body. (Crucifixion was not a punishment the Romans invented for Jesus. It was a common way of executing subjects of the Roman Empire, though it was not used on Roman citizens.)

Would someone suffering from awful injuries, who was barely alive, really have convinced his disciples he had risen from the dead? (And how would he have escaped from the tomb? It was sealed by a huge stone (Mark 15. 42 - 16.3).)

Theory 2.
Someone stole the body.

The Jews or the Romans could have stolen the body of Jesus. Or the disciples did.

If the Jews or the Romans did it, perhaps they wanted to stop the disciples themselves from stealing it. They wanted to prevent the disciples from faking Jesus' resurrection.

Or the disciples did it to do just that!

But:

- If the Jews or the Romans took the body, where did it go? The Jewish authorities hated the new religion of Christianity, and attacked it from the beginning. (The Acts of the Apostles in the New Testament gives the details.) The Romans did not like Christianity either.

  All they had to do to destroy the religion would be to produce the body. No missing body, no resurrection of Jesus. No resurrection of Jesus, no Christianity. End of story.

  But they didn't produce the body. This almost certainly means that they hadn't got it.

- The theory of the stolen body doesn't make sense for what we know about life in those days. It does not take account of the historical context. For Jews, dead bodies were revolting. Touching one made you religiously unclean, according to the Torah. The disciples were Jews. Their religious sense would have been too strong to allow them to fool around with a dead body. Moreover, the Jewish historian Josephus tells us that Jerusalem – quite a small town by today's standards – was absolutely packed with pilgrims during Passover. This was when Jesus was buried. Moving a dead body around unnoticed would have been impossible.

- The disciples would have believed in a general resurrection – that, at some fixed point in the future, *all* the dead would rise and be judged by God. Yet *no-one* believed that only *one* man would rise. So, they would not have believed that Jesus would rise from the dead, and would not have a motive to fake it. Mark's Gospel says

that they did not have the faintest idea what Jesus was talking about when he predicted his resurrection (Mark 9.9-10).

In fact, some scholars have suggested this point gives one good reason for saying that the resurrection *did* happen. No-one expected it, so no-one would fake it. The Messiah was expected to kill other people, not die and rise again. A good reason for making people change their view – and saying *one* man *had* risen – was that it happened!

- The natural reaction to finding an empty tomb would be to assume the body had been stolen. (John says this is what Mary Magdalene thought.) Careful study of the New Testament shows that faith in Jesus' resurrection was not originally based on an empty tomb. Paul, writing in AD 54 to the Church at Corinth, lists the people to whom he says the risen Jesus appeared (1 Corinthians 15.3-8). He says that most of them were still alive when he was writing (so presumably he's saying to his readers: go and ask them!). Paul bases his belief in the resurrection on the *appearances* of the risen Jesus. *He never mentions an empty tomb.* He did not think it was important.

  New Testament scholars say this shows belief in Jesus' resurrection was *not* based on the empty tomb. It was based on the idea that Jesus *appeared*.

  The concept of the empty tomb was only appealed to later, to back up the idea of the resurrection. This is the picture we find in the Gospels. An empty tomb alone would not make people believe the resurrection.

- Matthew says the Jewish leaders asked Pilate to set up a guard on Jesus' tomb to prevent the disciples from stealing the body (Matthew 27.62-66). If this detail is correct, how would the disciples have got past a squad of armed men?

Theory 3.
Someone else was crucified instead of Jesus.
Jesus then faked his own resurrection.

Once again, this makes Jesus a fraud and a liar. We have seen the problems with this idea.

And, once again, it makes the Romans total idiots. Jesus was well known. Wouldn't someone have noticed? John's Gospel says Jesus' mother and the 'other disciple' or 'the disciple who Jesus loved' (usually thought to be John) stood at the foot of the cross and were able to speak to Jesus (John 19.25-27). Surely they would have recognised him?

And when would the switch have taken place? The Jewish authorities had put pressure on Pontius

Pilate, the Roman governor, to have Jesus executed. Wouldn't they have protested at the Romans' incompetence when they saw it was not their enemy being executed, but someone else?

Theory 4.
The risen Jesus was actually someone else pretending to be Jesus.

But wouldn't they have noticed?! People were no more gullible then than they are now.

Theory 5.
The disciples believed they had seen the risen Jesus, but they were mistaken.

Perhaps, in their grief at Jesus' death, they made it all up. Or they hallucinated (perhaps they were on drugs).

Yet the risen Jesus did not behave like a hallucination. Hallucinations happen to individuals, not groups. They're usually incoherent, not coherent. Hallucinations can't be touched, and certainly can't cook you breakfast (Luke 24.36-39, John 21.1-14).

The disciples' being on drugs initially sounds more plausible. Magic mushrooms did grow in Israel.

There is only one drawback: there is no evidence that they used drugs.

And in any case, the accounts of the appearances of the risen Jesus are nothing like accounts drug users have written of their 'trips'.

The idea that the disciples made it all up is unrealistic. Professor E. P. Sanders draws attention to the Romans' usual practice. If you executed a troublemaker, you rounded up all his followers and executed them as well. That the Romans initially left the disciples alone shows that they did not regard Jesus as a very great threat. The disciples would have been terrified, believing that they were next. And they thought Jesus' execution was the end. He wasn't the Messiah after all, he was wrong, he'd died crying out to his God, who had abandoned him.

Men in that state of mind do not make up stories about their dead leader being alive again.

We also know that many of the disciples (including Peter) were executed for being Christians. Would they really be willing to die for something they had made up?

Jesus was killed on Friday. By Sunday evening, something had happened. Something which convinced broken men that Jesus had won, not lost. Something which they were willing to die for. Whatever had happened to effect this monumental change, it had to have been something absolutely extraordinary.

Theory 6.
Jesus was from outer space. Or he was a time traveller.

Jesus' superior technology made the disciples think he had risen from the dead.

It's pretty extraordinary that people suggest ideas like these, but they do. There is only one tiny problem with them: there is no evidence.

What makes most sense? What is most likely?

If we assume that nothing outside our own experience can possibly happen, we get nowhere. If it happened, the resurrection of Jesus *would be* outside our normal experience because, of the billions of people who have ever lived, *only one* rose from the dead. If it happened, it must be outside our normal experience. It only ever happened once.

History never allows us to be 100% certain. Henry VIII could have had a seventh wife whom he kept quiet about. We have to ask: what is the most likely explanation?

The Greek philosopher Aristotle said:

A plausible impossibility is preferable to an unconvincing possibility.

In other words:

an explanation which makes sense, but which we'd normally consider impossible,

     - can be more convincing than:

an explanation which is possible, but which is unconvincing.

What do you think? Does the resurrection of Jesus make more sense than the other explanations? Which solution best explains the evidence?

Either:

Write the following essay:
'The resurrection of Jesus is a historical fact.'
Outline the arguments for and against this view.
Give your own view and explain your reasons.
Or:
Motion for a class debate:
'This house believes that Jesus rose from the dead.'

18
Miracles (4):
Can you tell a false account from a genuine one?

We've got lots of stories about miracles, from all the world's religions. There are other accounts of things that are unusual, whether they're miraculous or not. Any major event produces deniers: conspiracy theories. There are people who say that Jesus was actually from another planet, or he was a time traveller, or he married Mary Magdalene and lived to a ripe old age in Rome. For more recent events, there are people who say that 9/11 was the work of the Americans themselves, or that the moon landings never happened.

How seriously should we take accounts of unusual events? Should we consider them seriously, or dismiss them without a thought?

When you were younger, you might have read C. S. Lewis' *The Lion, the Witch and the Wardrobe* (or have seen the film). Lewis was not just a novelist; he taught English at Oxford and Cambridge Universities and he wrote a huge number of books about Christianity.

In *The Lion, the Witch and the Wardrobe*, four children called Peter, Susan, Edmund and Lucy are staying in the large, rambling house of Professor Kirk. When they're playing hide-and-seek, Lucy hides in a wardrobe, which is actually the gateway to another world: Narnia. Lucy is nearly kidnapped by a faun, Mr Tumnus, but is allowed to go free, and she returns and tells the others about her experiences. She's very upset when they don't believe her. A little later, she gets back to Narnia, and her brother Edmund goes too.

Back in England, Lucy hopes that Edmund will back up her story. He doesn't, because he's a brat. He thinks it would be funny to say they'd

made it up, and he likes the idea of making his sister cry.

Lucy sticks to her story. Not knowing what to do, Peter and Susan go to see the Professor to ask his advice. We pick up the story at this point.

The result was the next morning they decided that they really would go and tell the whole thing to the Professor. 'He'll write to Father if he thinks there is really something wrong with Lu,' said Peter; 'it's getting beyond us.' So they went and knocked at the study door, and the Professor said 'Come in,' and got up and found chairs for them and said he was quite at their disposal. Then he sat listening to them with the tips of his fingers pressed together and never interrupting, till they had finished the whole story. After that he said nothing for quite a long

time. Then he cleared his throat and said the last thing either of them expected:

'How do you know,' he asked, 'that your sister's story is not true?'

'Oh, but —' began Susan, and then stopped. Anyone could see from the old man's face that he was perfectly serious. Then Susan pulled herself together and said, 'But Edmund said they had only been pretending.'

'That is a point,' said the Professor, 'which certainly deserves consideration; very careful consideration. For instance - if you will excuse me for asking the question - does your experience lead you to regard your brother or your sister as the more reliable? I mean, which is the more truthful?'

'That's just the funny thing about it, sir,' said Peter. 'Up till now, I'd have said Lucy every time.'

'And what do you think, my dear?' said the Professor, turning to Susan.

'Well,' said Susan, 'in general, I'd say the same as Peter, but this couldn't be true - all this about the wood and the Faun.'

'That is more than I know,' said the Professor, 'and a charge of lying against someone whom you have always found truthful is a very serious thing; a very serious thing indeed.'

'We were afraid it mightn't even be lying,' said Susan; 'we thought there might be something wrong with Lucy.'

'Madness, you mean?' said the Professor quite coolly. 'Oh, you can make your minds easy about that. One has only to look at her and talk to her to see that she is not mad.'

'But then,' said Susan, and stopped. She had never dreamed that a grown-up would talk like the Professor and didn't know what to think.

'Logic!' said the Professor half to himself. 'Why don't they teach logic at these schools? There are only three possibilities. Either your sister is telling lies, or she is mad, or she is telling the truth. You know she doesn't tell lies and it is obvious that she is not mad. For the moment then and unless any further evidence turns up, we must assume that she is telling the truth.'

Susan looked at him very hard and was quite sure from the expression on his face that he was not making fun of them.

'But how could it be true, sir?' said Peter.

'Why do you say that?' asked the Professor.

'Well, for one thing,' said Peter, 'if it was real why doesn't everyone find this country every time they go to the wardrobe? I mean, there was nothing there when we looked; even Lucy didn't pretend there was.'

'What has that to do with it?' said the Professor.

'Well, sir, if things are real, they're there all the time.'

'Are they?' said the Professor; and Peter did not know quite what to say.

'But there was no time,' said Susan. 'Lucy had no time to have gone anywhere, even if there was such a place. She came running after us the very moment we were out of the room. It was less than a minute, and she pretended to have been away for hours.'

'That is the very thing that makes her story so likely to be true,' said the Professor. 'If there really is a door in this house that leads to some other world (and I should warn you that this is a very strange house, and even I know very little about it) – if, I say, she had got into another world, I should not be at all surprised to find that the other world had a separate time of its own; so that however long you stay there it would never take up any of *our* time. On the other hand, I don't think many girls of her age would invent that idea for themselves. If she had been pretending, she would have hidden for a reasonable time before coming out and telling her story.'

'But do you really mean, sir,' said Peter, 'that there could be other worlds - all over the place, just round the corner - like that?'

'Nothing is more probable,' said the Professor, taking off his spectacles and beginning to polish them, while he muttered to himself, 'I wonder what they *do* teach them at these schools.'

'But what are we to do?' said Susan. She felt that the conversation was beginning to get off the point.

'My dear young lady,' said the Professor, suddenly looking up with a very sharp expression at both of them, 'there is one plan which no one has yet suggested and which is well worth trying.'

'What's that?' said Susan.

'We might all try minding our own business,' said he. And that was the end of that conversation.

Carefully read through the text again.
Explain:
- Peter and Susan's viewpoints (arguments)
- The Professor's viewpoints (arguments), especially when he says, 'Either your sister is telling lies, or she is mad, or she is telling the truth.' Why does he say this?
- Who do you agree with and why?
- We're considering the question of whether miracles are possible. If Peter and Susan had told the Professor that Lucy had witnessed a miracle, what might he say?

Notice that Peter and Susan are trying to evaluate *someone else's* experience. Lucy *knows* Narnia exists because she's had direct experience of it. (So has Edmund, but he's chosen to deny that experience.) Peter and Susan have to try and work out whether what Lucy claims is true. It can be much harder to work out whether someone else is telling the truth – to evaluate someone else's experience, than it is to evaluate your own.

Lewis would take seriously the reports of the miracles from the Gospels. His view is that the Gospel writers, like Lucy, are people who are concerned to tell the truth.

For an alternative view, let's look at the arguments of David Hume.

David Hume (1711 – 1776) was a Scottish philosopher; he was also an economist and historian.

One of Hume's many books was called *An Enquiry concerning Human Understanding.* There, he defined a miracle as:

'a transgression of a law of nature by a particular volition of the Deity, or by the interposition of some invisible agent.'

Not the easiest definition in the world to understand! We can translate this as:

A miracle is when God decides to breaks a law of nature. Or it can be when something else, something invisible, breaks a law of nature.

So, the key thing is that there are **laws of nature.** Most of us would probably agree with this. Hume says a miracle would be an occasion when God, or something else that can't be seen, breaks a law of nature.

Many people would argue that God exists because the universe exists. They'd say, for example, that the fact that there is a universe means someone has created it. Or they'd say that the universe looks as though it has been designed, which must mean that someone has designed it.

Hume would disagree with this. He said you can't prove God's existence from looking at the universe. Ordinary things don't prove God's existence.

But, said Hume, miracles might. Or at least, they'd be strong evidence that there is a God.

But Hume was very sceptical about the idea that miracles actually happen.

Why?

Well, Hume thought in terms of whether things were probable – or improbable. Most of the time, we think something has really happened because it's *likely.* This isn't Hume's example, but if I said the sun rose yesterday morning, you'd be inclined to believe me because it's *likely* it happened. You'd be less inclined to believe me if I said God cured me from being blind – because it isn't the sort of thing that often happens. So it doesn't sound likely.

Therefore, if we have a report of a miracle, it has to be investigated. It can only *really* be a miracle if another explanation for it sounds even more unlikely.

Hume is very dubious about the idea that any miracle ever happened. Why? Hume gives four reasons:

1. People often lie. They might lie about a miracle taking place, said Hume. This might be because they want to benefit their religion or because they want to be famous.
2. People will pass on miracle stories because they enjoy doing so. A false miracle story can still therefore be heard by lots of people, but it's still false.
3. Hume says miracles generally seem to happen in 'ignorant' and 'barbarous' times and places.
4. Hume notices lots of religions have their own miracle stories. Different gods are said to grant miracles. But miracle stories from different religions cancel each other out. Which god actually grants miracles? The God of the Bible? A god from ancient times? It looks more likely that none of them does. (You may not find this point terribly easy to understand. Not surprising; Hume's case seems pretty weak here.)

Is Hume right? Lots of people would go along with him. What do you think?

On the other hand...

1. Just because something's said by a famous philosopher doesn't mean it's true!
2. Hume can be criticised for his starting point: miracles are more or less impossible. He just

assumes this. It's where he's *starting* from, not where he's *reached* after looking at the evidence.

3. Hume assumes natural laws can't be broken. But if God exists, surely he can break his own laws? He designed them in the first place! If you can create a whole universe just by thinking it into existence, making a few loaves and fish will not be much of a challenge!

4. Miracles could just be rare. Is that the same as saying they're unlikely?

5. People often lie. True. But people often tell the truth, too. If some miracles stories are lies or are untrue, does it follow that *all* miracle stories are false?

6. Hume says that miracle stories happen in 'barbarous' and 'savage' societies. This sounds more like snobbery than judgement. It's very easy, for example, to say that Israel in Jesus' time was a savage and uncivilised society. But it is an assumption. Roman culture had its savage aspect but it was highly civilised in many respects; Israel was part of the Roman Empire. The Jewish society in which Jesus was brought up was very far from being 'barbarous' or 'savage'. It is nonsense to say 'past bad, present good.' Early twenty-first century Iraq, Zimbabwe or the Congo are far more savage societies than anything that existed in the ancient world. Snobbery is based on assumptions and assumptions are often wrong.

1. Give David Hume's definition of a miracle. (It's the bit beginning 'a transgression of a law...') What does this definition mean?

2. Hume gives four reasons why he is dubious that any miracle happened. What are these four reasons?

3. 'If God exists, God created nature. So God can break natural laws.' Do you agree? Give your reasons. Explain why someone might disagree with you and why you reject their viewpoint.

Talking point:

'People in the past were very dim. They believed all sorts of rubbish. They thought miracles happened. We know now that's not the case.'

19
Miracles (5):
Do miracles happen today?

What do you make of this account?

Studying at university generally involves a lot of lectures and classes. They vary in interest levels from being fascinating to being so dull that you want to gnaw your fist off. They're very rarely shocking. But I attended one that was.

I'd done my degree and was doing my PGCE. That's the one year course which qualifies you as a teacher. I was training in the RE department of the university. Most of us were Christians, though there were a few agnostics. Sally, our lecturer, decided we'd better have a couple of sessions on Christianity. She thought it would be worth our looking at an angle of Christianity that's not usually covered, so she invited along a Church of England priest who had a reputation of being a faith healer – in other words, a miracle worker.

I guess I was very closed minded in those days. I'd done well at school and university and thought I knew it all. The idea that this guy could work miracles seemed to me absolutely insane. Accordingly, when the priest – let's call him Peter – came in, we were not as polite as we could have been; to my shame, I can remember sitting there openly sneering at him.

Peter talked to us for a while about his work as a priest. He then made the claim that he had a special ministry of healing. In other words, he claimed that, working through him, God made people better. In his church, they organised special healing services.

Then it was time for questions. Time to show this guy up, I thought, as the nutcase he obviously is.

At the time, I was suffering from a heavy cold. And I mean a *really* heavy cold. The difference between this cold and a normal cold was like the difference between a nuclear reactor and a candle flame. I had a horrible cough, on top of feeling as though my head was full of glop up to just below my eyes (sorry to be revolting), and I had chest pains – the lot. Should have been in bed, really.

So, when we were asked for questions, I shot my hand up. 'Can you heal my cold, then?' I asked.

Suppressed laughter from the more cynical members of the group. Lecturer frowned warningly at me.

'Sure,' said Peter. 'Please could you come out to the front?'

A bit surprised, but not to be outcooled, I stood up and walked over to Peter. I still didn't believe a word of it, but was by now feeling a bit guilty about putting him on the spot. He was obviously going to fail and make a fool of himself and I wasn't being fair.

Peter and I were facing each other. He asked if it was OK for him to lay his hands on my head; I said it was. He closed his eyes and prayed, aloud. I remember him saying, 'Lord, I pray that you will heal this man'.

Remember I had the mother of all colds – and it was at its height. Normally, it would take at least a week to get better.

After Peter had prayed over me for a few seconds, my cold got better.

Not gradually. It disappeared. Vanished. Instantly. Just like that.

This is an account of something that really happened. It's hard to expect you, who are reading this, to believe me. If you knew me personally, you might be more inclined to believe me. The cure wasn't gradual. It didn't happen over a number of days, or even in hours or minutes. It was instant. If you could invent

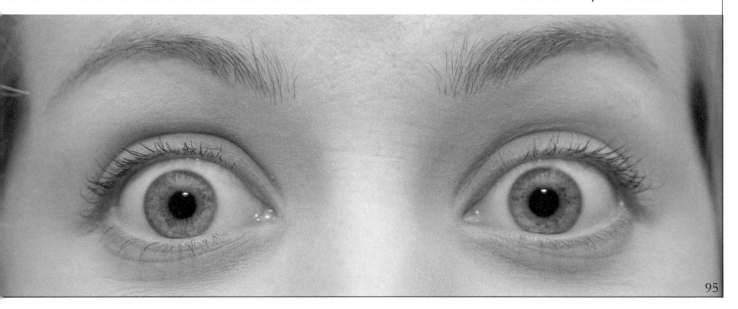

an over-the-counter cold remedy that worked so well, you'd make millions.

Something else was odd about the experience. I'd studied theology – ideas about God. I would have assumed that God had better things to do than to cure the cold of a privileged, middle class twenty-something. He'd want to intervene, to help, where it *really* mattered, in situations where people were really ill.

And yet, he cured my cold. That's the only explanation I can come up with for what happened.

Reports of miracles of healing are found in all the major Christian denominations. Not all Christians believe them, nor are they expected to. Things like this are negotiable: they're not at the heart of Christianity and people who find them difficult to accept don't have to.

This brings us to another question:

Why might accounts of miracles cause problems for Christians?

It's not just accounts of modern miracles that are a problem for some Christians today. Many are troubled by the whole idea of miracles.

Most Christians would say, though, that you have to believe in the resurrection of Jesus, the supreme miracle, if you're going to be a Christian.

(Actually, not everyone would agree with this. Some would claim to be Christians but think Jesus is dead and buried. However, they might say that Jesus' teaching or message is what's important. What do you think of this view?)

Suppose we take the other miracles of Jesus. Do you have to believe in those in order to be a Christian?

In fact, the answer's no. There's nothing in Christianity to say you must believe every single thing in the Gospels is historically accurate. So Christians are free to say that the miracles, or some of the miracles, did not happen.

Here are some of the problems Christians might have with miracles.

1. Miracles make it look as though God has favourites, or as though he is unfair. But God loves *everybody*. God wouldn't choose to cure the illness of a few ill or disabled people, just because they were lucky enough to have met Jesus, when he allows children to die of cancer in the world today. Miracles actually don't fit with God's goodness: if he's going to be good, he must also be fair, so he'd either cure everybody, or nobody.

2. Miracles like Jesus walking on the water or calming the storm look very like showing off. God is prepared to control the weather just to make Jesus look good. But he didn't stop the slaughter of around one million people in the Rwandan genocide of 1994. Can God have such a warped sense of priorities? He cannot be arbitrary in this way. So miracles don't happen. We don't know *why* God does not help; we only know *that* God does not help.

3. Some of the miracles in the Gospels involve demon possession. Some would say that, because science was then in its infancy, illness was said to be caused by demons. Today, we know it isn't. So some Christians would say the people were healed by Jesus, but the idea of demon possession is a first century one which has nothing to say to us today.

4. Some so-called miracles in churches today look like hysteria or self deception. And again, they raise the question of God having favourites.

1. If God exists, wouldn't we expect him to perform miracles today?

2. What are the problems miracles might cause for Christians today? Remember to give all four of them.

3. Some Christians might accept things as miracles that others would dismiss. Things like Jesus' face appearing on a pizza or statues weeping in churches. Are these more or less likely than miracles or healing – either in the Gospels, or in Christian communities today?

4. One place where miracles are reported to happen regularly is at the Catholic shrine of Lourdes, in France. Use a search engine to research more about Lourdes and prepare a short report on your findings.

Talking points:

- Look back at the previous chapter. What do you think the Professor in *The Lion, the Witch and the Wardrobe* would have to say about the modern account of the man who was cured of his cold?
- What do you think David Hume would have to say?

You may want to do this as a 'hot seating' exercise: one member of the class plays the Professor, and the rest of the class ask him questions. Do the same for David Hume. It will work best if 'Hume' and 'the Professor' prepare carefully for their roles by reading up the relevant bits in the previous chapter; and if people asking the questions work out what they're going to ask beforehand. Suggested props: pipe (Professor), tweed jacket (borrow one of the teachers'!), wig (Hume) – a jumper on the head will do. (What else might you want to use?)

Part Three

Religion and Science

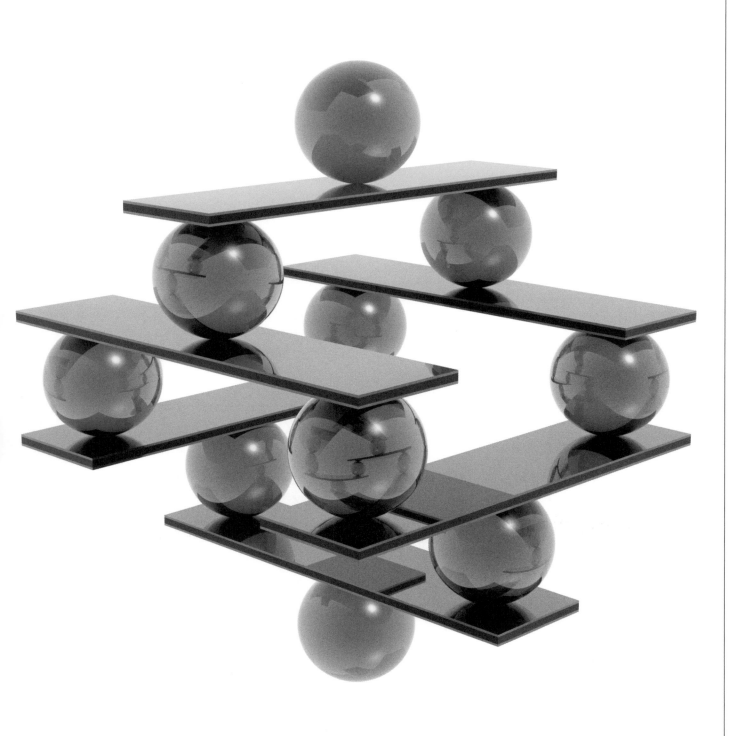

20
The Genesis creation stories (1)

This chapter starts a new section of *Philosophy of Religion for Today*, in which we examine the relationship between religion and science.

This topic surfaces frequently in the media. It can be presented in a very simplified fashion: all scientists are atheists and have all the answers; all Christians reject science, believe God made the world in six days and that the theory of evolution was invented by the Devil. Science proves the universe was created through the big bang and that life emerged through evolution. Christians believe in what the book of Genesis says about the creation of the world.

Of course, it's not as simple as that!

This section, then, examines the relationship between religion and science. We begin with a detailed examination of the accounts of creation from the book of Genesis, so that we can understand more about what Genesis is really saying.

In the beginning, God created the heavens and the earth.

(Genesis 1.1)

These words open the Bible. All Christians would agree with what they say: at the beginning of time, God created the universe. Most other religions would agree with this, too.

The disagreement among Christians, though, is over exactly how God did it.

Did God create the universe exactly as the Bible describes? Or was he behind the processes that are described by science? – the big bang and then, when billions of years had passed and the planets and suns had been formed, the emergence of life through evolution?

You may well know the creation stories from the book of Genesis: God created the world in one week, and the first humans lived in the paradise of the Garden of Eden until they disobeyed God and were cast out into the harsh world beyond the Garden. We've reprinted the stories on pages 101-104. They were originally written in Hebrew, as was almost all the rest of the Old Testament. We give an English translation.

In fact, Christians do not have to believe that Genesis is literally true: that it tells us exactly how things happened. This may come as a bit of a surprise. But the Bible contains lots of different types or genres of literature. It's not just history. There are also poetry, songs, parables, dreams and myths. We'll come back to myths in a moment.

Most Christians, and certainly those who have heard of the big bang and evolution, would accept that the methods God used to create the universe are described by science, and not by the book of Genesis.

The media, and some non-Christian writers, are not always fair in the way they present religion. There's a tried and tested technique in debate called a *straw man argument*. What this means is that you set up a caricature of your opponent's views – as though you're building a man out of straw. It's much easier to knock down a straw man than it is to knock down a real man. Christianity is often presented as though all Christians believe that the stories in Genesis are literally true. 'What a load of nonsense!' the opponents can then say. 'Haven't they heard of Darwin and the big bang?'

This is a straw man argument because it deliberately misrepresents the Christian viewpoint, in order to knock it down. It's a dishonest technique of debating. (And it's true, of course, that many atheistic writers and thinkers wouldn't use this sort of argument but would debate honestly and fairly with those they disagree with. But do watch out for straw man arguments. Politicians love them!)

So, if the accounts that open the book of Genesis aren't history, what are they?

Well, Old Testament scholars say the stories are just that: stories. The technical name for this sort of story is **myth**. In Biblical studies, a 'myth' doesn't mean a fairy tale. It's an attempt to get across religious truth in the form of a story. The *meaning* is what's true; the events described in the story are not true (and they're not intended to be).

Some people are unhappy with the term 'myth' because it sounds too dismissive. We could, then, suggest the term 'parable' instead. A parable is a story with a hidden meaning. There are lots of parables in the Old Testament and, in the New Testament, Jesus used them extensively when he preached. You probably know Jesus' parable of the good Samaritan (Luke 10.25-37). The point of the parable – the truth of the parable – is that human beings should treat each other with the same love and kindness that the Samaritan showed to the injured man. Jesus is not describing a real incident; he's not giving a news report. And it would totally miss the point to say that the parable has to be a narrative of something that really happened.

So, the Genesis stories are generally seen by Christians as myths.

It is true that some Christians – a minority – want to dismiss the findings of science and insist that Genesis tells us exactly how it happened. Christians who insist that the Bible is always literally true are

The Hebrew text of Genesis 1. You read it from right to left.

called fundamentalists. However, most Christians are not fundamentalists.

This is probably a good time for you to read the Genesis accounts.

Something you might have noticed is that there's a change of gear after Genesis 1 says God rested on the seventh day. We jump back, to before the creation of human beings. And God doesn't make lots of people at once, he makes just one. *Then* he makes the animals. But in the previous chapter, the animals were created *before* the humans. And God's suddenly called the LORD God, whereas up to now he's just been called 'God'. Also, the LORD God seems to be thought of in much more physical terms than he was in chapter one. He makes a statue out of mud, breathes on it, and it comes to life. He enjoys a stroll in the garden when the heat of the day has passed. But in chapter 1, there's no mention of his having a body: it's much clearer that he's omnipotent and just thinks (or speaks) things into existence.

- So, have we got one creation story in the book of Genesis, or are there two?
- And which part of Genesis 1-3 would you say is more sophisticated?

You've probably worked out that we're dealing with two creation myths, not one. Old Testament scholars say each comes from a different source. The Torah, the first five books of the Bible, is traditionally said to have been written by Moses. However, most experts now believe that there are four main sources used by the editor of the Torah.

They date from different times and given the initials of J, D, E and P. All were written well after Moses' death.

However, the material (traditions) which make up J, D, E and P may frequently be very much older than the documents.

So, some more details:

J

J uses God's name throughout. In Hebrew, this is written as YHWH or as JHVH; the Hebrew letters can be changed into our alphabet in either way. J is the first letter of JHVH / YHWH: hence the source's name. It's usually dated to the 9th and 10th centuries BC. (Remember that with BC dates, you're counting *backwards* from the birth of Christ. So, for example, 1000 BC is 900 years earlier than 100 BC.) In English, YHWH is translated as the LORD (with capital letters, to show it's translating the name of God). Saying 'Lord' instead of God's name follows ancient Jewish practice: the name of God was too holy to pronounce, so Jews would say 'the Lord' instead.

D

D is for Deuteronomy. The document was worked on between the 8th and 6th centuries BC.

The Torah

E

E stands for Elohist; 'Elohim' is the Hebrew word for 'God' and the source uses this name. It's less easy for scholars to identify E material than it is to identify the other sources. Some scholars therefore think of E as a number of different, small sources. E is probably from about the same period as J.

P

P, the last of the documents, dates from the 6th century BC. 'P' stands for 'Priestly'; the writer or writers seem particularly interested in matters to do with the ancient Jewish priesthood. P, or people who had the same ideas as P, produced the final version of the Torah.

Back to Genesis.

- The first creation story, Genesis 1.1–2.4a, is from P. This tells how God created the world in seven days.

- The second story, Genesis 2.4b-3.24, is from a combination of J and E. This may well be why God is called 'the LORD God', which is unusual in the Old Testament: 'LORD' or YHWH is what J calls him; 'God' or 'Elohim' is what E calls him – and the editor has just combined the two, so you get YHWH Elohim or, in English, the LORD God.

- The break between the P and the JE versions comes in Genesis 2.4, after the sentence in our translation which reads 'These are the generations of the heavens and the earth when they were created.'

The text of Genesis 1.1–3.24: the creation of the world.

In the beginning when God created the heavens and the earth, ² the earth was a formless void and darkness covered the face of the deep, while a wind from God swept over the face of the waters. ³ Then God said, 'Let there be light'; and there was light. ⁴ And God saw that the light was good; and God separated the light from the darkness. ⁵ God called the light Day, and the darkness he called Night. And there was evening and there was morning, the first day.

⁶ And God said, 'Let there be a dome in the midst of the waters, and let it separate the waters from the waters.' ⁷ So God made the dome and separated the waters that were under the dome from the waters that were above the dome. And it was so. ⁸ God called the dome Sky. And there was evening and there was morning, the second day.

⁹ And God said, 'Let the waters under the sky be gathered together into one place, and let the dry land appear.' And it was so. ¹⁰ God called the dry land Earth, and the waters that were

gathered together he called Seas. And God saw that it was good. ¹¹ Then God said, 'Let the earth put forth vegetation: plants yielding seed, and fruit trees of every kind on earth that bear fruit with the seed in it.' And it was so. ¹² The earth brought forth vegetation: plants yielding seed of every kind, and trees of every kind bearing fruit with the seed in it. And God saw that it was good. ¹³ And there was evening and there was morning, the third day.

¹⁴ And God said, 'Let there be lights in the dome of the sky to separate the day from the night; and let them be for signs and for seasons and for days and years, ¹⁵ and let them be lights in the dome of the sky to give light upon the earth.' And it was so. ¹⁶ God made the two great lights – the greater light to rule the day and the lesser light to rule the night – and the stars. ¹⁷ God set them in the dome of the sky to give light upon the earth, ¹⁸ to rule over the day and over the night, and separate the light from the darkness. And God saw that it was good. ¹⁹ And there was evening and there was morning, the fourth day.

²⁰ And God said, 'Let the waters bring forth swarms of living creatures, and let birds fly above the earth across the dome of the sky.' ²¹ So God created the great sea monsters and every living creature that moves, of every kind, with which the waters swarm, and every winged bird of every kind. And God saw that it was good. ²² God blessed them, saying, 'Be fruitful and multiply and fill the waters in the seas, and let birds multiply on the earth.'

The writer of Genesis 1 says God created the universe. But he didn't think of the universe in the same way as we do. This drawing is based on a reconstruction by Old Testament scholars; it shows how the Genesis writer saw the cosmos. As you read the story, think about how it matches the description of God's creation in the text.

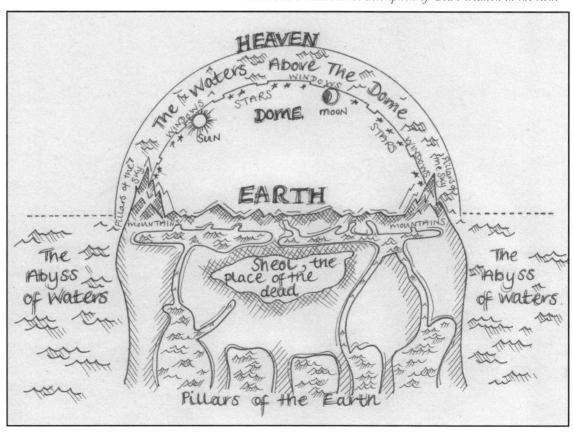

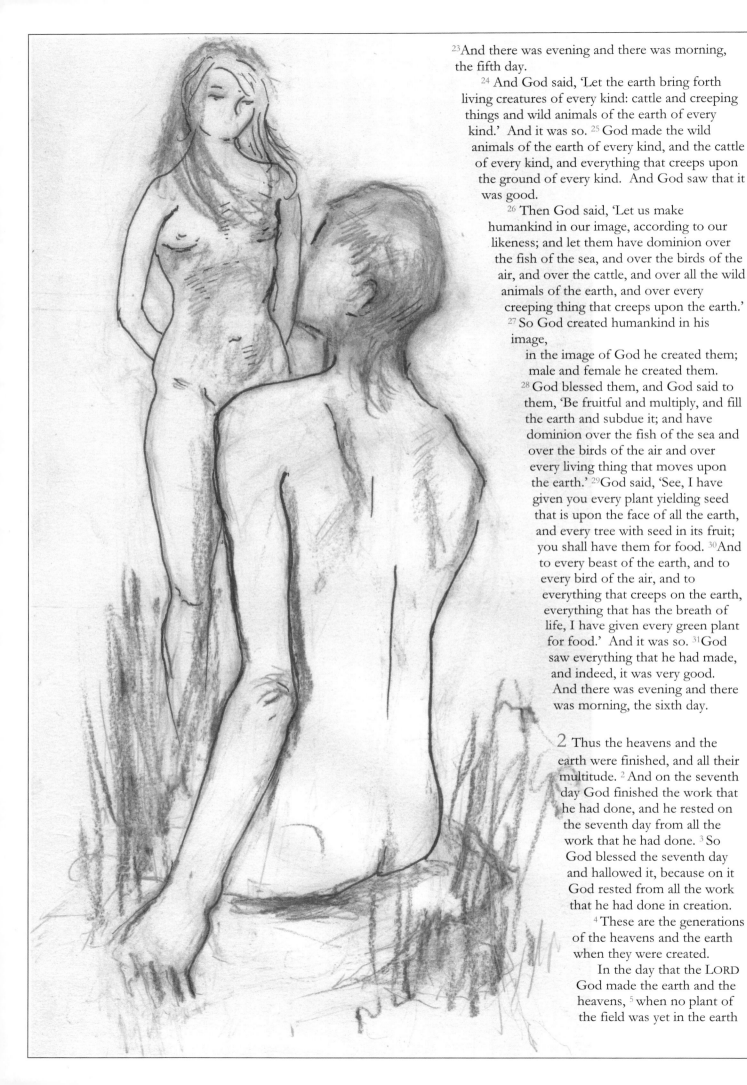

²³And there was evening and there was morning, the fifth day.

²⁴ And God said, 'Let the earth bring forth living creatures of every kind: cattle and creeping things and wild animals of the earth of every kind.' And it was so. ²⁵ God made the wild animals of the earth of every kind, and the cattle of every kind, and everything that creeps upon the ground of every kind. And God saw that it was good.

²⁶ Then God said, 'Let us make humankind in our image, according to our likeness; and let them have dominion over the fish of the sea, and over the birds of the air, and over the cattle, and over all the wild animals of the earth, and over every creeping thing that creeps upon the earth.' ²⁷ So God created humankind in his image,

in the image of God he created them; male and female he created them.

²⁸ God blessed them, and God said to them, 'Be fruitful and multiply, and fill the earth and subdue it; and have dominion over the fish of the sea and over the birds of the air and over every living thing that moves upon the earth.' ²⁹God said, 'See, I have given you every plant yielding seed that is upon the face of all the earth, and every tree with seed in its fruit; you shall have them for food. ³⁰And to every beast of the earth, and to every bird of the air, and to everything that creeps on the earth, everything that has the breath of life, I have given every green plant for food.' And it was so. ³¹God saw everything that he had made, and indeed, it was very good. And there was evening and there was morning, the sixth day.

2 Thus the heavens and the earth were finished, and all their multitude. ² And on the seventh day God finished the work that he had done, and he rested on the seventh day from all the work that he had done. ³ So God blessed the seventh day and hallowed it, because on it God rested from all the work that he had done in creation.

⁴ These are the generations of the heavens and the earth when they were created.

In the day that the LORD God made the earth and the heavens, ⁵ when no plant of the field was yet in the earth and no herb of the field had yet sprung up – for the LORD God had not caused it to rain upon the earth, and there was no one to till the ground; 6 but a stream would rise from the earth, and water the whole face of the ground – 7 then the LORD God formed man from the dust of the ground, and breathed into his nostrils the breath of life; and the man became a living being. 8 And the LORD God planted a garden in Eden, in the east; and there he put the man whom he had formed. 9 Out of the ground the LORD God made to grow every tree that is pleasant to the sight and good for food, the tree of life also in the midst of the garden, and the tree of the knowledge of good and evil.

10 A river flows out of Eden to water the garden, and from there it divides and becomes four branches. 11 The name of the first is Pishon; it is the one that flows around the whole land of Havilah, where there is gold; 12 and the gold of that land is good; bdellium and onyx stone are there. 13 The name of the second river is Gihon; it is the one that flows around the whole land of Cush. 14 The name of the third river is Tigris, which flows east of Assyria. And the fourth river is the Euphrates.

15 The LORD God took the man and put him in the garden of Eden to till it and keep it. 16 And the LORD God commanded the man, 'You may freely eat of every tree of the garden; 17 but of the tree of the knowledge of good and evil you shall not eat, for in the day that you eat of it you shall die.'

18 Then the LORD God said, 'It is not good that the man should be alone; I will make him a helper as his partner.' 19 So out of the ground the LORD God formed every animal of the field and every bird of the air, and brought them to the man to see what he would call them; and whatever the man called each living creature, that was its name. 20 The man gave names to all cattle, and to the birds of the air, and to every animal of the field; but for the man there was not found a helper as his partner. 21 So the LORD God caused a deep sleep to fall upon the man, and he slept; then he took one of his ribs and closed up its place with flesh. 22 And the rib that the LORD God had taken from the man he made into a woman and brought her to the man. 23 Then the man said,

'This at last is bone of my bones
    and flesh of my flesh;
this one shall be called Woman,
    for out of Man this one was taken.'

24 Therefore a man leaves his father and his mother and clings to his wife, and they become one flesh. 25 And the man and his wife were both naked, and were not ashamed.

3 Now the serpent was more crafty than any other wild animal that the LORD God had made. He said to the woman, 'Did God say, "You shall not eat from any tree in the garden"?' 2 The woman said to the serpent, 'We may eat of the fruit of the trees in the garden; 3 but God said, "You shall not eat of the fruit of the tree that is in the middle of the garden, nor shall you touch it, or you shall die." ' 4 But the serpent said to the woman, 'You will not die; 5 for God knows that when you eat of it your eyes will be opened, and you will be like God, knowing good and evil.' 6 So when the woman saw that the tree was good for food, and that it was a delight to the eyes, and that the tree was to be desired to make one wise, she took of its fruit and ate; and she also gave some to her husband, who was with her, and he ate. 7 Then the eyes of both were opened, and they knew that they were naked; and they sewed fig leaves together and made loincloths for themselves.

8 They heard the sound of the LORD God walking in the garden at the time of the evening breeze, and the man and his wife hid themselves from the presence of the LORD God among the trees of the garden. 9 But the LORD God called to the man, and said to him, 'Where are you?' 10 He said, 'I heard the sound of you in the garden, and I was afraid, because I was naked; and I hid myself.' 11 He said, 'Who told you that you were naked? Have you eaten from the tree of which I commanded you not to eat?' 12 The man said, 'The woman whom you gave to be with me, she gave me fruit from the tree, and I ate.' 13 Then the LORD God said to the woman, 'What is this that you have done?' The woman said, 'The serpent tricked me, and I ate.' 14 The LORD God said to the serpent,

'Because you have done this,
    cursed are you among all animals
    and among all wild creatures;
upon your belly you shall go,
    and dust you shall eat
    all the days of your life.
15 I will put enmity between you and the woman,
    and between your offspring and hers;
he will strike your head,
    and you will strike his heel.'
16 To the woman he said,
'I will greatly increase your pangs in childbearing;
    in pain you shall bring forth children,
yet your desire shall be for your husband,
    and he shall rule over you.'
17 And to the man he said,
'Because you have listened to the voice of your wife,
    and have eaten of the tree
about which I commanded you,
    "You shall not eat of it",
cursed is the ground because of you;
    in toil you shall eat of it all the days of your life;
18 thorns and thistles it shall bring forth for you;
    and you shall eat the plants of the field.
19 By the sweat of your face
    you shall eat bread
until you return to the ground,
    for out of it you were taken;
you are dust,
    and to dust you shall return.'
20 The man named his wife Eve, because she was the mother of all who live. 21 And the LORD God made garments of skins for the man and for his wife, and clothed them.

22 Then the LORD God said, 'See, the man has become like one of us, knowing good and evil; and now, he might reach out his hand and take also from the tree of life, and eat, and live for ever' – 23 therefore the LORD God sent him forth from the garden of Eden, to till the

ground from which he was taken. [24] He drove out the man; and at the east of the garden of Eden he placed the cherubim, and a sword flaming and turning to guard the way to the tree of life.

1. Your exam specification may well require you to learn some or all of the contents of Genesis 1-3.
Write your own questions to help you remember the text.
You need to have a question for each major point of the story.
We've done the first 3 for you:

1. In the beginning, God created – what?
2. How is the earth described?
3. What swept over the face of the what?

Swap questions with another member of the class and test each other!

2.a) What does it mean to say the creation stories in the book of Genesis are myths? (You need to give a detailed answer.)
b) Why would a fundamentalist say the creation stories are not myths?
c) Do most Christians accept the fundamentalist viewpoint?

3.a) Name the four sources of the Torah, with their dates.
b) Which source contained the account of God making the universe in a week?
c) Which source contained the Adam and Eve story?

If you need to learn the text for the exam, this is a good technique to help you.

Read it! (It may help to concentrate your mind on the story by reading it aloud.)
Then read it through again, carefully, the next day.
And the next.
And the next.
Do it for a week. Test yourself, using your questions.
Then highlight the details you've forgotten and / or make a note on them and learn them.
Once you know the text, come back to it once a week or so just to keep your memory topped up.
This sort of learning – little and often – is less stressful and more efficient than trying to cram it all in in one sitting.

21

The Genesis creation stories (2)

Here's a question which could be asked:

Did the writers of Genesis think they were recording how creation actually happened?

There are certainly Christians and Jews who would say they did. However, this may not be the case:

- The stories are very different. If they're trying to describe how things actually happened, wouldn't the editor have tried to iron out the differences? He doesn't seem worried by the fact that the order of creation in the stories is different, or that God is described in much more human terms in JE than he is in P. Surely he would have noticed!

- The Genesis stories are not the only creation myths from the ancient world in the area around Israel (the Near East). Old Testament scholars have studied other myths from other cultures – and the writers of these other myths seem perfectly happy to rewrite and change them. So it does look as though people from that time, unlike us, were quite happy with having different accounts of the same events. It's as though they're saying, 'Here's a way of thinking about this' and 'Here's another,' rather than 'this is how it happened.'

What do you think?

To a large extent, the stories speak for themselves. Here, though, are a few notes to help. It's worth reading the accounts again. (As a general tip, it's always good to re-read any set texts you have, for any subject. The more often you read them, the more they'll stick in your memory: useful if you're going to have to sit an exam when they might come up!)

The P story (Genesis 1.1-2.4a)

- The idea of having water as a symbol of chaos was common in the ancient world. Why do you think they hit upon this image?

- God certainly seems omnipotent (all powerful) in this story. He also seems to be omnibenevolent (all good) too. Everything he makes is 'very good'. The universe is not hostile or evil; it's good and it's beautiful.

- You probably know about the Jewish food laws, which basically categorise different types of food. A similar sort of categorising runs through this story. There are different types of plants, according to what seeds they have; different types of animals; there's a difference or a distinction drawn between the waters under the dome from the waters above the dome.

- From this story, and from other parts of the Old Testament, scholars have tried to see how P understood the universe that God created. He didn't think of the universe – 'the heavens and the earth' – in the way we do today. If P had been asked to draw what he thought the universe was like, he'd probably have drawn something like the picture on page 101. In the story of Noah's ark, it's the waters under the earth and above the dome that are unleashed to flood the land (Genesis 7.11).

- The writer C. S. Lewis comments that people in the ancient world did not think of the universe in terms of *distance*, as we do today. We'd say the

sun is 91 million miles away and the next nearest star is about four light years distant. But people in the ancient world thought of the universe in terms of *height*. The stars, the sun and moon, were not so much a long way away as very, very high up.

- The sun, moon and stars are made by God. This is a bit of an attack on the polytheistic (many gods) religions of the other nations, who often thought the sun, moon or stars were gods. They're not. They're lights, and they're made by God.

- The 'great sea monsters' in verse 21 aren't things like plesiosauruses. People in P's time didn't know about dinosaurs (as far as we know). P seems to believe in sea monsters, unless he's thinking of things like whales. Again, P's probably having a go at other religions here. The Babylonian creation story is called Enuma Elish. In it, the god

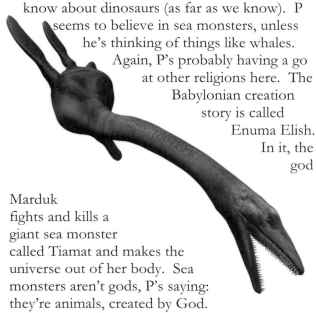

Marduk fights and kills a giant sea monster called Tiamat and makes the universe out of her body. Sea monsters aren't gods, P's saying: they're animals, created by God.

- The climax of the story is at the end, on the sixth day. God creates human beings. They, not the plants or the animals, are made 'in the image of God'.

  Frequently, in the ancient Near East, the king alone was called the image of (a) god. In the non-Biblical creation stories, ordinary human beings were made by the gods as scum. When Marduk makes human beings, he makes them as 'savages' and slaves for the gods.

  There is a huge contrast to this in P. Every human being is made 'in the image of God', as though every human being is a king or queen. Moreover, there doesn't seem to be any difference in status between men and women (though there is in the JE account). God makes people in his own image, whether he makes individuals to be male or female.

- That God says 'Let us make' is a bit puzzling. Why doesn't he say 'Let me make'? It's not certain, but this may be a 'plural of majesty' – in other words, it's like a king calling himself 'we' rather than 'I'. (In fact, the Hebrew word for

'God', Elohim, is plural, but it means 'God' and not 'gods'.)

- The original human beings are vegetarian (1.29) and it looks as though P thought God intended people to be vegetarian. Later in P, humans are allowed to eat meat. This comes after the flood, when God's recognises that people are often sinful, so he moves away from his original intentions (Genesis 9.3).

- P explains the origin of the Sabbath, the Jewish holy day (2.2-3). In fact, the Sabbath was already being observed by the time P wrote. Maybe P thought that God would have wanted to keep his own rules, and so he too rested on the Sabbath.

The JE story (Genesis 2.4b-3.24)

If you put aside everything we've been saying so far, and just read this as a story, it's actually a very, very good one. There's a baddie, there's the 'will they / won't they?' suspense as to whether they'll eat the fruit or not, and there's the sadness and terror of God's curses at the end.

Interesting, too, that a 3000 year old story still has people saying, 'It wasn't me, it was him,' and 'It's not my fault!' You sometimes wonder whether human nature changes all that much.

Some comments:

- In contrast to P (which hadn't been written yet), JE has Adam created first, then plants, then animals, then the woman.

- The Hebrew for 'man' is 'adam', and he's made from earth: 'adama'. The words are closely related. He's adam because he's made from adama.

- The man's forbidden to eat the fruit of the tree of the knowledge of good and evil. In the Garden of Eden, the man and the woman are totally innocent when they are made; they're almost like little children. God does not want them to lose that innocence.

- Marriage is part of God's creation. It was part of God's design for human beings, in Paradise; it was not invented later.

- The snake is not meant to be the Devil, even

though later Christian writers thought that's who he was. He's just a particularly sneaky snake.

- The LORD God's punishments are severe:
  - The snake will crawl on its belly. (Presumably, JE thought he had legs before this?) Human beings and snakes will always hate each other.
  - Childbirth will be painful for the woman, and the man will be her ruler.
  - Adam's fault curses adama: it will not be easy to make the soil bear crops, and agriculture will mean toil and sweat.
- Now that Adam and Eve have lost their innocence, they may try to eat the fruit from the tree of life. But only God should live for ever. So the LORD God banishes them from paradise, and bars their way by the flaming sword and by the cherubim. Cherubim aren't cute, chubby little boys with wings here; they're mythological monsters. Sadly, JE does not describe them, but there are similar creatures in the mythologies from elsewhere in the ancient Near East.

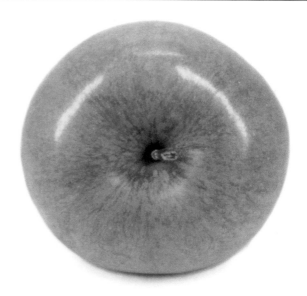

Three ways Christians today understand these stories

1. The fundamentalist view: they are literal accounts of how things actually happened. (This is a minority viewpoint.)

2. They are myths.

3. They can be reconciled (brought together) with what science tells us about the origin of the universe.

We haven't examined this third view yet. People who hold it would say:

- The stories do describe the big bang and evolution, in simple ways that the people of the time could understand. For example:
- When God says, 'Let there be light,' (1.3), this could mean the big bang.
- The six 'days' don't mean literal days of twenty-four hours. Each 'day' stands for millions, even billions, of years.
- The order of creation in Genesis 1 is the same as evolution tells us things developed. First planets, then animals, then human beings.

The problem with this viewpoint is that things get much more difficult when you get to Genesis 2 and 3. It's almost impossible to bring together evolution and the Adam and Eve story. One way round this is

to see Adam and Eve as a sort of parable of what happens to everybody. We want to be good, to be perfect, but we're tempted, we give in, and we fall away from the perfection God wants for us.

What do you think? Are the P and JE stories best understood:
- as accounts of how things actually happened;
- as attempts to get across scientific ideas to ancient, non-scientific people;
- or as myths?

Christian beliefs and the creation stories

Christians disagree about what type of story the creation narratives are, but they would all agree the creation stories contain the following truths:

- God created the universe. This is true, regardless of whether he did it in six days or used the big bang and, billions of years later, evolution.
- God loves what he created, and his creation is ultimately good. He did not create the universe and then not bother about it (this view is called *Deism*). Creation is a gift, and it's given to living things, including the animals and, especially, human beings.
- Human beings are made in the image of God. This does not mean they look like him. (P does not seem to think of God as a physical being, unlike JE.) Like God, human beings have a capacity for goodness, for creativity, and they have a mind, personality and intelligence. Every human being is a person, and God is a person too.
- As they are made in the image of God, human beings are of infinite value and must be treated as such. Jesus told a parable about the fate of those who do, and those who do not, treat other

human beings as their brothers and sisters, made in God's image (Matthew 25.31-46).

- Human beings have an enormous capacity for messing things up. They do not always choose goodness. As a result, God has to save them from themselves. Christianity teaches that God does this by becoming human as Jesus Christ, by dying and by rising from the dead.

1. Write your own notes on the P and JE stories. You need to include the following words:

P
water
sun, moon and stars
sea monsters
'it was very good'
'in the image of God'
Sabbath

JE

adam / adama
marriage
the snake
God's punishments
cherubim

2. Look at the section 'Christian beliefs and the creation stories'. Make your own notes on the five points we give. (The point about human beings' being made in the image of God is particularly important. You'll need to ensure you learn this point, too.)

3. 'The creation stories in Genesis were trying to explain the big bang and evolution to people who couldn't understand science.' Do you agree? Give reasons for your answer, showing that you have thought about more than one viewpoint.

4. Draw the diagram of the Hebrew conception of the universe from page 101. (Better still, make a model of it!)

Talking points:

'The writers of Genesis believed they were recording history: they were writing records of exactly how things happened.' Do you agree?
'If the writers of Genesis had known about the big bang and evolution, it would not have troubled them.' What do you think?

Extension work: *Enuma Elish*, the Babylonian creation myth, is actually well worth reading. It's easily available on the Internet. Use a search engine to locate it and then read it!

The Bible and the natural world: Good stewardship

This is another way that modern Christian belief and practice relates to the book of Genesis.

The earth is beautiful. Genesis says that when God made it, 'he saw that it was very good.' But it's been spoilt by people's opting not for beauty and sharing, but for greed and selfishness. Today, we're all very aware of the things people have done which now threaten not only the beauty of nature, but perhaps the very existence of the natural world as we know it.

Sometimes people have done these things because they did not realise what they were doing. At other times, their actions have been much more blameworthy.

Christianity shares with Islam and Judaism the idea that the world is God's creation. It is not part of God. Nor did the universe just happen by accident one day. Rather it is filled with purpose and meaning, and it reflects God's goodness.

We can see these ideas very clearly in the Bible, and particularly in the poetry of the Old Testament:

The earth is the LORD's and the fullness thereof,
the world and those who dwell therein;
for he has founded it upon the seas,
and established it upon the rivers.

Psalm 24.1-2

O LORD, our Lord,
how majestic is thy name in all the earth! …
When I look at thy heavens, the work of thy fingers,
the moon and the stars which thou hast established;
what is man that thou art mindful of him,
and the son of man that thou dost care for him?
Yet thou hast made him little less than God,
and dost crown him with glory and honour.

Psalm 8.1, 3-6

Texts like these are among the oldest parts of the Bible. Many of them were written at a time when the people of Israel were tempted to adopt the religions of the countries around them, especially the religion of the Canaanites, whose country they had largely taken over.

One of the interesting things about Canaanite religion is that it was very much concerned with trying to get what you wanted from the natural world. There were different gods for different natural phenomena – and by worshipping them, you tried to bribe them into giving you a good harvest, for instance.

This was very different from the religion of Israel. The Old Testament prophets and writers repeatedly insisted that **the natural world belonged to one God, who was the creator of everything. God had put men and women in charge, but the ruler of everything was God.** This idea appears in the Psalms and in the creation stories in Genesis.

But being in charge of the world does not mean people can do what they like with it and try to get as much out of it as they can, for two reasons:

- Trying to manipulate the world for your own advantage was a characteristic of pagan religion, as we have seen. The Israelites' attitude was to be different: it was to be one of humble awe before God's creation, the sort of attitude expressed in the Psalms.

- The idea that, when you're in charge, you can do what you like is totally different from the Bible's teaching. The kings of Israel were not allowed to be tyrants, like their neighbours in Egypt. They were God's stewards, his deputies, who were

looking after things for him. They are meant to rule fairly, as God himself rules, and obey his laws of justice.

We can sum this up by saying:

The Bible teaches that people's attitude towards the natural world should be one of

good stewardship.

109

22
Hindu Creation Myths

There are various creation stories in Hinduism. We'll consider two of them in this chapter.

One of the best known comes from the **Rig Veda.** It is difficult to date this myth with certainty, though it's at least 3000 years old.

The myth in the Rig Veda tells of the **Purusha** – the primordial, cosmic Man. Purusha was later identified as Vishnu; Vishnu is one of the ways Hindus think of God (see page 24).

Purusha, says the myth, was gigantic. He had a thousand heads, a thousand eyes and a thousand feet. 'Everything that existed in the past,' says the Rig Veda, 'and that will exist in the future' is the Purusha.

Purusha was sacrificed by the devas, the higher beings or beings of light. The ghee or clarified butter that resulted produced 'birds flying in the air, wild animals of the forest, and domesticated animals of the villages.' The sacrifice also produced the poetry and rhythms of the Rig Veda.

Purusha's sacrifice also produced:
- the moon, from his mind;
- the sun, from his eyes;
- the air, from his breath;
- the devas, such as Indra, Agni (Fire) and Vayu;
- the antariksha, the space between the earth and the heavens, was produced from his navel;
- heaven, from his head;
- and earth, from his feet.

The Purusha's sacrifice produced caste:
- From Purusha's face came the Brahmans, the priests;
- From his arms came the kshatriyas, the warriors;
- From his thighs came the vaishyas, the merchants;
- From his feet came the shudras, the labourers.

We need to explore a byway at this point, because **caste** is an aspect of Hinduism that has been massively misunderstood in the West. To explain, we'll hand over to Seeta Lakhani, who writes:

'The Purusha myth states that just as different parts of the body fulfil different functions for the benefit of the one body, people with different skills should use their diverse skills for the benefit of

society as a whole, just as a person with the skills of a bricklayer should work as a bricklayer; a person with the skills of a brain surgeon should work as a brain surgeon, for the benefit of society. We now contrast this with the "hereditary caste system": a stick used for beating up Hinduism in the West.

'Hereditary caste teaches that the profession of a person is not dictated by the skills he possesses, but by birth. If a person is born into a carpenter's family he is only fit to be a carpenter. The best example of the hereditary caste system operating in the UK is the royal family. A person who is born into the royal family automatically becomes the heir to the throne. He might not be suited to this task but he is not only placed at the head of the state but is also made the head of the Church of England! This is a prime example of hereditary caste system operating in the UK. The reason why we have offered a very English example of hereditary caste is to draw attention to

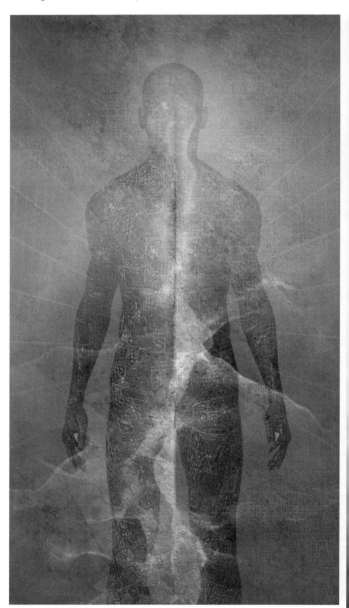

the fact that the hereditary caste ascribed to the Hindus is *not* a religious institution but a *socio-economic one,* visible in every society.

'The idea of classifying people at birth as being higher or lower, or only fit for certain professions, has no basis in the scriptures of authority of Hinduism. The *Bhagavad Gita* states that "A person's caste is determined by the qualities he possesses" (18.41). In the next verse, it defines the qualities of a person suitable to be a Brahmin as "one who exhibits self-restraint, purity, forgiveness, uprightness, and love of knowledge and belief in God." There is no mention of a *hereditary* caste system. The *Bhagavad Gita* does *not* define a Brahmin as "one who happens to be born into a Brahmin family"!

'Every modern proponent of Hinduism has sharply rebuked the practice of a hereditary caste system. All of them have condemned the hereditary caste system as an *atrocity* in the name of religion. Just as the Crusades* are an atrocity in the name of Christianity, but cannot and should never be promoted as Christianity, the Hindu hereditary caste system *cannot and must never be* taught as Hinduism.'

* Crusades: the anti-Muslim wars fought by Christians in the 11th, 12th and 13th centuries.

The Purusha myth and the book of Genesis

The Purusha myth is very different from the two Hebrew myths of creation.

They're not only different in terms of their stories, but in terms of their ideas.

Creation out of nothingness?

Christian interpretations of Genesis 1 (the P myth) have generally said that it shows creation *ex nihilo*. This means that God created the universe out of nothing. In the Purusha myth, this is not the case: something that already exists is re-organised.

However, some Biblical scholars today suggest that creation *ex nihilo* isn't actually in the P myth; it's been read into it. The point goes like this. Genesis 1.1-2 reads:

In the beginning God created the heavens and the earth. The earth was without form and void, and darkness was upon the face of the deep; and the Spirit of God was moving over the face of the waters.

When it says the earth was formless and empty, and there were waters over which God's Spirit hovered, are these things to be taken as images of nothingness? Or are they meant to be some sort of

Vishnu

pre-existent matter? The first sentence can actually be translated, 'When God began to create the heavens and the earth...' which makes it even less like creation *ex nihilo*.

(Creation ex nihilo doesn't seem to feature one way or the other in the JE myth.)

God and the universe

In the Purusha story, there's a much closer connection between God and creation than there is in the Genesis accounts, where God is wholly separate from what he creates.

Purusha *becomes* the universe. This *can* be taken as an image of **pantheism.**

(*Pan* is Greek for 'all' and *theos* is Greek for 'God', so pantheism is 'all-God-ism': everything is God.)

However, if you look back to chapter 4, you'll understand why Hindus would be unhappy with the idea of Hinduism being defined as pantheism.

Hinduism is better called '**pan*en*theism**': 'God-in-everything-ism'. ('En' is Greek for 'in'.) Panentheism is very close to the idea that God is omnipresent (everywhere); it's a stronger version of it, if you like: rather like the difference between grape juice and wine: same thing, just stronger! In fact, you could define 'panentheism' as 'omnipresence, but taken seriously!'

Most modern Hindus do not take the Purusha

myth to be an account of how the universe was actually created – just as most modern Christians do not take the Genesis myths to be historically accurate accounts. These Hindus and Christians are quite happy to accept the findings of scientific investigation into the origin of the universe.

Looking deeper: God giving up his Godhead

Let's consider some deeper meanings in the Purusha myth and look at a second Hindu account of creation. Again, we'll hand over to Seeta Lakhani for this section.

'It's true that the Purusha myth or Shukta tells of how different parts of the universe were made from the Purusha's body. This is mythological, though: it shouldn't be taken literally. There's a better and more subtle way of understanding what the myth is saying.

'The Purusha Shukta discusses a sacrifice. In the Vedic scriptures, the more simple meaning of sacrifice is making offerings (oblations) to the fire. The less obvious meaning of 'sacrifice' is 'giving up'. This is symbolically repeated during the process of sacrifice by saying, 'Swahah,' which means 'I give up.'

'The Purusha Shukta is symbolic of something being given up for the creation to come into being. What is being given up is the Godhead of God. It is God (as Purusha) who has to give up his Godhead to be manifested as the creation, which includes the physical, mental, and human realms.

'Underpinning this idea is an interesting theological concept of the Hindus which insists that, before you can have evolution, you have to have involution (becoming involved). Something that was

pure and pristine (the spirit or Purusha) sacrificed this perfect state and took on limitations to become the creation. It is *perfection* that is being sacrificed in the Purusha Shukta.

'To handle the puzzle of how this creation came into being, Hindu philosophers point to the Nasadiya Sukta.

Nasadiya Shukta (Rig Veda 10.129)
The idea of God as the cause of the universe is suspect!

'There is another Rig Vedic hymn that has perhaps greater bearing on Hindu understanding of creation. It is called the **Nasadiya Shukta** (literally meaning neither existence nor non-existence). This is a more poetic but also a more philosophically satisfying creation story for the Hindu philosopher. It suggests creation is a play of existence and non-existence. It even suggests that the idea of God is secondary, with a very cutting comment at the end: 'He who surveys in the highest heaven, He surely knows or maybe he does not!' This suggests that the spirit (Brahman) manifesting as the creation will continue to challenge every kind of explanation. (See chapter 4.)

Here is a full translation of the Nasadiya Shukta:

At first was neither Existence nor non-existence.
There was not air nor yet sky beyond.
What was wrapping? Where? In whose protection?
Was Water there, unfathomable deep?
There was no death then, nor yet deathlessness;
of night or day there was not any sign.
The One breathed without breath by its own impulse.
Other than that was nothing at all.
Darkness was there, all wrapped around by darkness,
and all was Water indiscriminate. Then
that which was hidden by Void, that One, emerging,
stirring, through power of Ardour, came to be.
In the beginning Love arose,
which was primal germ cell of mind.
The Seers, searching in their hearts with wisdom,
discovered the connection of Being in Nonbeing.
A crosswise line cut Being from Nonbeing.
What was described above it, what below?
Bearers of seed there were and mighty forces,
thrust from below and forward move above.
Who really knows? Who can presume to tell it?
Whence was it born? Whence issued this creation?
Even the Gods came after its emergence.
Then who can tell from whence it came to be?
That out of which creation has arisen,
whether it held it firm or it did not,
He who surveys it in the highest heaven,
He surely knows - or maybe He does not!

1. Outline the *Purusha* myth. In your answer, give the source and possible date of this story. Illustrate your answer by drawing the outline of a man, and labelling it according to which parts of Purusha's body became which phenomena. (For example, the sun comes from his eyes.) Drawing little pictures of the sun, moon and so on will help you to remember the myth. It may sound silly: it isn't, and it really will help you remember the story!

2. Do Hindus believe the *Purusha* myth is historically true?

3. 'The *Purusha* myth means that Hindus have to believe in a hereditary caste system.' Explain why this statement is incorrect.

4. What is:
a) pantheism, and
b) panentheism?
Is Hinduism best understood as being pantheistic, or panentheistic?

5. 'The *Purusha* myth is about how God gives up the Godhead in order to become manifested as creation.' What does this mean?

6.a) What is the *Nasadiya Shukta*?
b) What ideas are contained in the *Nasadiya Shukta*?

7. Christianity cannot be pantheistic. Why not? Could Christianity be seen as panentheitic? Explain your answer.

8. 'Creation myths are old fashioned and were written before science gave us the facts. They have nothing to say to us today.' Do you agree? Give reasons for your answer, showing that you have considered more than one viewpoint.

This translation of the *Nasadiya Shukta* on page 112 is by Professor Raimon Pannikar. It appears in his book *The Vedic Experience* and is used with his kind permission.

23
Religion and Science (1)

Religion and science have huge impact in today's world and frequently people get very worked up about the relationship between them. Here are some things people believe:

- Modern science gives us all the answers we need about the Universe. We don't need the idea of God any more.
- The Church and the organisations of non-Christian religions have held back the advance of proper scientific knowledge.
- The Bible says the universe was created in six days but today we know about evolution. This means all the Christian (and Jewish) scriptures must be rubbish. Probably the scriptures of the other religions are as well.

But on the other hand...

- People experience things which science has a big struggle explaining. You can't look at the ability to choose between good and evil, or the meaning of art, in a test tube.
- A very large number of scientists today are religious. They seem to have had no trouble combining being religious with being passionate about science. These people are very far from being stupid.
- Modern research into the scriptures has suggested that the ancient creation stories in the book of Genesis may never have been intended to be taken literally at all.

Writing contains meaning without being literally accurate. This is particularly true in poetry. The Scots poet, Robbie Burns (1759 -1796) wrote of his sweetheart:

O my Luve's like a red, red rose
That's newly sprung in June:
O my Luve's like the melodie
That's sweetly play'd in tune.

Burns doesn't mean that his girlfriend has thorns, petals and a fragrant flower. But by the imagery he uses he conveys to us a truth.

Many scholars say that the stories of creation are like this. And we know that some of the writers of the Old Testament were great poets, because they have left us collections of their works. Perhaps people who have taken the creation stories literally have been naïve, and may even have lost the real 'meanings' or 'truths' which the stories contain.

The Beginnings of Science

It's astonishing how much ancient people knew about mathematics and science. For instance, well before 2000 BC, the Ancient Sumerians (who lived in what's now modern Iraq) had already worked out how to divide a circle into 360°. The Babylonians who followed them knew how to calculate accurate positions from observing the stars and laid the foundations of astronomy. Ancient people applied advanced geometry to build huge structures like the pyramids of Egypt and the temples of their gods.

Eventually, ancient **Greece** became a great centre of learning and discovery. Many of the great mathematicians whose work we still rely on today came from there. For instance, you probably know how to calculate the length of the long side (hypotenuse) of a right angled triangle from its other two sides. The man who discovered this was an ancient Greek, Pythagoras, and we still call his discovery 'Pythagoras' theorem.'

As they learned all this mathematical and scientific knowledge, people asked questions about the world around them and the nature of truth. In

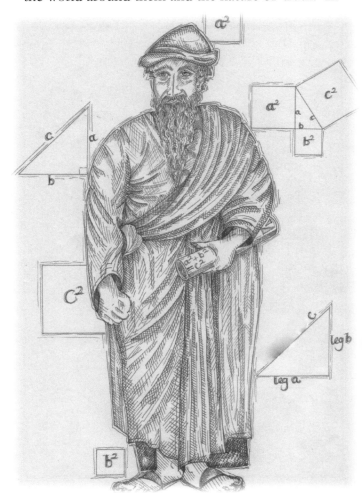

other words, they did philosophy.

Two very important philosophers of this time whose works have come down to us were **Plato** and **Aristotle**. Both of them thought it was superstitious to believe in the many gods worshipped by people of that time. Instead they thought that the moral and scientific laws of the universe pointed towards one God who was in some way responsible for those laws. This was rather similar to the beliefs of the Jews, who thought there was only one God who had guided them throughout their history.

In the course of time and in far away Italy, **Rome** expanded her borders until eventually she became a superpower. Large numbers of formerly independent countries were drawn into her Empire, which in Europe lasted for just over four hundred years (27 BC – 476 AD.) The Romans already had a great respect for Greek learning, and after they had conquered Greece they continued to use Greek philosophy, mathematics, art, poetry and science – what we call **classical learning**. Very frequently, Greeks were employed as private teachers and university lecturers. In this way, the great advances of science and philosophy were spread about the Empire. Even today, many of our modern laws, EU languages, architecture and philosophy are still rooted in the Roman Empire's way of doing things.

When Christianity started, it suffered terrible persecutions from the Romans. But by the middle of the fourth century AD, it was strong enough to become the official religion of the Empire. The Church was beginning to be very powerful in politics and education. It borrowed heavily from Roman ideas and so in this way the **classical tradition** of learning (Greek philosophy and science) passed into the outlook of the Church and into its schools and monasteries. The Church and the philosophers who followed Plato – and most philosophers did – both agreed there was one God, so that made the process easier.

The Roman Empire didn't last for ever. In Europe, it completely fell apart in 476 AD. The **Dark Ages** had begun, when fierce northern tribes, many still worshipping their own gods, descended on what was left of Roman Europe with one invasion after another. This was a time of huge threat to education and existing knowledge.

What saved classical learning in Europe was the Christian monasteries. (In the Arab countries and for different reasons, the new religion of Islam was going to do the same job). In the Christian monasteries that survived during the Dark Ages, the ancient books were copied out, and the tradition of knowledge learned from Greece and Rome was able to continue. The monasteries ran schools, trying to teach the message of Christ and to hold up the light of classical education in a dangerous and difficult time. And slowly but surely one European tribe after another became Christian (although sometimes this was difficult to tell from their behaviour).

Eventually, most of the people of Europe were Catholic Christians. This was the time of the Middle Ages, and the Church had never been more powerful. It had time to provide many of the things we now expect our countries to provide for us: a health service, schools, a dole for the poor. Great Universities were founded: in the UK, Oxford, Cambridge, St Andrew's and Glasgow. Here, classical learning and philosophy were continually discussed, along with Christian theology.

Some wonderful things were done by scholars and the Church in the Middle Ages, but there were serious problems

- All the knowledge that had survived the Dark Ages was so precious that they relied very heavily on it for their ideas.
- This meant that they didn't do any scientific experiments for themselves. If someone from classical times said the sun went round the Earth, they tended to believe it.
- Because the Church had got so powerful and important, many people who weren't really very interested in the teachings of Jesus used it for their own advantage. There was a lot of corruption, and people were beginning to say that radical reform of the Church was needed. But as you can imagine, many in positions of power had no intention of allowing this to happen. They were very resistant to change.

Towards the end of the Middle Ages and at the beginning of the sixteenth century, a new type of scholar appeared. They didn't just accept what the scholars of the Middle Ages had said about philosophy, or how the Church during the same period had interpreted the Bible. They studied the classical writers for themselves and drew their own conclusions. Then they searched for the best manuscripts of the scriptures, in their original languages, and studied them. We call them the **Christian humanists**. They wanted to see the Church reformed and they yearned for a simpler society based on Christ's original teachings. In England, St Thomas More is the best known of them.

At the same time in Germany, **Martin Luther** was beginning the Reformation. He owed a great deal to the Christian humanists. Luther was so outraged by the corruption in the Church that he said it had no authority at all. He had always been a biblical scholar, and now he believed that **the Bible was the absolute Word of God** and that was that. This started the birth of the Protestant Churches. Some of Luther's ideas were going to have very serious consequences for the relationship between religion and science later on.

The important thing about the Christian humanists is that they had introduced a new way of looking at questions. They weren't interested in taking things on trust and **went back to the original root of things**.

What the Christian humanists had done – going back to the root of things – was to make a huge impact in science. People looked again at what the classical writers had written, and began to ask questions for themselves. Scholars began to do **experiments,** instead of just relying on the classical writers. In this way, they found out more and more about the world around them and the universe. The beginnings of modern scientific method had been born. But it wasn't an easy birth for some. Certainly not for Galileo Galilei.

Galileo Galilei (1564 - 1642)

Galileo was an Italian Catholic scholar who specialised in astronomy. He was a personal friend of Pope Urban VIII and he had a brilliant mind. He was also a lively character who spent a fair bit of time hanging around in pubs. He made enemies easily and his ideas unsettled people, but had the protection of his friend the Pope.

Galileo proved by observation and mathematics that **the earth revolved around the sun**, and not the other way round. This was deeply shocking to most people of his time. The vast majority of people assumed that the Earth was the centre of the universe. Two of their reasons came from the classical and religious traditions they had grown up in:

- The book of Genesis has the earth in the middle;

- The ancient Greek mathematician Ptolemy had put it there as well.

There was another reason why it was very difficult to accept what Galileo was saying. In people's daily lives they didn't go about their business as though they were moving around the sun. It seemed a profoundly odd idea. And of course in our daily lives we do it too. When evening comes, we say 'the sun's going down' when of course it is doing nothing of the sort: our side of the earth is turning away from it. To say otherwise is strongly *counter-intuitive* (something which appears to be against common sense).

Thinking about the universe as being centred on the Earth is called having a *geocentric universe*. Galileo proved that the Sun is the centre of our solar system (*heliocentric*), an idea already put forward as a theory by Copernicus in 1543. It took many years before science developed to a point where the immense vastness of space and time could be appreciated.

Galileo seemed to be turning the whole way people thought about the world inside out. The earth was no longer in the middle of everything, as the centre of God's creation. To many people, especially Galileo's enemies, it seemed like heresy (believing in dangerously false ideas about God).

Pope Urban had reservations about what Galileo was saying, but he was a fair man and encouraged Galileo to publish a book. This was the ***Dialogue Concerning the Two Chief World Systems*** (1632). It was meant to be a fair discussion of the evidence for a universe with the earth as its centre (the classical idea) and his own idea that the Earth revolved around the sun. Unfortunately, Galileo ridiculed the classical idea. The character he invented to defend it he called 'the simple one' (*Simplicio*) – rather as we might talk about 'Simple Simon'. And, almost unbelievably, he put the words of the Pope, who had been brought up in the classical tradition, in the mouth of Simplicio.

Not surprisingly, Galileo soon found himself on trial in Rome. He was put under house arrest and was told that he had to go back on everything that he had said. In fear of his life, he agreed, and he died, still under house arrest, in 1642. Catholics were told not to read his books and their printing was banned in areas the Church could control until 1741, almost exactly a hundred years after his death.

Galileo isn't just important because of the scientific truths he discovered. He is important because what happened to him was the final death spasm of the old world of the Middle Ages, when classical learning, the authority of the Bible and the teaching of the Church had been seen as the reliable ways to truth. Now a modern, scientific way of doing things by **experimentation** had entered the field. For this reason, many people see Galileo as **the father of modern science.**

1. Write some notes on the following key words:
   Plato
   Aristotle
   Classical learning
   Christian humanists

2. Look at the section 'The Beginnings of Science.' This examines the development of ideas up to Galileo's time.
   From that period:
   Can you choose what you consider to be the two most important ideas?
   Why have you selected these?

3. 'True scientists must be atheists.' Do you agree? Explain your reasons. Why might someone disagree with you?

Talking points:

'What the Church did to Galileo shows that religious people will always attack science.' Do you agree?
Do you think modern Christians would approve of the way the Church treated Galileo?
'Before the development of science, human beings knew basically nothing.'
Can Science itself be a religion?

24
Religion and Science (2)

Charles Darwin

Galileo had astonished people in the seventeenth century by proving that the sun stood at the centre of the universe. Three hundred years later, the English naturalist Charles Darwin was to have a similar impact. What he said was to start an argument which still rumbles on today in religious communities in more than one part of the world.

In 1859, Darwin published a book called **On the Origin of Species.** It isn't a particularly snappy title so it needs a bit of explaining.

Until Darwin wrote *The Origin of Species,* the usual idea Christians had about animals was that God had created each of them directly. So for instance, he had made polar bears to live in the Arctic and gorillas for the tropical jungles of Africa: they had absolutely nothing to do with one another. Each of them were quite unique, beautiful original creations which were made directly by God, who had given them marvellous equipment to deal with where they were meant to live. Not only that, but God was meant to have done all this shortly after the creation of the world itself. This sort of thinking chimed in very well with the creation stories in the book of Genesis. The resulting wonder and beauty of the animal kingdom, it was felt, showed how marvellous God was.

The Origin of Species upset all of that. In it, Darwin suggested that the different species of animals were not the product of God's direct involvement at the moment of creation. Instead, they were the end result of a very long period of **evolution**. Over vast amount of time, animals had evolved from one another.

Darwin pointed out that farmers and people who keep pigeons regularly bred new types of animal to get the best results. Darwin said that evolution was slowly doing the same to the animal kingdom.

Much of Darwin's research was undertaken on the Galapagos Islands

118

So, for instance, the fact that some birds have beaks which look as though they'd been created especially to open shellfish had nothing to do with God's interfering in creation in the way people had thought. The real reason was that, over millions of years, that species of bird, distantly related to all other birds, had evolved to make the best use of some available food.

Lastly, and most importantly, Darwin said that humans were themselves the product of the same kind of evolution. He pointed out the huge similarities between us, the great apes and monkeys, and said that we had evolved from them.

The idea that mankind was not the pinnacle of God's creation and was simply another part of the animal kingdom – and descended from, above all things, monkeys – was deeply shocking. People responded in different ways to Darwin and his ideas. He was sometimes ridiculed by religious people who knew little about science. Other people simply lost their faith in Christianity as a result of what he said. The poet Matthew Arnold wrote about this in his poem *Dover Beach*, which was published eight years after *The Origin of Species*:

The Sea of Faith
Was once...at the full, and round earth's shore
Lay like the folds of a bright girdle furled.
But now I only hear
Its melancholy, long, withdrawing roar,
Retreating, to the breath
Of the night-wind, down the vast edges drear
And naked shingles of the world.

Ah, love, let us be true
To one another! for the world, which seems
To lie before us like a land of dreams,
So various, so beautiful, so new,
Hath really neither joy, nor love, nor light,
Nor certitude, nor peace, nor help for pain;
And we are here as on a darkling plain
Swept with confused alarms of struggle and flight,
Where ignorant armies clash by night.

Darwin's views on religion

Darwin's teachings (**Darwinism**) caused trouble, just as Galileo's had done before him. Darwin himself had once been training to be an Anglican clergyman, but his ideas about religion changed and developed during the course of his life. This seems to have caused him considerable distress, and he had many private discussions about it with his family and friends.

So, for instance, in *The Origin of Species* he talks about 'the Creator' being behind the process of evolution and that evolution was a better model for God's activity than **creationism**. ('Creationism' is the idea that the creation stories of Genesis are historically accurate.) But even in 1850, well before its publication, he would go for a walk while his family attended church, something that upset his wife Emma very badly. Soon he admitted privately that although he believed in a God he wasn't a Christian any more. After he died, his autobiography was published and that showed that he had taken a step further and become an agnostic.

What was Darwin's problem with religion? After all, very many Christians quickly accepted his scientific ideas. Darwin's difficulties with religion were these:

- The God of the Old Testament often seems a vengeful, unforgiving character. Once you accept that the creation stories of Genesis aren't historically true then you can see this more easily.

- In the summer of 1850, his ten year old daughter Annie died from scarlet fever. Although we probably shouldn't have favourites among our children, Annie was certainly Darwin's, and it is extremely probable that her death undermined his belief in a God who was good.

- The existence of cruelty in the animal kingdom meant that it didn't, after all, reflect the designs of a benevolent God.

- Religions all over the world – and those of the people he calls 'savages' – have miracle stories like the ones about Jesus in the New Testament. No sane person would be expected to believe in the miracle stories from the cultures of the 'savages', so the same must apply to those in the New Testament.

The last one of these points reflects the racism which Darwin shared with most Europeans of his time. But look carefully at the other three. While it is probably true to say that science opened Darwin's mind and helped him to break free from the traditional Protestant Christianity of his upbringing, none of them are really *scientific* arguments. Instead, they are to do with Darwin's struggle to believe in a good God in the face of evil in the world. (We look at this issue in the next section of this book.)

Here are some quotations from Darwin's autobiography that might interest you:

> I had gradually come, by this time [1836], to see that the Old Testament, from its manifestly false history of the world, with the Tower of Babel, the rainbow..., etc., etc., and from its attributing to God the feelings of a revengeful tyrant, was no more to be trusted than the sacred books ... or the beliefs of any barbarian.

> What advantage can there be in the suffering of millions of the lower animals throughout almost endless time? This very old argument from the existence of suffering against the existence of an intelligent first cause [God] seems to me a strong one.

Other people, however, welcomed what Darwin had to say. Less than two years after the publication of *The Origin of Species,* the leading Roman Catholic theologian in England, Cardinal Newman, said that the idea of evolution was 'a new idea of modern times which is superseding the old' and that it fitted in fine with Catholic teaching. In his view, the Bible didn't set out to explain *how* God went about creation, just that what he did, out of nothing, was good.

So it was that many Catholics were able to accept the idea of evolution without too much trouble. You may know that Catholic teaching is based not merely on the Bible but the teaching of the Church and on philosophy as well. Because of that, Catholic Christians (and many Anglicans) were able to draw on more than one way of thinking to see them through at a time when many Protestants saw the whole Bible – the basis of their idea of religious authority – as being under attack.

Particularly in America, however, a huge number of these Protestant Christians found Darwinism simply too hard to take. At the time Darwin was writing, the West was being taken from the Native Americans by the white man with his gun in one hand and, to read in his time off, a Bible in the other.

Many Americans believed themselves to belong to a special people who had been chosen by God to inhabit this 'new' land of America, just as the Bible said that the Jews were God's chosen people who had been given Canaan, the land of milk and honey.

These were very conservative Protestants who believed that every word of the Bible was literally true. For them, Darwinism undermined both their faith and the way they thought about their place in the world. So in America, there grew up a tradition which we still have today. We call it **Protestant Fundamentalism.** These Christians reject the idea of evolution completely and believe the creation stories of Genesis to be historically true. This attitude to the creation of the world and its species is creationism. Needless to say, it is dismissed outright by the whole of the scientific community and almost all European theology, but nonetheless it remains a very powerful force in American politics and education. Many people would say that this is an example of an unnecessary conflict between personal religion and known science.

The Debate Today

If we have modern Protestant Fundamentalists on one end of the scale, there are also people on the other end of it.

These are a group of modern scientists, mainly specialising in biochemistry, who argue that all life and its experiences are merely the effect of bits of DNA trying to replicate themselves in the struggle for survival.

These scientists are called the **Neo-Darwinians** because they say that they are following in Darwin's footsteps. The most famous of these thinkers is Professor Richard Dawkins, who has set out his ideas for non-scientists in two famous books, *The Blind Watchmaker* (1986) and *The God Delusion* (2006). Dawkins describes himself as a 'militant atheist' and claims that religion is a sort of evolutionary mental illness.

But of course there are problems with this. Most of all, Dawkins tries to describe how everything in the universe evolved, but he cannot seem to tell us why it is there and why there shouldn't be just nothing.

Creationism is still a force in the argument. A modern form of creationism is called **'Intelligent Design'.** This rejects the scientific discoveries of Darwin and others, and claims that the biological study of organisms shows each to have been directly designed by God. The people behind the idea of 'intelligent design' came up with this term because it didn't have the 'baggage' of 'creationism' – but in fact it's actually a variation of the same idea.

People who advocate 'intelligent design' are very influential in the United States. They continue to try to get their ideas taught in science classes in US schools, and at one stage had the backing of President George W. Bush in this. But the US courts ruled that 'intelligent design' was unscientific, on the basis that the scientific community as a whole said it simply didn't hold water.

There are, from time to time, attempts to have 'intelligent design' taught in science classes in UK schools as well, but these are unlikely to come to anything. (Do you think it's something you should learn for your science GCSEs?)

People tried to introduce 'intelligent design' into Belgian schools too. It wasn't successful: the Belgians felt that there was no point in changing the curriculum – because the Catholic Church had no problem with the theory of evolution!

Note:

Don't confuse *intelligent design* with *the argument from design* (the *teleological argument*):

- Intelligent design is a modern restatement of creationist views.
- The argument from design / the teleological argument does *not* need creationism to work. You can still believe in evolution and the big bang and accept the teleological argument.

Final thoughts

You can see that the relationship between religion and science has been a very complicated one. No doubt as we make more and more scientific discoveries, we will be challenged and astonished by the phenomenon that is our universe. History seems to teach us that religion is best off when it comes to terms with genuine science, as most Christians and those of other faiths do today. As for scientists themselves, their work can lead to terrible as well as wonderful results – think about the hydrogen bomb and chemical warfare. Perhaps their science needs to be informed by spiritual questions which are too often dismissed.

One last thought. Something we can definitely say is that over its long evolution the universe has begun to understand itself and to ask questions. We know that because it happens in every one of us, and we are part of the universe, self-conscious beings who are each made from the dust that was once part of a star.

Where did the Universe come from to start with?

The short answer to this question is that we don't really know. This is because science after Galileo has always insisted that in order to establish something as a fact, we have to be able to reproduce it in an experiment. We can't do this for starting up a universe! So in some very fundamental ways the question 'Where did everything come from?' can't be a strictly scientific question. However, scientists can still make some observations about the Universe as it is now and draw conclusion. Here are some very important examples:

- We know that objects are moving away from Earth very fast. We can *conclude* from this that in the past things were a lot closer together.
- The universe is not *absolutely* cold. In fact, it has a temperature of 2.7 degrees Kelvin. Though this is colder even than liquid helium, the fact that it is 'warm' is surprising. The fact that the galaxies are moving apart implies that at some time they were closer together. In a similar way, the fact that the universe is not completely cold implies that at some time it was much hotter. After that it then cooled down during its process of expansion, since expansion of something generally reduces its temperature.

So it seems that at the start of the universe, it was very hot and very compressed. Most scientists think that there was then a sudden critical explosion of space, time and matter which started everything off. This is usually referred to as the **big bang** idea. It has helped us with the calculation of, for instance, the amount of hydrogen, helium and lithium isotopes in interstellar space.

But the big bang idea holds problems. When we look at galaxies far away in space, their light takes a long time to reach us. Some of these galaxies are so far away that the radiation they send to us takes us to within a few seconds of creation itself. But those first few missing seconds are crucial to a scientific understanding of where the universe came from, and we are not certain what happened in them. Similarly, we can observe and calculate how much matter there is in the universe and therefore how much it should weigh. But unfortunately by calculation we know how to 'weigh' the universe – and it weighs far too much! This has led to the idea that there exists a huge amount of heavy 'dark matter' which we cannot observe. Other scientists think we have just got our sums wrong.

This is not to say scientists are wrong about the big bang. It's just that the evidence for the big bang is not quite as certain as is sometimes thought. The big bang fits the evidence we have – but we don't have all the evidence.

So things seem to be a bit up in the air, and we certainly don't seem to be any nearer the answer to the question, *why* is the universe there in the first place?

1.a) What was the title of Darwin's book?
b) What did Darwin say about evolution?
c) What was the usual idea Christians had about animals before Darwin wrote his book?
d) In what different ways did people react to Darwin's findings?

2. 'Darwin did not believe in God because of evolution.' Is this correct? Explain your answer.

3. What is:
a) creationism
b) intelligent design?

4. What does Professor Richard Dawkins say about religion?

5. What was the big bang?

6. 'If evolution is true, then humans are part of the animal kingdom. That means we must treat animals with respect.' What do you think?

Talking points:

'Scientists don't have all the evidence they need to prove the big bang happened. So we need to look for an alternative explanation. And that alternative explanation is that God created the world in six days.'

'The big bang fits in much better with God's omnipotence than the book of Genesis does!'

'Atheistic scientists start from the position that God doesn't exist and then look for evidence to prove their opinions.'

Part Four

God and evil

25

The problem of pain (1)

'When you look at the misery in the world, the evil, suffering and death, it seems pretty obvious that God does not exist.'

This is a common viewpoint. In theology (God talk), the fact that there is suffering is a real problem if you want to believe in God. It is sometimes called the **problem of pain.**

What is the problem of pain?

The problem of pain is also called:

the problem of evil

or

theodicy.

It has three main aspects:
- Where does suffering come from?
- Can you believe in a God who is good when the world is so full of suffering?
- Can suffering have any positive value or meaning?

We'll examine each of these questions in turn.

Where does suffering come from?

Most Christian writers say the answer depends on the kind of suffering you are talking about. It could be said that there are –

two types of suffering:

Suffering caused by human wickedness. Some examples are the horrors of war, murder, people trafficking and exploitation. This is given the technical name of

moral evil.

Suffering which apparently 'just happens'. This includes the suffering caused by natural disasters, illness, and the sufferings of the animal kingdom. The technical name for this is

natural evil.

Sometimes, natural and moral evil can overlap, as when an earthquake (a natural disaster) causes the collapse of houses which have been built unsafely because of the greed of a property developer.

Traditional Christian theology says a great deal of suffering is caused by sin.

The idea goes like this:

God gives people **free will:** they are not God's puppets; they can genuinely choose how to live their lives. So people have a real choice to do or not to do things that are wrong and alienate them from God: sins.

Because God is wholly good, wrong choices lead further and further away from him and from perfection. The imperfection resulting from sin results in suffering, both for the sinner and for his or her victim.

Christians have sometimes tried to explain natural evil in this way as well. Here, the sins of human beings are seen to have affected the whole of creation, corrupting what was once a prefect world. This idea, in its crude form at least, is not as popular as it once was. It is hard to believe that the suffering of the dinosaurs when they became extinct was directly caused by a species which was not going to evolve for millions of years!

Modern science has helped us understand that some natural evil seems to be necessary for the world to carry on at all. If volcanoes did not occasionally erupt, enormous pressures would build up under the earth and blow it apart. If animals did not die off, there would be no room for new individuals and no evolution. Even cancer cells and disease are risks that have to be taken for biological life to be sustained. But it still seems unfair on people who live under volcanoes or who get cancer.

Is it possible to believe in a God who is good when the world is so full of suffering?

For many people, the existence of suffering is the biggest reason for not believing in God and for disliking religion altogether.

If there is a God, why would he invent childhood leukaemia or meningitis? Why didn't he intervene to stop the 1994 genocide in Rwanda, when a million men, women and children were murdered?

If God is good, why does he allow suffering?

The devastation caused by the 2005 Indonesian tsunami

Let's examine this in more detail. The argument goes like this. According to Christianity:

1. God is absolutely good (onmibenevolent);
2. God is able to do anything (he is omnipotent);
3. God knows everything (he is omniscient).

BUT suffering exists and God (if he exists) seems to do nothing about it.

So, either:

- God knows about the suffering in the world. He could help but he doesn't want to. In that case, he can't be good: he must enjoy people's pain.

Or:

- God knows about the suffering in the world and wants to help but is unable to. In this case, he is not omnipotent, and does not seem to be much use as a God any more.

Or:

- God could and would help if he knew about suffering but he does not know. In this case, it is God's omniscience which has gone out of the window. Once again, he is pretty useless as a God like this.

Many people would conclude that the whole idea of a God just contradicts itself. An all good, all powerful and all knowing God would want to end suffering – but he does not end it. Therefore, God does not exist.

Providing an answer to an argument like this is going to be a hard job for anyone who still wants to say that there is a God.

Many Christian theologians point out that although God is omnipotent – he can *in theory* do anything – there may be some types of action which God *could* do but which would change the nature of

the world. It would stop being a real creation with its own independent existence.

Something like this may be happening with suffering. If God kept interfering with the universe, if he kept intervening to take away all suffering, the universe's whole nature would change. It would become part of God, people would not have free will, and there would have been no point creating it in the first place. So although God could in theory act to remove all the suffering in the world, in practice his hands are tied.

Even so, God is not powerless. He can work through people: doctors fight disease, charities work for developing countries. By using their freedom to choose the right things, people can co-operate with God to remove suffering. Christians would say that God can inspire them if their lives are open to him. But that may be about the limit, if the world is not going to become a puppet theatre with God pulling the strings.

Think about this for a moment. Imagine you lived in a world where every time we were going to experience pain or cause pain to someone else, God prevented it from happening. Sometimes, this would mean stopping you from doing things you had chosen to do. Would you have been able to grow up? Would you ever be really free?

This brings us to our final question:

Can suffering have any positive value or meaning?

Some suffering has a practical and very important value. Most physical pain warns us that something's

Finally, Christianity teaches that there can be spiritual value in suffering. Most important of all, there is the suffering of Jesus on the cross. Christians believe that, when Jesus was crucified, God entered into the world and reconciled humanity to himself. One way Christians have of thinking about this is to say that, by his death, Jesus paid the penalty for the sins of the whole world.

When Christians suffer, they are encouraged to think that, in some way, they are sharing in Jesus' suffering and are learning to empathise with others who suffer. In the Roman Catholic tradition especially, suffering, particularly illness, is seen as an important sign that the world is imperfect and in need of God.

wrong. If you touch a flame and it burns, you pull your hand away. This limits the damage. So pain of this sort is a defence mechanism.

In the same way, mental pain can spur us on to do things that need doing. Being worried is unpleasant, but it can make us do the revision we have to do. Or our being upset by others' suffering can spur us on to help.

So some suffering seems to be unavoidable, even important. But this is not always the case. Although physical pain is a warning mechanism, a disease or injury can go on hurting long after the pain is useful. Mental suffering can turn into the nightmare of mental illness. Some suffering seems particularly terrible and pointless because of its victims. It is very hard to see what meaning there can be in the suffering of children.

Christianity does not say that all suffering is meaningful. Some things that happen in the world are against God's will. They are cruel, meaningless and nothing else.

Yet in the new life beyond death, Christianity teaches there will be no pain or suffering. In this extract from the New Testament, an early Christian writer describes what he has seen in a vision:

Then I saw a new heaven and a new earth... I heard a loud voice call from the throne. 'Look, here God lives among human beings. He will make his home among them; they will be his people, and he will be their God, God-with-them. He will wipe away all tears from their eyes; there will be no more death, and no more mourning or sadness or pain. The world of the past has gone.   (Revelation 21.1-4)

Original sin

Not all Christians believe in this. It used to be thought that all human beings shared in the punishment of Adam and Eve, which was passed on from generation to generation.

It's much more difficult to believe in original sin now that most Christians accept the Adam and Eve stories are not historical. Whose sin would we be punished for? On top of that, the whole concept rests on old fashioned and unpleasant ideas of God. You end up with a God who's quite prepared to punish people for something done by one of their remote ancestors. Hardly their fault.

However, 'original sin' has been reinterpreted by some theologians to mean a bias towards evil, which is in all of us. We have free will, but it's hard to do the right thing. Doing wrong seems much more interesting than doing right. Casual cruelty like laughing at people and wounding their feelings can seem much more entertaining than befriending them.

Do we have a bias towards evil? I don't know, but I sometimes wonder. In my home town, two fifteen year old boys were recently found guilty of murder. They had been wandering along the river, and there happened to be a tramp sitting by the water. They beat him to death. There was no reason for it; at their trial, it became clear that they had just done it for fun.

Do we have a bias towards evil?
What do you think?

Soul making

The theologian **John Hick** (born 1922) is particularly associated with the idea of soul making. **Very roughly, 'soul making' means that suffering helps us to develop spiritually.**

People who believe in soul making would argue like this:

If we never suffered, we would never get better as people. Our spiritual selves, our souls, would not develop. So **God allows suffering because he wants us to develop.** We could say suffering allows us to become more caring and loving human beings: mature, not shallow; people who care for others rather than stay wrapped up in ourselves. At the end of the day, pain and suffering are not really bad. In fact, they're good, because they make us better people. We need them, to build up virtues like compassion, patience and courage.

(Can you see any problem with this view?)

Hick did not believe in original sin, saying the concept makes no sense today. He argued that all religions are culturally conditioned: their ideas are influenced by the culture in which they grew up. So no one religion is totally true, and that includes Christianity. Hick said Jesus was not God: he was a human being, even though he was a great man.

A number of commentators do not regard Hick's views as Christian ones. Cardinal Joseph Ratzinger took this view. Joseph Ratzinger is now Pope Benedict XVI. As a result, it would be difficult for Roman Catholic Christians (who actually form the majority of Christians in the world today) to accept soul making as a defence for the existence of evil.

It's been pointed out that it's not so much *suffering* that can effect soul making, as *when suffering stops*. For example, if I'm selfish and mean, I might offend all my friends and then have no friends at all. It's only when I stop and think about it – and not before – that I decide I'm going to stop being selfish and mean and be kind instead (and then I might get my friends back!). But when I'm being nasty, when I'm hurting myself and other people, I'm not getting better as a person. The suffering has to stop before I can grow from it.

Moreover, if someone's suffering has no end, it can't effect soul making. If I'm starving, and I starve to death, how does that help me become a better person? The suffering is agonising, I can't see beyond it, and then it kills me. How can someone who's dead become a better person as a result of the agony they've experienced?

And why should I be allowed to inflict pain on other people just to make me a better person? What's it got to do with them? ('I forgive you for making my life hell for the past two years because,

hey, it's made you a better person and it doesn't matter about me!')

Soul making may help explain some aspects of evil. But the evil inflicted by human beings sometimes seems almost limitless: way beyond what's needed for soul making.

And how can soul making explain natural evil?

What do you think?

127

1. Which three questions summarise the problem of pain?

2.a) What is the difference between natural evil and moral evil?
b) Give five examples of suffering caused by moral evil, and five caused by natural evil.

3. How does Christianity account for the existence of moral evil? What do you think of this explanation?

4. What religious value might Christians see in suffering?

5. What is original sin?

6.a) What did John Hick say about soul making?
b) 'Soul making is the best answer to the problem of evil.' Do you agree?

Talking points

'When you look at the world, it's pretty clear that either God is evil or he doesn't exist at all.'

'At the end of the day, there's no total answer to the problem of evil. I don't know why God allows suffering. But I still believe in him because the arguments in favour of God's existence are stronger than the arguments against.'

Activity

God is on trial. The counsel for the defence and the counsel for the prosecution have to prepare their closing speeches to the jury.

Divide the class into an even number of small groups. Each group produces a speech. Half the groups have to work out the defence speeches, and half the prosecution speeches. Each then elects a speaker, who presents the group's speech to the class.

Films and Further Reading

It's well worth trying to see the following **films**. They're all available on DVD.

Shadowlands. This is a true story about C. S. Lewis, who, when he was in his sixties, fell in love with and married a woman who was dying. Remember Lewis is a Christian writer, whose books still sell in their millions. His wife's death led him to question the goodness of God.

The Crucible. Another true story, this time about the American witch hunts in Salem in the 1690s. It explores the nature of evil. The film is based on the play, which is well worth reading. The writer, Arthur Miller, was an atheist.

The World at War: Genocide. An upsetting but incredibly important documentary about the extermination of the Jews.

A Clockwork Orange. Very good. Tells the story of a teenager addicted to 'ultra-violence' but be careful because, as a result, the film is extremely violent. The book's better; the film changes the ending. The writer, Anthony Burgess, said it was about original sin. See what you think.

And this **book** is worth reading:

The Screwtape Letters by C.S. Lewis. A very funny collection of letters from a senior devil to his bungling nephew. We've used one of the letters on page 56.

26

The problem of pain (2): Karma

by Seeta Lakhani

Karma is a concept found in Hinduism, and it's also a concept that's often misunderstood. We need to look at the background to the idea and consider what Karma has to say about the problem of pain.
As Karma is connected with the Hindu teaching about life after death, we start by considering this.

Hindus believe that we are born again and again. This theory is called the theory of reincarnation.

Samsara is the cycle of rebirth and suggests the continuity of our existence beyond death. Krishna states in the *Bhagavad Gita* that 'as the soul passes in this body through childhood, youth and old age, it also passes through death and takes rebirth in another body' (B.G. 2.13). The only thing that accompanies us into our new life is the character we have built up.

There is no eternal heaven or hell in Hinduism. Just as when we go to sleep and conjure up a dream-world and live in it for a short while, the individual may spend some time between rebirths living in a mental heaven or hell of his own making. There is also reference in the Hindu scriptures that we sometimes share this world with our ancestors (*pitriloka*), or with higher beings (*devaloka*). All such interludes are temporary and we continue to be reborn on earth until we attain *moksha*.

Moksha: the cycle of rebirth only comes to an end with moksha: liberation from the cycle of rebirth. The word 'moksha' derives from two Sanskrit roots: *moha*, meaning delusion, and *kshaya*, meaning destruction. So, moksha is the destruction of delusion that takes place when the individual becomes enlightened. Moksha is the process of merging with God, or, as some would prefer to say, recognising our identity with God.

Evolution: Hindus believe that at the beginning of the cycle of rebirth, we all started off as 'lower beings', originally as a single cell. Over many lifetimes, we undergo evolution, as we are reborn into the animal kingdom and then eventually as humans. After the development of human characteristics it would be unlikely (though not impossible) that we may be reborn as an animal or plant. After being born human, the individual keeps being reborn as human, unless his actions were so bestial as to warrant his being reborn as an animal.

The positive aspect to the theory of reincarnation is that we can view life as more just. Missed opportunities in one lifetime can perhaps be achieved in another, and rewards not earned in this life may be reaped in another life. The hard work put towards building up character in one life becomes our asset in the next life.

The drawback with this theory can be that people may adopt a laid-back approach in this life, hoping to do better in their following lives. Moksha is guaranteed for everyone, so some people may not bother to make spiritual progress in this life. This sort of attitude can slow down our spiritual progress.

Karma

Most books on Hinduism have seriously misinterpreted karma. They say that the law of karma is the cause of suffering in the world.
This is quite wrong.
Let's explore what karma actually *does* mean.

The law of karma is also called **the law of action and its consequences.** Hindus believe that the law of cause and effect is embedded in the structure of the universe. It affects all of us, even at an individual level. We have to bear the consequences of our activities or karma.

In some cases, the consequences become evident immediately. In others, it may take some time for the consequences to come to fruition. For example, heavy smoking may not produce immediate results but may cause serious illness in a few years' time.

Hindus take this idea further and say that every action we will do produces consequences. Some of these consequences will only become evident in our next life or lives. This theory is called the law of karma. We reap what we sow and must therefore act with great care. Poor behaviour will produce harmful consequences and disciplined behaviour will produce beneficial results. Recognising a link between our actions and its consequences is a very logical way of promoting better behaviour.

Consequences of belief in the law of karma:

- **We are put in charge of our destiny.** The endearing aspect of this theory is that it puts every individual in charge of his or her destiny and makes us behave in a focused manner.

- **God does not sit in judgement over us.** This concept also eliminates the idea of God sitting in judgement. Hindus cannot accept the idea of God sitting in judgement and dishing out punishment at the end of our lives. At worst, we can blame God for creating the law of cause and effect but then we are put in charge of our destiny and made responsible for what we do. We have to be ready to bear the full consequences of all our actions.

- **The problem of indifference.** The law of karma, *if it is misunderstood,* can have detrimental effects on people's behaviour. For example, it can make one indifferent to the suffering of others. Misinterpreting the law of karma can result in people not helping others in distress, who supposedly 'deserve to suffer' due to their past wrong actions. This indifferent attitude to others' suffering can inadvertently have negative effects on one's own karma.

The correct interpretation of the law of karma would require one not to ignore the suffering of others, but help to alleviate it, thus acquiring good karma for oneself in the process.

- **Fatalism:** The law of karma can also be misinterpreted in another way. Some individuals may become indifferent to their *own* suffering. They may not attempt to recover from their unfortunate circumstances but wallow in them, since they 'deserve to suffer' for their former misdeeds.

This apathy towards improving one's condition is called **fatalism.** The correct interpretation of the law of karma does not advocate any such idea. On the contrary, it would suggest that rather than blame one's past karma, one should fight back and negate the results of earlier bad karma by performing good karma.

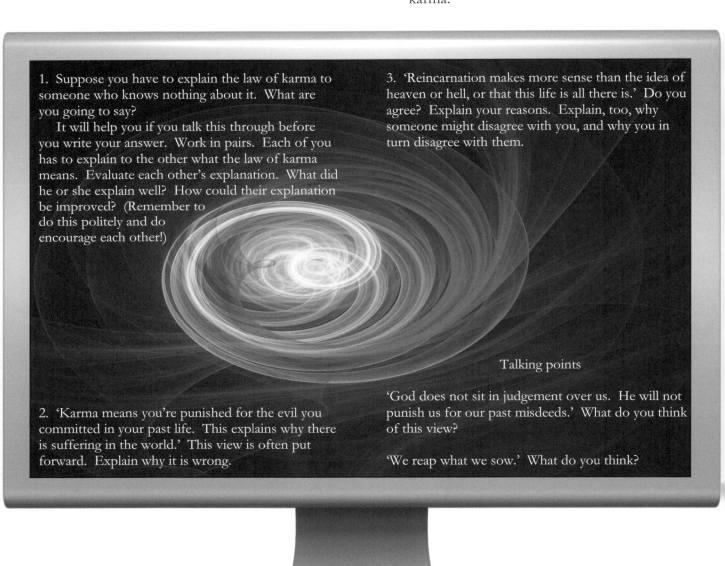

1. Suppose you have to explain the law of karma to someone who knows nothing about it. What are you going to say?

It will help you if you talk this through before you write your answer. Work in pairs. Each of you has to explain to the other what the law of karma means. Evaluate each other's explanation. What did he or she explain well? How could their explanation be improved? (Remember to do this politely and do encourage each other!)

2. 'Karma means you're punished for the evil you committed in your past life. This explains why there is suffering in the world.' This view is often put forward. Explain why it is wrong.

3. 'Reincarnation makes more sense than the idea of heaven or hell, or that this life is all there is.' Do you agree? Explain your reasons. Explain, too, why someone might disagree with you, and why you in turn disagree with them.

Talking points

'God does not sit in judgement over us. He will not punish us for our past misdeeds.' What do you think of this view?

'We reap what we sow.' What do you think?

27
(D)evil?

Then war broke out in heaven. [The Archangel] Michael and his angels waged war upon the dragon. The dragon and his angels fought, but they had not the strength to win, and no foothold was left them in heaven. So the great dragon was thrown down, that serpent of old that led the whole world astray, whose name is Satan, or the Devil – thrown down to the earth, and his angels with him.

Revelation 12.7-9

One way of explaining the evil in the world – or at least some of it – is to say that it is caused by the Devil.

The extract that opens this unit comes from Revelation, the last book of the Bible. Revelation is also known as the Apocalypse. The author's name was John (probably not the same John who wrote the Gospel) and it was one of the last New Testament books to be written. In his book, John claims to have been given a series of visions by God.

Revelation – it's sometimes mistakenly called 'Revelation**s**' but that's wrong: there's no 's'! – says that the Devil / the Dragon was the leader of a group of angels. They battled against the good angels, who were led by the Archangel Michael. The Devil lost and was thrown down to the earth.

Christian beliefs about the Devil:

1. The traditional Christian view

Most Christians believe in the Devil. They would say that much of the evil in the world can be laid at his door. This is in part a solution to the problem of pain, the question of how an omnibenevolent (infinitely good) God could allow suffering. It gives the answer that much of the suffering in the world is caused by the Devil.

But Christians don't believe that God and the Devil are equal and opposite powers. In Christian tradition, the Devil is an angel, not a god – and there's a huge difference there. Some Christians would see the Devil as a tremendously powerful figure who can directly cause disasters and untold suffering.

Others would see him as almost an irritant: a nasty little being who gets a kick out of trying to tempt human beings to do wrong – from acts of petty spite to far worse things. On this view, it's possible, though not perhaps always easy, to tell the Devil to get lost. (St Thomas More, who was at one time a friend of Henry VIII, said that the Devil could not bear to be mocked. Some Christians think that the best way to get rid of the Devil is to laugh at him.) The Devil is rather a pathetic figure, so wrapped up in his own pride and hatred that he is imprisoned by his own evil. The early Christian writer Origen thought that, in the end, even the Devil would be saved and re-enter heaven.

2. An alternative Christian view: the Devil is a *symbol* of evil

Many Christians, though, do not believe in the Devil. Not literally, anyway. They would say that the Devil is not a being, but a *symbol* – a symbolic representation of evil.

That doesn't mean it's a symbol which shouldn't be taken seriously. Evil and suffering can sometimes be so great that they do seem almost to be personal – as though someone's gloating about the pain inflicted on human beings. But human beings themselves are capable of the most appalling acts of cruelty. Ten minutes of watching a film about the holocaust shows that to be the case. You don't need to appeal to the Devil to explain evil. We're quite capable of doing it all ourselves.

Moreover, saying it's the Devil's fault can be a way of avoiding responsibility, as though people were saying, 'It's not my fault, it's the Devil's.'

On the other hand, people who believe in the Devil would say that doesn't let people off the hook. You have to say 'yes' to him – and if you do, you're very much to blame, because you could have said no.

The liberal view is partly based on study of the Bible. In much of the Old Testament, the Devil or Satan doesn't appear at all. He only starts featuring in the later Old Testament books. In the story of the Garden of Eden (Genesis 2.4-3.24), Eve is tempted by the snake to eat the fruit from the tree of the knowledge of good and evil. Later Christian thought identified the snake with the Devil. In the original story, though, he's simply a talking snake: nothing more. So, the Devil doesn't actually appear in the book of Genesis.

Before the later Old Testament books were written, then, suffering was believed to have come from God himself. The Lord punished people who disobeyed him. The Old Testament writers thought that the Lord's punishments were the cause of much war, famine or disease.

Zechariah is one of these later Old Testament books, yet it is also one of the earliest to feature Satan. In Zechariah, Satan is the prosecuting counsel in a court in heaven. He's not yet considered an evil angel, and he's simply called Satan (which means 'the opposition') – he's not yet considered to be the Devil. The idea of Satan's being evil comes later still. (Zechariah was written in the sixth century BC.)

Some biblical scholars have suggested that the concept of the Devil is an import from a polytheistic (many gods) religion.

By the time of the *New* Testament, the idea that God is totally good has become firmly fixed. So it's more difficult to say that God causes suffering. Therefore, the concept of the Devil explains where suffering comes from. He and his followers, the individual demons or devils, are constantly at war with humankind. The Jews and Christians in the first century believed that disease and mental illness were caused by demon possession. As a result, when Jesus healed people, he is said to have done so through exorcism: casting out demons (see, for example, Mark 5.1-20 and 9.14-29).

Even so, the New Testament accepts that people are responsible for their own actions. They can't blame it on the Devil.

One story in the Gospels tells how Jesus encountered the Devil.

This was when Jesus was about thirty; he'd given up making his living as a carpenter and was about to start his ministry, his real work. Before he did so, he underwent some rigorous spiritual preparation in the desert. He wanted to be alone, with God. Unfortunately, an uninvited guest showed up.

Then Jesus was led up by the Spirit into the wilderness to be tempted by the devil. And he fasted forty days and forty nights, and afterward he was hungry. And the tempter came and said to him, 'If you are the Son of God, command these stones to become loaves of bread.' But he answered, 'It is written,

"Man shall not live by bread alone,
but by every word that proceeds from
the mouth of God."'

Then the devil took him to the holy city, and set him on the pinnacle of the temple, and said to him, 'If you are the Son of God, throw yourself down; for it is written,

"He will give his angels charge of you," and
"On their hands they will bear you up,
lest you strike your foot against a stone."'

Jesus said to him, 'Again it is written, "You shall not tempt the Lord your God."' Again, the devil took him to a very high mountain, and showed him all the kingdoms of the world and the glory of them; and he said to him, 'All these I will give you, if you will fall down and worship me.' Then Jesus said to him, 'Begone, Satan! for it is written,

"You shall worship the Lord your God
and him only shall you serve."'

Then the devil left him...

Matthew 4.1-11

The Jews were waiting for the coming of the Messiah, the chosen King who God would send to lead them. This story is about the kind of Messiah Jesus is going to be.

The Devil holds out three temptations:
- To turn stones into bread. This is trying to get Jesus to concentrate on relieving physical poverty by making sure people have enough to eat. While making sure people have food is important, it's far from the whole story. The Devil is trying to make Jesus forget the spiritual and concentrate just on the physical. But people need more than just food.

Yet Jesus again corrects him. Miracles are part of Jesus' work but they're not the whole thing. Jesus' work is to teach, and to suffer and die to save people from their sins and from death itself. The Devil's purpose in the temptations is to neutralise Jesus: to make him lose sight of the bigger picture, and to be what, at the end of the day, would be a pretty useless Messiah. A hero is a good thing to be, but it's far, far less than the Saviour of the World.

- To worship the Devil and to gain political power. Not a chance. Lots of people were expecting the Messiah to be a warrior, to set up a new Jewish empire and to drive the Romans out of Israel. This is partly what Jesus is being tempted to do. But it would also mean saying that the Devil is greater than God. Jesus will not follow evil rather than good, and sends the Devil packing.

There are different ways of understanding this story, and they are linked to Christians' different views about the Devil.

1. Some (perhaps most) Christians would see this as a narrative of a historical event: it's something that really happened to Jesus.
2. It is an attempt to put into words an experience or experiences Jesus had. Jesus really had temptations like these. But they were things he wrestled with inside his own mind, and the temptations may or may not have come from the Devil. Perhaps he struggled with such temptations through the weeks he was in the desert. But they are Jesus' internal experiences, not things happening outside of him. (Using more technical language, they were subjective rather than objective.)
3. It is a myth: a story which is told to get across religious truths. It didn't happen, in any sense. But it explains why Jesus is not the sort of Messiah that people were expecting.

You might think that Christians would only be allowed to accept the first option. In fact, they could accept any one of these. Christians are not required to believe every single thing in the Bible really happened.

What do you think? Do you think the story of the temptations is best understood as:
- a historical account;
- an attempt to describe a psychological experience of Jesus; or
- a myth?

- To perform a dazzling miracle. Interesting that the Devil has a go here at quoting the Bible. But his purpose is evil. Whether this is a true story or not, it's certainly a very good story. The Devil tempts Jesus by offering him things that appear attractive – and, more, importantly, that have some good in them. It *is* important to relieve hunger. And you certainly could argue that amazing people by surviving a leap off the Temple is backed up by the Old Testament quotation. The Devil is characterised as being clever, subtle. He doesn't say, 'Here's something really nasty: go and do it'; he tries to persuade people that there are morally good reasons for acting badly.

Other ways to understand evil

There is **the view that God himself is evil.** Or, at least, he is morally corrupt; he is spiteful and arrogant and does not deserve to be called 'good'.

This idea is expressed in a poem by the writer Kingsley Amis (1922-1995). Amis is best known as a novelist (and a very funny one too: try *Lucky Jim* or *Take A Girl Like You*. Be warned: some of his work is very rude!)

Amis was once asked whether he was an atheist. His reply was, 'Well, yes, but it's more that I hate him.' He expands this view in the poem. The person speaking in the poem is God. (The spelling mistakes and other mistakes in English are deliberate. See if you can work out why.)

To a Baby Born Without Limbs

This is just to show you whose boss around here.
It'll keep you on your toes, so to speak,
Make you put your best foot forward, so to speak,
And give you something to turn your hand to, so to speak.
You can face up to it like a man,
Or snivvle and blubber like a baby.
That's up to you. Nothing to do with Me.
If you take it in the right spirit,
You can have a bloody marvelous life,
With the great rewards courage brings,
And the beauty of accepting your LOT.
And think how much good it'll do your Mum and Dad,
And your Grans and Gramps and the rest of the shower,
To be stopped being complacent.
Make sure they baptise you, though,
In case some murdering bastard
Decides to put you away quick,
Which would send you straight to LIMB-O, ha ha ha.
But just a word in your ear, if you've got one.
Mind you DO take this in the right spirit,
And keep a civil tongue in your head about Me.
Because if you DON'T,
I've got plenty of other stuff up My sleeve,
Such as Leukemia and polio,
(Which incidentally your welcome to any time,
Whatever spirit you take this in.)
I've given you one love-pat, right?
You don't want another.
So watch it, Jack.

- What's your reaction to the poem?

- What do you think of the poem's view of God? Is it fair?

There is also the view of **polytheism.** Polytheism – belief in many gods – used to be very common in the ancient world. It's easier to explain evil if you're a polytheist: you just say it's all caused by an evil god. Other gods are on the side of goodness and of virtue.

In ancient Egyptian mythology, the god of evil was called Sutekh or Set. In Egyptian art, he was often shown as having a human body and the head of an animal called the 'Typhonic beast': a mythical creature with a curved snout, square ears and a forked tail. He's pictured on the next page and has agreed to pose for us in modern dress.

135

1. Copy out the sentences below, correcting them when necessary. Be careful, because not all of them need correcting: some have got it right!

a) The book of Revelations in the Bible says that the Archangel Steve defeated the Devil in a war in heaven.
b) All Christians believe in the Devil.
c) Christians believe the Devil and God are equal and opposite powers.
d) All Christians believe the Devil is tremendously powerful and can cause untold evil.
e) The Devil is believed to be a god.
f) The Devil does not feature in the earliest books of the Bible.
g) The snake in the Garden of Eden story is meant to be a snake and nothing more.

2. 'The best solution to the problem of evil is to say that evil is caused by the Devil.' Do you agree? Give reasons for your answer. You must show that you have considered more than one viewpoint.

3.a) 'We don't have to accept suffering, either our own or other people's. We can do something about it.' What sort of things could people do about suffering?
b) 'God allows suffering because it gives us the opportunity to do good.' What do you think?

Talking points:

Do you believe in the Devil? Why?

'Belief in the Devil is actually immoral. It lets people off their responsibility for their own behaviour.' What do you think?

There is such a thing as temptation. Some of the things we're tempted to do are plain childish: silly or spiteful. It certainly feels as though there's someone at your elbow saying, "Go on, go on: it'll be a laugh." The best way to explain these things is to say the Devil exists and he's genuinely tempting us.' Do you agree or disagree? Why?

How might an atheist explain the suffering in the world?

Further reading:

At the risk of this book's becoming the journal of the C.S. Lewis fan club...

Perhaps the best depiction of the Devil in any form of fiction is in C. S. Lewis' novel *Perelandra*. This is part of his science fiction trilogy. Dr Ransom, a university teacher, arrives on Perelandra, which we call Venus, as life begins to emerge there. He is met there by his adversary Professor Weston, a scientist who has perfected space travel. But Ransom begins to realise that this is not really Weston at all, and that something else is inhabiting Weston's body.

All three of Lewis' science fiction novels – *Out of the Silent Planet, Perelandra* and *That Hideous Strength* – are superb and well worth reading. There's nothing wrong with starting with the middle one, either. Sites like Amazon sell them second hand for just a couple of pounds.

136

Sutekh, the Lord of Death. Yesterday.

Part Five

The Undiscovered Country

28
Do ghosts exist?

Quite a lot of us would probably just say, 'Yes!' or 'Don't be daft!' without thinking about the question too deeply. It's actually worth examining, because:

If you think about it, what's behind the question is another one:

How can we tell whether any report is true or false?

People who study this sort of question say there are a number of tests we need to apply:

1. How reliable is the source of the report?
2. Does the source of the report – a person, or a written report – have another motive for making the claim?
3. Can the report be checked?
4. Are there other factors which could explain what was claimed to be witnessed?
   (These could include:
   - misinterpretation – giving an incorrect meaning to what was experienced
   - exaggeration
   - imagination)
5. What might the experts say?
6. How easily are we taken in by reports like this? Are we gullible?

Let's examine these questions in more detail.

1. How reliable is the source of the report?

Would we be more likely to believe something if it was reported:
- on the BBC's main news programme, or

- if it was on a programme called *Britain's Weirdest Wackiest Weirdo Events*, broadcast on a satellite channel with a reputation for running any old trash just to get the ratings?

This isn't trying to be snobby. It's just that BBC News has a *reputation* for telling the truth – which doesn't mean they don't make mistakes. On the other hand, sensationalist stuff sells newspapers and makes people laugh, but it just doesn't have a serious reputation.

What about when the report comes from a person – perhaps a friend or someone we know well?

This is where you need to go back and read the extract from *The Lion, the Witch and the Wardrobe* on pages 91-92. It's about how you evaluate someone else's experience. Read it through and think about how it could be applied to alleged experiences of ghosts.

2. Does the source of the report – a person, or a written report – have another motive for making the claim?

Suppose I write a book called *Real Ghost Sightings* and my publisher agrees a fee of a million pounds. If you knew I'd been paid that, would you be more or less likely to believe me?

So, *motive* is going to come into it. It might not be a nasty motive; it could just be wanting to say something interesting, maybe to liven up a dull conversation.

3. Can the report be checked?

Which of these would you say gave the best evidence?
1. One person claims to have seen a ghost walking through the churchyard.
2. A group of friends claim to have seen a ghost walking through the churchyard.
3. There are written reports of sightings of a ghost walking through the churchyard. They date from various different times, but go back 300 years. They all describe the same thing.

You've probably worked out that the third is the strongest evidence – or, least, the least bad evidence. It's far from being cast iron; there are other possible explanations for the report. For example, the later accounts could be based on the first 'sighting' and could be made up.

Moreover, lots of things do happen which only one person saw. In other words, we only have that person's evidence. But it's rather different if someone says, 'I saw a swan in the park' (when they were alone) and 'I saw a ghost in the park' (when they were alone). Can you explain the difference?

The larger the number of people who saw an event, the stronger the evidence, broadly speaking, that it really happened.

Again, a problem with alleged experiences of ghosts is that they're often seen by only one person. In addition, there may be other factors which would make us dubious about the report.

4. Are there other factors which could explain what was claimed to be witnessed?

If we're going to believe an experience of a ghost, we'd probably have to rule out things like:

1. **Misinterpretation.** The witness misunderstood what was seen. For example, what they actually saw was a barn owl flying past in the fog.

2. **Exaggeration.** Something we're all prone to do to make a story more exciting! If the exaggeration is stripped away, what are you actually left with?

3. **Imagination.** If the witness has just been watching a DVD double bill of horror films, this might have frightened or 'spooked' them. Imagination could then work on this feeling and make someone think there was something there, when it really existed only in their heads.

5. What might the experts say?

If there's disagreement about an idea, we would usually listen to what the experts had to say. For example, if we wanted to know whether there was a tenth planet in the solar system, we'd ask an astronomer. Or if my car was making funny noises, I'd ask a mechanic what was wrong with it.

Asking the experts is something we'd normally be able to do. It's more difficult with a subject like 'do ghosts exist?' because there aren't any real experts. (There may be people who claim to be, but how seriously we should take their qualifications is another matter.)

Also, experts in one subject may not be experts in another. I might ask my doctor her opinion of why I keep getting headaches. However, her guess is as good as mine as to why my TV won't get channel 5!

So, there aren't any experts in ghostology.

On the other hand, if we can find people who can think clearly, who can offer wise advice in general, their opinion would be worth thinking through. (Rather like Peter and Susan in the extract from *The Lion, the Witch and the Wardrobe*. They asked the Professor what he thought because they knew he was clever and that he thought clearly – that he was unbiased.)

6. How easily are we taken in by reports like this? Are we gullible?

We believe what we want to believe.

This isn't always true. There have been atheists who didn't want to believe in God who have come to believe in him. C. S. Lewis himself is an example.

However, if we'd like to believe in ghosts, we're more likely to believe accounts of experiences of them.

And if we don't want to believe in ghosts, we're more likely to dismiss such accounts.

And a few final thoughts:

- Christianity has nothing much to say on the subject of ghosts one way or another. If anything, Christian teaching about life after death would seem to rule out the idea of ghosts. So, Christians would be as sceptical or credulous (believing) about ghosts as anyone else.

- There's a difference between superstition and religion – even if some noisy people shout that they're the same thing! Believing in things like ghosts without examining the evidence *really* thoroughly is probably superstition. This isn't to say people who are superstitious are nasty people, it's just saying that ideas have to be tested rather than just accepted uncritically. ('Uncritically' means 'without thinking something through or testing it'.) A religion that's worth anything has to have evidence for it. Otherwise, it is just superstition.

So, do ghosts exist?

For what my opinion is worth, I have to say it seems very unlikely. However, if the only explanation of a reported experience of a ghost – once we'd ruled out all the other possibilities – was that it really *was* a ghost, then we'd probably have to accept it. At least, we'd have to accept it until a better explanation came along!

But then, I could be wrong.

What do you think?

Do ghosts and séances prove that there is life after death?

Many people, throughout the centuries, have claimed to have had experiences of ghosts.

There are sects, some of them semi-Christian, some not, who claim to be able to contact the dead at meetings called séances. A 'medium' leads the meeting; he or she is claimed to be the person through whom the dead get in touch with the living.

Things like ghosts and séances are sometimes called the paranormal: things that are beyond the scope of normal investigation.

Some would claim ghosts and séances show that there is life after death.

We've seen what Christianity has to say about ghosts. As far as mediums are concerned: while some religions accept them, it has to be said that it is not part of mainstream religion. Most atheists would dismiss the paranormal as superstitious nonsense and here, Christianity on the whole would agree with them. The kind of shadowy, ethereal, rather miserable existence envisaged by the paranormal is nothing like the 'life in all its fullness' promised by Christ to his followers – and it's certainly not evidence of heaven. It'd be hard to see why you would want to swap being in heaven for drearily wandering around on earth, not doing very much of interest. And a God who punished people by condemning them to live as ghosts would be cruel – and, again, Christian promises for life after death are very different.

The fact that so many mediums have been proved to be fakes, preying on sad and easily led people, and that so many accounts of ghosts are pretty obviously untrue, means that there would have to be very good evidence indeed before such things were accepted as realities.

If (a very big 'if'!) we could say that an experience of a ghost was a real experience, we'd then have to interpret the experience.

Just suppose that such an experience was shown to have really happened. What would the ghost be?

A person – even if it's a dead one? But how would we know it was a person and not something else? Could we have a conversation with it?

There have been suggestions that ghosts may be some sort of impression made upon a place by a very powerful personality, or a particularly strong event (like a violent death). They'd be natural phenomena rather than supernatural ones, even if they're very unusual natural phenomena.

Some have suggested that contact is genuinely made at (non faked) séances, but it isn't contact with the dead. It's contact with the subconscious of other members of the group. The subconscious part of the mind isn't the nicest place to be, and getting in touch with the subconscious of a disturbed individual doesn't sound like a bundle of laughs.

Well. Maybe. All this does sound a bit like scrabbling around for explanations. *If* a ghostly experience or a séance could be shown to have been real, then maybe it's best not to claim to know *what*

actually was experienced. It's too big a leap to say 'this ghost report is true' and then to say, 'So this proves Sir Roger de Nasty is paying for his crimes by wandering the house and making funny noises.'

And it depends on whether any experience of ghosts or séances could be said to be genuine, in any case.

1. We've given six tests that could be used to see whether or not a report of ghosts was genuine.
a) Put these into a spider diagram.
b) How fair do you think these tests are? Are there any you want to add?

2. Suppose you're investigating an account of an experience of a ghost. What sort of evidence would you need to convince you it was genuine?

3. 'Ghosts and séances prove that there is life after death.' Do you agree? Give reasons for your answer, showing that you have thought about more than one viewpoint.

4. 'If there is life after death, then there must be ghosts, and séances would work, as well.' What do you think?

Further reading:

A brilliant (and very funny) ghost story is *The Green Man* by Kingsley Amis. It's about an alcoholic who meets the ghost of the deeply unpleasant Dr Underhill, a priest who was also a murderer and sorcerer. Health warning, though: it's very rude in parts!

This is a photograph of some smoke in sunlight.

If I had said it was a photo of a ghost, would anyone have been convinced?

29
Life after death (1)

In these chapters, we're going to consider different ideas about life after death, and whether there is any evidence for it.

The great religions of the world teach that there is life after death. The details vary but broadly speaking, religious people believe that there are either:

- **Two lives**: life in this world, and eternal life with God after death. Judaism, Christianity and Islam teach this.
  or:
- **Many lives: reincarnation.** After death, you are reborn as someone (or something) or else. This is essentially the view of Buddhism and Hinduism. After the cycle of reincarnation, the individual becomes one with God (Hinduism) or with Nirvana (Buddhism). Sikhism also believes in the loss of individuality after death; Sikhs, too, hold that the individual becomes one with God. (This is all over-simplified as usual. We'll come back to it later.)

Atheism, by contrast, holds that there is only **one life**: this one.

Christian beliefs about life after death

Christianity is one of the three semitic religions; the others are Judaism and Islam. These faiths teach that after death comes judgement, then heaven or hell. We'll look in some detail at the teachings of Christianity on all this.

What do Christians today believe about life after death?

For a start, they would claim not to know about the details. God does not inform people about the furniture of heaven or the temperature of hell.

However, Christianity teaches that people will still be themselves after they die. They will remain individuals. There are two ways in which this idea is expressed: **the resurrection of the body** or **the immortality of the soul.**

The resurrection of the body

Another term for this is simply 'the resurrection'. Just as Jesus had a body after he rose from the dead (although one which was transformed in some way), so everyone else will have a body. God will raise all the dead some day in the future. This will happen on the *Day of Judgement*, which used to be called *Doomsday*

('doom' here means 'judgement'). The Day of Judgement, the resurrection of the dead, will take place when Jesus returns at the end of time.

Some Christians take these ideas literally: the dead really will rise, their bodies will be transformed and made eternal – and this will not happen until the second coming of Christ. Others take it as imagery for saying that Jesus' judgement follows death, and that we shall remain individuals in the next life – but what this life will be like, we don't know.

Some of the early Christian writers speculated at great length about what our bodies would be like at the resurrection. Origen (c. 185-254 AD) was at the more eccentric end of this speculation. He came up with the rather wonderful idea that our resurrection bodies would be entirely spherical. As the next life was to be perfection, the resurrection body would have to be the perfect shape – and Plato said the sphere was the perfect shape. (Plato, the Greek philosopher, was enormously influential on the development of early Christian thought.)

Rather sadly, Origen's ideas did not catch on. Christians today do not believe that the resurrection body will be spherical.

St Augustine (354-430 AD) was rather more influential. He followed St Paul in saying that the risen Christ was the first human being to rise from death – but not the last. We're not God, as Jesus was, but Jesus was 'the first born from the dead', the first human to reach the resurrection state. So, said Augustine, you can work things out about our own resurrection body by studying what the Bible, and especially Paul, says about the risen Jesus.

In his first letter to the Corinthians, Paul says a good deal about all this:

> So it is with the resurrection of the dead. What is sown [Paul means when you die] is perishable, what is raised is imperishable... It is sown a physical body, it is raised a spiritual body... Just as we have borne the image of the man of dust [Adam], we will also bear the image of the man of heaven [Jesus]...
>
> For this perishable body must put on imperishability, and this mortal body must put on immortality.
>
> (1 Corinthians 15.42ff. The quotation 'the first born from the dead' is also from this passage.)

Augustine picks up on what Paul says, especially the line, 'we will also bear the image of the man from heaven.' He speculated like this.

Jesus was about thirty years old when he died. So, when we rise from death, we'll also be about thirty. This applies to people who die as children, or who die in old age, or as babies, or who die before they're born. Everybody. But physical imperfections will vanish. People who are too fat will be slimmed down; those who are too thin will fill out a bit. If you've lost a limb in life, it'll be back when you rise from the dead. Things like warts, scars or wrinkles will vanish. Our resurrection bodies will be

recognisable as us, but we'll all be physically beautiful. And the body will last for ever.

Augustine's ideas are more acceptable than Origen's to Christians who believe in the resurrection of the body. However, they are speculations, and shouldn't be taken to be what all such Christians believe. Many would say they believe in the resurrection of the body, but we simply don't know what our risen bodies are going to be like.

Other Christians would say that all talk of the resurrection of the body is simply imagery. It means that we shall survive death as individuals, and that we shall be judged by Jesus.

The immortality of the soul

This is another way of saying we shall survive death as individuals.

It comes down to what you believe human beings to be.

- Many say that the real human being is the soul. Bodies are just machines. They rot when we die but our souls survive. Thus we can talk about **the immortality of the soul.**
- On the other hand, many would say that the body *is* part of what makes us human beings. Therefore, if we're still going to human beings in the next life, we're going to have to have bodies – because without a body, you're not human.

We need to unpack this a bit further.

Different Christians have different ideas about what exactly the soul is. It is usually taken to be those aspects of human beings which are not physical. Things like the mind, personality, memories, intelligence – the things which make a human being truly human.

We mentioned Plato earlier. Plato wasn't a Christian; he lived well before Christ's birth, from 428 or 427 to 348 or 347 BC. Yet, as we said, Plato was enormously influential on early Christian thought. He said the relationship between the soul and the body was like the relationship between a charioteer and the chariot. The one who's doing all the thinking and controlling is the charioteer (the soul). The chariot (the body) is just a thing, which follows instructions. So the vital bit is the charioteer, not the chariot.

And the soul, said Plato, is the real human being. The body is simply its vehicle.

Science fiction gives us a good parallel for this idea. Think about the Daleks in *Doctor Who*. In the series, when people say 'Dalek', they usually mean the upturned metal beaker with a domed top, three rods, flashing lights, and various metal patterns on its sides.

But that isn't actually a Dalek. It's a machine. The *real* Dalek is the creature that lives inside the machine, which is pretty hideous, gets very cross, and resents anyone who's better looking than it is. The metal container, which is popularly called a Dalek, is just a mobile life support system and an artificial body.

What you see on the outside is a travel machine. The real Dalek is within.

So, when you look at a human being, what you see on the outside is a travel machine. The real human being is within. And that's the soul.

This idea, that a human being = a soul + a body, is called **dualism** (two-ness). If we believe in dualism, then it is the travel machine only that can die. The soul cannot die but continues for ever.

However, the Biblical writers didn't see it that way at all. They thought of a human being as a **psycho-somatic unity.** This is a long winded way of saying that soul and body are one. The human body *is* part of the human being; it isn't just a vehicle or a chariot or a machine. It's as much a part of the human being as the soul is.

If you think about this idea, there's a lot to be said for it. You might want to discuss these questions:

- If your body had been different, and you'd grown up in a different body, would you still be the same person?
- The soul is usually taken to include what we call the mind. The physical function of the mind is contained in the brain. Suppose we take two of you in your class, and swap your brains over, so that you're in each others' bodies. Would you still be the same people? Would you continue to be so?

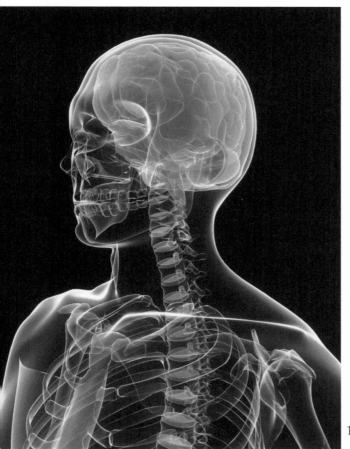

Something else to think about: doctors now appreciate that a lot of physical illness can be caused by mental suffering. The actor and comedian John Cleese had flu-like symptoms for a long time, which would not go away. He then had therapy for depression, and it was discovered that this was affecting his body. As his depression was treated, the flu symptoms disappeared.

You can probably think of times when you've been worried – maybe before exams – and you've felt it physically. Other feelings, like anxiety, fear or anger, can be felt in our bodies, not just in our minds. (Remember that, for Plato, the mind was an aspect of the soul.)

There are good grounds, then, for saying that a human being is a psycho-somatic unity.

→ If you take this view of a human being,
→ and if you believe that human beings survive death,
→ then you're going to have to have a body after death
→ because having a body is part of being human.

If, on the other hand, you believe in the immortality of the soul, you could say that we survive death, but not in a physical way. Christians who think like this might say that the Day of Judgement takes place for each individual at the moment of death.

Or we could say:

Both the resurrection of the body and the immortality of the soul are different images or pictures. They are basically saying the same thing. Humans survive death as individuals, and are judged. The reason for there being different images is that we cannot put into words what life after death will be like. All we can use are pictures. And after all, we simply do not know the details.

Reincarnation - Seeta Lakhani

We have touched on this topic already, in chapter 26. It is worth reading that chapter again.

The theory of reincarnation is one of the key beliefs in all Indian religions. It states that all individuals participate in a cycle of birth and death. The cycle continues until we find God, or as some Hindus would say, we identify ourselves with God.

Why don't we remember our past lives? The greatest criticism laid against this theory is that it sounds too preposterous. If we have lived many times in the past, why don't we remember any of our past lives?

In response, Hindus say that the transition from one life to another is extremely traumatic. In order not to relive that pain, the mind blocks out the memory of previous lives. Otherwise, the memory of earlier lives with all the people we have loved would overwhelm us.

Is there hard evidence of reincarnation?

Professor Ian Stevenson of Virginia University in the USA has carried out a great deal of research on the theory of reincarnation. He has recorded thousands of cases of children from all around the world, who have been able to provide detailed accounts of their previous lives. In many cases, it has been possible to check these accounts against known events. Professor Stevenson concludes that these facts can best be explained through the theory of reincarnation.

Measured rewards for measured risks: One of the endearing aspects of the theory of reincarnation is that it offers measured rewards for measured risks

we take. Individuals get what they deserve. The Hindu law of karma (see page 129) states that everything we do will have consequences in this life or the next. Therefore, all the good work we may have done in this life does not go to waste when we die; it comes to fruition in our future life or lives.

Phobias explained: The theory of reincarnation provides a wonderful explanation as to why people suffer from phobias. For example, someone may be afraid of heights because, in one of his or her previous lives, he or she may have died by falling from a great height. That fear remains in the psyche of that person and manifests itself as a phobia in the next life.

Geniuses: The theory also explains why we have geniuses. It suggests that, over many lifetimes, individuals may have worked hard to develop certain skills, for example in music. These skills have become ingrained into the psyche of that person and reveal themselves at an early age when they are reborn. The classic example is Mozart: he started composing operas at the age of seven!

1.a) Explain what is meant by 'the resurrection of the body'. You've got two sentences to do this in!
b) What is the difference between the resurrection of the body and the resurrection of Jesus?
c) Do all Christians believe in the resurrection of the body?

2. What did St Augustine say about the resurrected body?

3.a) What is meant by 'the immortality of the soul'? (Again, you've got two sentences!)
b) 'The soul means a light, fluffy cloud that floats away from your body when you die.' Is this right? If not, how could you define the soul?
c) What did Plato say about the relationship between the soul and body? (If you illustrate your answer, it will help. It's not meant to be patronising; it genuinely will help you to remember it.)

4. Consider these two statements.
'Human beings are lumps of matter. They are creatures which have evolved over millions of years. Any idea of having a soul is nonsense. You are a lump of meat, and that is all.'

'Your true self is your soul. That is the part of you that you need to develop, to improve. You body can get in the way of this spiritual progress. So you should ignore it as much as possible. You should detach yourself from physical cravings and avoid overeating, sex and physical pleasure. Only by doing this will you improve your true self – your soul.'

What do you think?

5. 'The ideas of resurrection of the body and immortality of the soul are basically saying the same thing. They are images, picture language.' What does this mean?

6.a) What is reincarnation?
b) What evidence is given in favour of the idea of reincarnation?

7. 'Reincarnation is more convincing than other ideas about life after death.' Do you agree? Give reasons for your answer, showing you have thought about more than one viewpoint.

'Heaven' literally means 'the sky', and there was a time when people thought that heaven was a place above the sky. No-one believes this now. 'Heaven' is a shorthand used for the state of living with God, for ever. Talking about 'heaven' as a place, or saying people 'go up' to heaven, is using imagery. It could be said that heaven is not a 'place' at all, but a way of existing – something that is 'beyond' time and space. Talking about it as a 'place' just helps people to understand it. Those who 'go' to heaven enjoy eternal happiness 'in' 'paradise', with God and with the other people who are there. Heaven may be experienced in a body, if we believe in the resurrection of the body. Or we may experience it as a soul, if we believe in the immortality of the soul. (Other Christians would just say we don't know how it will be experienced!)

Heaven is said to be for ever. If we think of eternal life as being endless life, going on and on for ever, it becomes rather a horrible idea. If nothing else, it would become terribly boring! Millions upon millions of years of existing, with no end in sight, would be a frightening prospect. So some have said that eternal life is not really 'life which goes on and on for ever'. Eternity is 'bigger than' time, not 'endless time'. For heaven not to be just endless existence, people there must have a different awareness of time. We simply do not know what this is like, it is said, because we have not experienced it.

Who do Christians believe goes to heaven? It depends who you ask. The problem is striking a balance between two aspects of God. 'God is love,' says the first letter of St John (1 John 4.8). But God is also said to be just, and to punish evil (Matthew 25.31-46). The more conservative Christians are, the more they tend to shift the balance towards God's justice. The more liberal they are, the more they shift the balance towards God's love. So, fundamentalist Christians say that only Christians go to heaven, and only true Christians at that. More liberal Christians accept that non Christians also go to heaven. Some believe it's having a Christian faith that gets you to heaven, whereas others believe it is how you behave.

Some Christians suggest that people can be followers of Jesus without realising it. Anyone who tries to do what is right, to be kind, and to care about others, is really a follower of Christ, even if they would not use those words, or do not realise it. There is truth in the other religions. God cares more about how people treat each other than he does about what they believe. The Roman Catholic Church holds that salvation is not limited to Christians, and that the Kingdom of God is not the same as the Church.

The Roman Catholic Church also accepts the doctrine of **purgatory.** (This idea is rejected by the other Christian denominations.) Purgatory used to be thought of as a *place* where people are purged of their sins before they are fit to enter heaven. It was thought to take many thousands of years to do this, and the purging was thought to be very unpleasant.

Some Catholics still think of purgatory like this. Others think of it as not so much a place, but a process. Human beings, they would say, have some nasty things lurking in their psychological make-up, however hard they try to control them. Rage, hatred, greed, lust, resentment – they're all there, even if they're buried pretty deep. It would be a shame to have to cart all this around for the rest of eternity. So purgatory is the process which gets rid of the unwanted baggage.

What happens to people who do not enter heaven? Christians usually say that they go to hell.

We have to be careful here. The picture of hell as an everlasting torture chamber is not an idea found anywhere in the New Testament. It is a medieval view, and a savage one at that. The more brutal aspects of medieval life were projected onto people's views of religion, hell included. The word Jesus uses for 'hell' is 'gehenna', which was a rubbish dump outside Jerusalem. No concept of a torture chamber is found in the teaching of Jesus himself.

The medieval view of hell cannot be squared with the God of love. A loving God could not possibly sentence anyone to everlasting torture. Although some – though not all – fundamentalist Christians still believe in the medieval concept of hell, other Christians tone the concept down.

Perhaps hell means extinction. (Gehenna was a rubbish tip, and the rubbish was burnt. If you burn something, it is destroyed. Perhaps fire is an image of extinction rather than a method of punishment.)

Perhaps God *sends* no-one there; everyone is offered the chance of salvation, but some refuse it.

God respects their freedom of choice, and will not force his presence upon anyone who does not want it. It is hard to see how people as evil as Hitler, or other, more modern tyrants, could enter heaven or could even want to. (Perhaps there are many others who are as evil, but on a lesser scale because they have less power. Tyranny in a home or in an office is still tyranny.)

Even here, perhaps caution is necessary. At the end of Graham Greene's novel *Brighton Rock*, one of the characters comments that there is 'an appalling strangeness in the mercy of God'. In C. S. Lewis' *The Great Divorce*, hell is pictured not as a torture chamber, but as a wet Saturday afternoon, waiting in the drizzle for a bus which never comes. (Both books are well worth reading.)

The details of life after death are not given in the New Testament. But this is what St Paul says in his Letter to the Romans:

Who shall separate us from the love of Christ? Shall trouble or hardship or persecution or famine or nakedness or danger or sword? … No, in all these things we are more than conquerors through him that loved us. For I am convinced that neither death nor life, neither angels nor demons, neither the present nor the future, nor any powers, neither height nor depth, nor anything else in all creation, will be able to separate us from the love of God that is in Christ Jesus our Lord.

Romans 8.35, 37-39

Justification by faith

For many Christians, though not for all of them, it's **having faith** that saves you. This means the Christian faith; having another faith is of no use. People who have a Christian faith are members of the Kingdom of God and it is they who will go to heaven.

Behind this doctrine (religious teaching) is a question: What makes people OK with God?

Is it:

- having faith?

or

- doing good things

The problem is that you can argue from both points of view from the New Testament. Jesus says, 'I am the Way and the Truth and the Life. No one comes to the Father except through me.' (John 14.6) This seems to mean that the only way to God the

Father, and therefore to heaven, is through Jesus Christ. In his letter to the Romans, Paul says:

I am not ashamed of the gospel [the good news about Jesus]; it is the power of God for salvation for everyone who has faith, to the Jew first and also to the Greek. For in it the righteousness of God is revealed through faith for faith; as it is written, 'The one who is righteous will live by faith.'

(Romans 1.16-17. In the last sentence, Paul quotes from Habakkuk 2.4 in the Old Testament.)

Paul means the Christian faith here; when he talks of 'the Jew' and 'the Greek', he means those Jews and Gentiles who become Christians.

On the other hand, Jesus says to his disciples:

> Truly I tell you, whoever gives you a cup of water to drink because you bear the name of Christ will by no means lose the reward.
>
> (Mark 9.41)

This seems to mean that God will reward people for the smallest act of kindness. There's no mention of their faith. The example here is of a kindness given to Jesus' disciples, so it seems to mean the people doing the giving are not Christians. In the parable of the sheep and the goats (Matthew 25.31-46), people are judged by Jesus at the end of time. But they're not judged on their faith. They're judged on their behaviour.

So there's a real tension here in Christianity. Protestant Christianity has tended to go for Paul's idea: only Christians go to heaven. Let's explore this a bit further.

The technical terms for 'being OK with God' are:

- being **justified** ('made just' – 'just' in the sense of 'justice')
- being made **righteous.**

In the sixteenth century, **Martin Luther** picked up on Paul's ideas and developed them. Luther is still one of the most important thinkers in Christian history.

Luther said that no one could become righteous by doing good things. You could never do enough. God is perfect; people are not, never can be, and will only fail if they try to be. You can't earn a place in heaven (be justified) by totting up enough good actions. You will only fail if you try to.

It has to be said that Luther was also influenced by the fact that the Catholic Church at the time had devised some rather silly systems of doing 'good works'. Lots of these were to do with performing rituals rather than loving your neighbour. (Also, giving large amounts of cash to the Church was of course said to be one of the good works!) Moreover, Luther's own psychological state has to be taken into account. He was terrified of being judged by God. He had tried the religious systems of the time; he'd tried to amass enough good works, and felt he had failed. He despaired and became ill.

Luther said, then, that a place in heaven was a free gift. You can't earn it. God gives it to those who have faith in what he was doing through Jesus Christ.

The technical term for this doctrine is **justification by faith.**

Luther found in his own life that he was freed from despair. He no longer had to worry about being good enough. He never would be. Yet because he had faith, he knew God had accepted him. Every Christian, in Luther's words, is 'always a sinner, always just.' The whole idea took an enormous burden from his mind.

Most Protestants and many Anglicans believe in justification by faith. Many Christians would go on to say that faith itself is a gift from God, and God *chooses* not to give it to everybody.

However, justification by faith is not accepted by all Christians. It basically ignores those teachings of Jesus which say salvation is to do with how we've behaved. And the major problem is that it seems to exclude non Christians. (Hence the desire by many Christians who accept the doctrine to go and convert to Christianity people who come from different faiths.)

But isn't God supposed to love everybody? If God's omniscient, isn't his understanding of social science, of sociology and history, going to be superb? If you're brought up in a Muslim or Jewish family, it's very unlikely that you're going to become a Christian – especially if you live in a country or community where Islam or Judaism are the norm. If justification by faith is true, doesn't that mean that God's unjust? It would actually mean people who live in countries like India, Libya or Saudi Arabia are far less likely to go to heaven than are Europeans or Americans – and that's ridiculous. (As well as immoral. As far back as the book of Genesis, Abraham said, 'Shall not the Judge of all the earth do what is just?' (Genesis 18.25))

147

Previous page: stained glass window of Paul, St Peter and St Paul's church, Appledore, Kent. In art, saints are often shown with the thing that killed them: Paul was beheaded.

As we have said, the Roman Catholic Church teaches that it is not only Christians who will be saved. Many other Christians accept this idea too.

Two things to think about:

- There are very surprised atheists in the Kingdom of God.
- Some Christians say we shouldn't be obsessed with our own salvation, as though religion is a giant game of snakes and ladders. Jesus has given us a job to do on this earth: to love others. As far as eternal life is concerned, we should put the idea on the back burner, trust in God's mercy and love – and get on with what Jesus wants us to do now.

1. What do different Christians believe about –
a) heaven,
b) hell,
c) purgatory?

2.a) What does 'justification by faith' mean?
b) Why did Martin Luther say you couldn't get to heaven by doing good things?
c) Do all Christians believe in justification by faith?

Talking points

'People who believe in life after death are just weak minded. They're just frightened of dying.'

'Only Christians go to heaven.'

'There might be a hell, but you don't have to believe that anybody's there.'

'God wouldn't keep people alive in hell. Hell must mean non-existence.'

'Some things are so evil that everlasting punishment is the only fair sentence to give.'

31
Life after death (3)
Wishful thinking?

If Christ was not raised, then our gospel is null and void, and so is your faith.

(1 Corinthians 15.14)

This is what Paul says in his first letter to the Church at Corinth. The resurrection of Jesus underpins Christianity. If it didn't happen, Christianity falls apart.

The whole thing does. Including what Christianity teaches about life after death: life after death is guaranteed because Jesus rose from the dead. He was the first to rise from death and he promised it for other people.

Paul continues:

We turn out to be lying witnesses for God, because we bore witness that he raised Christ to life, whereas, if the dead are not raised, he did not raise him. For if the dead are not raised, it follows that Christ was not raised; and if Christ was not raised, your faith has nothing in it and you are still in your old state of sin... If it is for this life only that Christ has given us hope, we of all men are most to be pitied.

1 Corinthians 15.15-19

Paul had lots of problems with the Christians at Corinth. Here, he's trying to put them right about an idea that some of them had been circulating: Jesus rose from the dead, some were saying, but there's no life after death for anyone else. Paul's view is that Jesus' resurrection shows there's life after death for other people. It works the other way round, too. If there's life after death, then Jesus must have risen. They go together. Jesus can't have been raised from the dead unless there's such a thing as life after death.

There's no proof.

Maybe not – although it depends what you mean by 'proof'.

If we were asked, we'd probably say that 'proof' means absolute, 100% certainty. The sort of certainty you can apply to things in mathematics: that 2 + 2 = 4 is absolutely certain.

But in fact, we accept much less certainty a lot of the time and we don't think it's odd. You could still call this proof, even if it's not 100% proof.

In a criminal court, you have a jury. Everyone accused of a crime is innocent. They have to be *proven* guilty. That's what the law says, and that's where the jury comes in. But the jury doesn't have to be absolutely certain that the accused is guilty. They have to be sure 'beyond reasonable doubt'. Reasonable doubt's allowed – but a verdict's still held to be sound enough to send someone to prison.

At other times, you can act on even less proof. Civil law deals with disputes between individuals or bodies of people like companies. In civil law, the standard of proof isn't 'beyond reasonable doubt'; it's the 'balance of probability'.

If you study history, you'll probably know that it's very difficult to prove 100% that things happened – but we tend to accept them when the

149

arguments for their having happened are good. Maybe proof is like gold. 24 carat – (almost) pure gold – is wonderful stuff, but 18 carat gold is still gold.

What this all shows is that we don't always demand 100% proof. We'd frequently quite happy to accept things as true when there isn't 100% proof.

Religious people might therefore say to their atheist friends, 'It's a bit unreasonable to expect me to give you 100% proof when you don't usually need 100% proof!'

Well. Maybe only 100% proof can really be called proof. In the other cases given above, we could say that there's evidence – very solid, pretty solid or quite solid – for things being true. In this sense, we can say there's evidence for Christian claims about life after death.

It is claimed there are **two types of evidence** here:

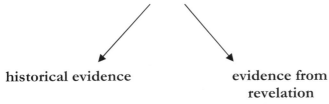

historical evidence   evidence from revelation

Historical evidence

In chapter 17, we studied the evidence for saying that the resurrection of Jesus is a historical event, something that really happened. Whatever conclusion we reached, there's a strong case for saying that it did actually happen.

If it did, then certain things follow:

- It shows that there is such a thing as life after death.
- It shows that what Jesus said was true. He wasn't a deluded dreamer; he was shown to be right.
- Jesus taught that eternal life was on offer. That must be true, too.

This is similar to what Paul was saying all those years ago in 1 Corinthians.

Evidence from revelation

The argument here is:

We know that there is life after death because God tells us so.

One way he does this is by raising Jesus from the dead. Another way he does this is through what Jesus taught: about his own death and resurrection, and about life after death for others.

In Mark's Gospel, Jesus says:

The Son of Man [Jesus] did not come to be served:
he came to serve
and to give his life to redeem many people.

Mark 10.45. 'Redeem' literally means 'to buy back'. It has come to mean 'to save' or 'to rescue'.

Jesus' teaching about life after death, then, is linked to his own death. He predicted this was going to happen:

They were on the road, going up to Jerusalem, Jesus leading the way; and the disciples were filled with awe, while those who followed behind were afraid. He took the Twelve [disciples] aside and began to tell them what was going to happen to him. 'We are now going to Jerusalem,' he said; 'and the Son of Man will be given up to the chief priests and the doctors of the law; they will condemn him to death and hand him over to the foreign power. He will be mocked and spat upon, flogged and killed; and three days afterwards, he will rise again.'

Mark 10.32-34. If you're not familiar with the story, the earliest account of it we have is in Mark 14.1 to 16.8. You may wish to read this up.

Christians believe what Jesus and the rest of the New Testament teaches: Jesus died to overcome the sin which separates men and women from God.

What do they mean by this?

They would say that no matter how hard we try, we cannot really be as good as we ought to be. If the world was judged tomorrow in a kind of cosmic law-court, none of us would do very well. But according to Christianity, God did not want this to happen. The love and obedience Jesus had in dying can still somehow make up for everything that men and women do wrong.

The idea that Jesus' death puts everything right between God and the world is called the **atonement** (at-one-ment: making things one). It also means human beings are saved from death, so Jesus' death means **salvation**. And it means they're bought back or **redeemed** from being imprisoned by sin and death. So another term for salvation is **redemption**.

How exactly the atonement works is another question. Various suggestions have been offered; all of them use imagery taken originally from life in

Jesus' time:

- Jesus' death was like a **sacrifice.** In the first century, the Jewish Temple still stood in Jerusalem. There, people offered animal sacrifices to God. (It was the only place in the world that Jewish law allowed Jews to do this. The Romans destroyed the Temple in AD 70 and it has never been rebuilt. Hence Jews today do not sacrifice animals.) Jesus and all his disciples were Jews and they would have known about the idea of sacrifice. There were various reasons sacrifices were offered, including *to take away sin.* So Jesus' death was said to be like a sacrifice, only much greater than the animal sacrifices. It didn't take away the sins of a few; it took away all the sins of all the world.

- Jesus said his death would 'redeem many people'. In English, 'many' suggests 'many but not all'. This isn't the case for the Greek word for 'many', which can mean everybody. (The New Testament was written in Greek.) The Greek for 'redeem' can mean paying a fine as punishment for a crime. So Jesus' death is like **paying a fine as a punishment**. But we don't have to pay the fine ourselves; we don't have to be worried about paying the punishment for our sins. Jesus has paid it on our behalf.

The problem with all images is they only get us so far. You can't push them too hard. If you say 'the Lord is my rock and my salvation', you can't then ask, 'Is he granite or sandstone?' If you push the images of the atonement too far, you end up with an enraged God who demands the death of Jesus to calm him down, because he's so furious with human beings' wickedness. But Christianity teaches God is love.

All of these ideas, then, tell Christians something about the meaning of Jesus' death. They form a sort of picture language which helps them to understand the atonement. But all of them fall short of a complete picture, perhaps because what went on in the atonement is just too big to put into ordinary words. Perhaps it helps to remember that, in Christian teaching, God was actually present in Jesus. Many modern writers talk about God's entering into the suffering of the world on the cross and offering people a way out of it. But this is still only one idea among many.

The Temple as it was in Jesus' time

What else did Jesus teach about eternal life?

I am the good shepherd. The good shepherd lays down his life for the sheep.

I am the resurrection and the life. Those who believe in me, even though they die, will live, and everyone who lives and believes in me will never die.

When a rich man asked him, 'What do I need to do to inherit eternal life?' he replied: 'You know the commandments: "Do not kill, Do not commit adultery, Do not steal, Do not bear false witness, Do not defraud, Honour your father and mother."

Anyone who hears my word and believes him who sent me has eternal life, and does not come under judgement, but has passed from death to life.

All who see the Son and believe in him may have eternal life; and I will raise them up on the last day.

Come to me, all who labour and are heavy laden, and I will give you rest

Truly I tell you, whoever gives you a cup of water to drink because you bear the name of Christ will by no means lose the reward.

152

References: John 10.11, 11.25, Mark 10.19, John 5.24, 6.40, Matthew 11.28, Mark 9.41

Christian Death Rites

The religious rituals (rites) to do with death are connected to Christianity's beliefs in life after death. There's also strong emphasis on compassion and care for those who are left behind, in accordance with Jesus' teaching.

For an example of Christian rites associated with death, we'll look at what happens in the Roman Catholic Church.

When someone's dying, he or she may receive three sacraments to prepare for death and the next world. A sacrament is a visible sign or ritual, through which God acts.

- The sacrament of reconciliation, which used to be called confession. The priest listens to the person's account of their sins and pronounces God's forgiveness.

- The sacrament of the sick. The dying person receives the laying on of hands, and his or her hands and forehead are anointed. The Catholic Church teaches that the sacrament of the sick unites the sick person with the suffering of Christ and gives them the peace and courage to endure their own suffering. If they were unconscious, and therefore unable to receive the sacrament of reconciliation, the sacrament of the sick also has the effect of forgiving sins.

- The viaticum ('food for the journey'): the final time the person receives the sacrament of the Eucharist, the 'bread' and 'wine' that are the body and blood of Jesus. The Church teaches that Jesus is genuinely present in the 'bread' and 'wine', and that he's present in the same way in both of them. For practical reasons, then, the dying person receives the sacrament 'in one kind': the 'bread' only is used.

There are usually prayers very soon after the death, led by the priest. These normally happen before the body's moved from home or from the hospital. The prayers are for the person who's dead, but also for those who are left behind. Christians have a special responsibility for them, not least because Jesus said those who mourn were especially close to God (Matthew 5.4).

The body is then received into the church and there's a vigil service: a chance for the parish community to pray with the family, usually the night before the funeral.

And then there's the funeral. For Roman Catholics, this will usually be a special Mass, though it does not have to be. As the Mass celebrates the death and resurrection of Jesus Christ, it's particularly

helpful for a funeral. Christians are promised that like Christ, they will die and rise again to eternal life.

There is then the committal: burial or cremation. Some or all of the mourners will move to the graveside or the crematorium. They may sprinkle earth or holy water (water that's been blessed by a priest) onto the coffin. Until 1965, Catholics were not allowed to be cremated. Cremations are now allowed, though the Church prefers if the ashes are buried (the Church recommends biodegradable containers) rather than scattered. Burying is simply more traditional, even though it's now increasingly common to bury the ashes rather than the body.

1a) What is the atonement?

b) 'The death of Jesus is like a sacrifice or a fine.' What does this mean?

c) 'You can't push the images of the atonement too hard.' What does this mean?

2. What did Jesus teach about eternal life?

3. **Either :** describe the Roman Catholic Church's rites for someone who has died;

or find out about a different Christian denomination's rites for the dead. (On a search engine, you could enter key words like 'Church of England' and 'funerals'.)

4. Look up the following passages in the Bible. They're parables, stories with a meaning, that Jesus told about life after death. (If you don't have a Bible, it's easily available online.)

    Luke 12.15-21

    Luke 16.19-31

    Matthew 25.31-46

Think about the quotations from Jesus on page 152 as well.

Now answer about this question:

'If you believe in life after death, how should that affect the way you live now?'

(It's probably a good idea to discuss your answers before you start to write.)

5. 'Christian promises about life after death are just make believe. You can't prove they're true.' Do you agree? Give reasons for your answer, showing that you've considered more than one point of view.

Talking points:

'It's immoral to do good things when you're just doing them to get to heaven. If you're kind to someone just to make sure you're saved, that's actually a form of selfishness.'

'What do we mean by "proof"?'

32

Life after death (4)
A tale told by an idiot?

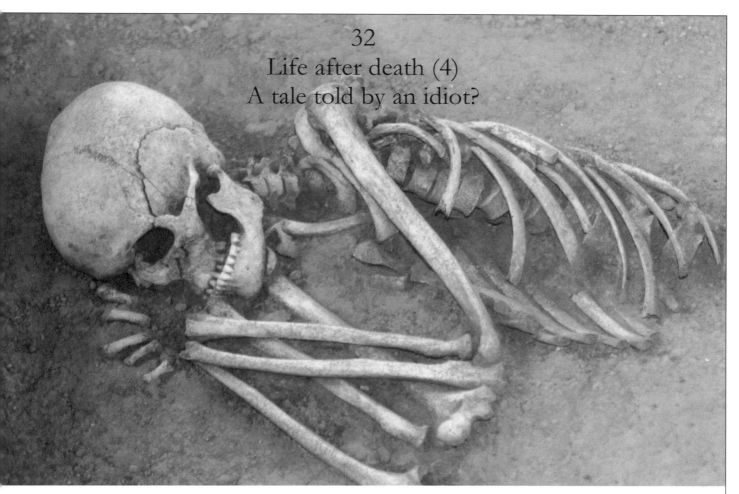

It is a fact that the human organism terminates at death. The heart stops, breathing ceases, and the brain dies. The consciousness of the organism ceases. In normal conditions, the body soon starts to decay.

Those are the facts. That's what science can tell us. So why look any further? Death is the end. To talk about 'life' afterwards is a contradiction in terms. You can't be dead and still alive, just as you can't both exist and not exist.

Religion was invented by human beings to help them to face their fear of death. And death, for many, is terrifying. People need reassurance, comfort. Unfortunately, the comfort religion brings is a false comfort. You could even say it's a cruel one because it's offering illusions. It's like lying to a cancer patient that you've got a drug that will make them better – when in fact their cancer's terminal. Far better not to give them false comfort, but to let them accept that they will die, and then come to terms with it.

We are no longer superstitious. We no longer have to believe in nonsense. The scientific fact is that we die. There is no scientific evidence for anything afterwards. Full stop.

This is pretty much what atheism has to say on the topic of life after death.

Some atheists take the view that what they leave behind can be worthwhile and can help other people. This legacy may be material: it could mean passing your property down to your children, or to a charity, or donating your organs for transplant or research. Or it may be a different sort of legacy: perhaps leaving behind you the contribution you've made to society – which could be in the things you've achieved, the love you've given people, and so on.

Others take the view that death shows existence to be totally meaningless. We come out of nothingness and we return to nothingness. Whether we achieve something or achieve nothing, ultimately our lives have no importance whatsoever. The universe will go on just the same: cold, unfeeling and unsympathetic, whether we live or die.

Let's consider the idea that what we leave behind may be worthwhile and can help others. This idea is the theme of George Eliot's poem *O May I Join the Choir Invisible*. George Eliot is the pen name for Mary Anne Evans (1819-1880), one of the leading Victorian novelists. She was brought up as a Christian but later – and very reluctantly – she rejected Christianity, not least because of Darwin's discoveries. *O May I Join the Choir Invisible* is an attempt to make sense of an atheistic view of death. It's saying that we live on in other people's minds and thoughts. Our achievements help those who come after us to live better lives. Here it is:

O May I Join the Choir Invisible

O may I join the choir invisible
Of those immortal dead who live again
In minds made better by their presence; live
In pulses stirred to generosity,
In deeds of daring rectitude, in scorn
Of miserable aims that end with self,
In thoughts sublime that pierce the night like stars,
And with their mild persistence urge men's minds
To vaster issues.

So to live is heaven:
To make undying music in the world,
Breathing a beauteous order that controls
With growing sway the growing life of man.
So we inherit that sweet purity
For which we struggled, failed and agonized
With widening retrospect that bred despair.
Rebellious flesh that would not be subdued,
A vicious parent shaming still its child,
Poor, anxious penitence is quick dissolved;
Its discords, quenched by meeting harmonies,
Die in the large and charitable air;
And all our rarer, better, truer self,
That sobbed religiously in yearning song,
That watched to ease the burden of the world,
Laboriously tracing what must be,
And what may yet be better – saw rather
A worthier image for the sanctuary
And shaped it forth before the multitude,
Divinely human, raising worship so
To higher reverence more mixed with love –
That better self shall live till human Time
Shall fold its eyelids, and the human sky
Be gathered like a scroll within the tomb
Unread forever.

This is life to come,
Which martyred men have made more glorious
For us who strive to follow.

May I reach
That purest heaven – be to other souls
The cup of strength in some great agony,
Enkindle generous ardour, feed pure love,
Beget the smiles that have no cruelty,
Be the sweet presence of a good diffused,
And in diffusion ever more intense!
So shall I join the choir invisible
Whose music is the gladness of the world.

George Eliot (1819-1880)

The other point of view is to say that death renders life meaningless.

One of the best expressions of this viewpoint is in Shakespeare's *Macbeth*. Towards the end of the play, Macbeth utterly rejects the idea that human existence has any meaning whatsoever. This is what he says. (We've also given a modern 'translation', which is nothing like as good as the original!)

Tomorrow, and tomorrow, and tomorrow,
Creeps in this petty pace from day to day,
To the last syllable of recorded time;
And all our yesterdays have lighted fools
The way to dusty death. Out, out, brief
  candle!
Life's but a walking shadow, a poor player,
That struts and frets his hour upon the stage,
And then is heard no more. It is a tale
Told by an idiot, full of sound and fury,
Signifying nothing.

Tomorrow. Then the next day. And the next.
  They creep in pettily, day after day – to the final syllable of time. All our own yesterdays have just lighted for fools the way to death, to dust. The candle of life should be snuffed out.
  Life: just a walking shadow.
  It's a bad actor, overacting. He makes a lot of stupid noise on the stage. Then he's heard no more.
  It's a tale told by an idiot. It's full of sound, full of fury
  And it means:
  Absolutely *nothing*.

Two views, then. If we decide that God does not exist, and therefore there is no life after death, which view makes better sense? Does atheism give a hopeful outlook on life and death, or is despair more realistic?

Near death experiences

Near death experiences or NDEs are generally taken seriously by scientists. The experiences themselves are real in the sense that the people who have them are not making them up. NDEs have been investigated by numerous researchers, particularly medics, and they are far too common and consistent to be written off.

You may have seen programmes on TV about NDEs or you may have read about them. There are individual differences but they generally follow a pattern (though not always). The early stages are more common than the later stages. The experiences usually happen to people who are close to death or who have clinically died (their heart or breathing has stopped, for example). However, they can be experienced by people who have taken certain drugs, or by people who are very tired or, rarely, by people who are doing nothing unusual. There is no link, either, to mental illness.

A number of stages are common to NDEs, though they're not necessarily all experienced:

- The first thing noticed is an unpleasant sound. This is followed by:

- A realisation that you are dead, which, surprisingly, is accompanied not by terror but by feelings of calm and peace.

- There's then an out of body experience: a vivid sensation of looking down on your own body. Many can then accurately recall what was said and done by the medical team after they were 'dead'.

- Floating up a tunnel, which has a very strong light (or garden) at the end.

- Meeting a 'being of light'. Sometimes this being is Christ, though it can be God or a spiritual being for members of other faiths.

- Looking back over your life, over everything you've done.

- Having to return to your body, which many people who've had NDEs said they did not want to do.

It would be tremendously exciting if NDEs were proof of life after death. Certainly, many people have taken them to be just that. However, they may be part of *this* life, rather than the next.

This isn't to belittle them; many people have been profoundly affected by their NDEs and they have changed their whole outlook on life. However, many investigators, regardless of whether they are themselves religious, think they tell us nothing about life after death, one way or the other. It has been suggested that they may be part of a 'program' in our brains, usually triggered by the onset of death, to make the experience of dying less unpleasant and frightening to the organism.

From a religious viewpoint, although NDEs are interesting, they don't fit in very closely with, say, Christian views of the afterlife. For Christians, this is a major problem with taking them as evidence of heaven. Jesus' teaching is the bedrock of Christian belief; what he said is revealed by God, and it is on this, not on NDEs, that Christian teaching is based.

Some Christian thinkers would therefore agree with the view that NDEs are part of the body's preparation for dying. This also explains why, if a spiritual being is experienced, it seems to be culturally conditioned. Life after death comes afterwards.

Many people of other faiths would agree with this view.

Still, many who have had an NDE say it has taken away their fear of death. If it is the case that our own deaths will be accompanied not by pain and terror, but by an experience of peace, calm and acceptance, that is something to hold on to.

1. Use a computer – or your own artistic skills! – to design a presentation piece. Use a title like 'Atheistic views on existence.' One part of the display gives the positive approaches. Another gives the negative approaches.

Look again at *O May I Join the Choir Invisible* and the quotation from *Macbeth*. Select some quotations and add them to your display.

You may also wish to look at Philip Larkin's poem *Aubade* (an aubade is a poem or song about dawn). You may find it in the school library; it's also easily available online. Read it carefully (it's very good) and select some more quotations.

You could also consider: if you were going to use music to accompany your visuals, what would you choose?

2. What is meant by a near death experience, and what are the typical features of an NDE?

3. 'NDEs show that there is life after death.' What do you think? Why?

4. 'Birth, life and death. That is all there is.' Do you agree? Give reasons for your answer, showing that you've considered more than one opinion.

Talking points

'Religion makes a lot of false promises. That's just cruel.'

'Scientifically, it's true that the body ceases at death. But to say this proves there's no life after death is going too far. There are lots of things that science just can't tell us.'

'There are good reasons to believe in life after death.' [It's worth looking back over the chapters in this section and thinking about them.]

'If God exists, it must follow that there is life after death. God wouldn't be so uncaring as to create human beings and then let them rot.'

It's often said that religion was made up to comfort people who are afraid of dying. In fact, we know that the earliest forms of Judaism *did not* believe in life after death – though people carried on believing in God. The same view was taken by the Sadducees, a Jewish religious group in Jesus' time. So religion *doesn't* necessarily believe in life after death.

Given this, can it still be said that religion is just made up to comfort people who are frightened of death?

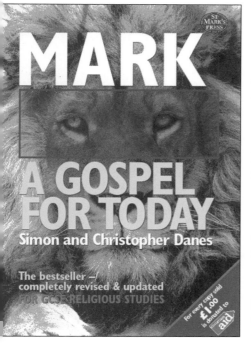

Mark: A Gospel for Today
Simon and Christopher Danes

Mark: A Gospel for Today is a standard and highly acclaimed textbook for GCSE Religious Studies. It has enjoyed wide success in schools throughout the United Kingdom for many years.

Originally issued in 1989, the first two editions were published by Lion / LionHudson. This new, third edition from St Mark's Press has been completely revised and updated for the needs of today's classes.

Whether for class use or for use by individual students for revision, *Mark: A Gospel for Today* provides everything the busy student and teacher needs for this option at GCSE – and much that will be useful for students studying the topic of modern Christianity.

£1 donation to Christian Aid for every copy sold.

'A first class textbook which brings the pages of *Mark* to life. Many generations of students have been inspired by *Mark: A Gospel for Today* – a *must have* textbook for anyone taking GCSE Religious Studies.'

Gill Smith, Head of RS at King's School, Ely

Today's Issues and Christian Beliefs
Simon and Christopher Danes

New edition of the bestselling and highly commended textbook, formerly published by Lion: over 100,000 copies have been sold worldwide. A book to get students interested, which never sells them short, and encourages them to think for themselves.

- Full and in depth coverage
- Includes first person accounts from people who were actively involved in the issues, including:
  - Racism: an account from an escapee from the Treblinka death camp
  - Punishment: a campaigner and former prisoner tell their stories
  - Asylum: a Baptist minister on his church's work with asylum seekers
  - Families: a teacher writes on her experiences of being adopted
- Feedback from students themselves on *Today's Issues* is very positive: they like this book!

£1 donation to Christian Aid for each copy sold.

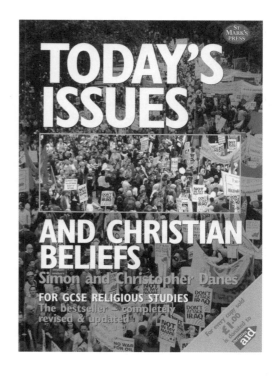

Mark's Gospel on double CD
NIV text, read by Peter Wickham   Ideal for students' individual revision or for classroom use

Peter Wickham's reading is superb. An experienced film and TV actor, Peter has recorded over 250 audio books and he brings his great experience to this double CD of Mark. So many talking books of the Bible are flat and dull; Peter invests this work with strong characterisation, pace and energy. Discounts are available for class sets.   £1 donation to Christian Aid for each copy sold.

Mark: A Gospel for Today Teacher's Book – Simon Danes

As well as co-writing *Mark: A Gospel for Today*, Simon Danes has been teaching the Gospel at GCSE almost since GCSE began. The Teacher's Book draws on this experience, on advice from colleagues who've used the textbook – and, most important of all, from students. It covers: how best to revise the Gospel for the exam; best practice in teaching Mark; planning a scheme of work; suggestions for fun activities, geared to different learning styles; notes on each unit of *Mark: A Gospel for Today*; scholarly comment for non-specialists. £1 donation to Christian Aid for each copy sold.

Books by William Barclay

The Gospels and Acts – (two volumes)   The Mind of St Paul

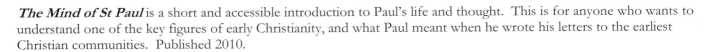

It's hard to read Barclay without being gripped. You can't help but marvel at his immense knowledge and wise analysis. They're books for the general reader: highly accessible and simply a good read. They'll be enjoyed by anyone interested in the Bible and in Christianity.

The Gospels and Acts, previously published by SCM, isn't to be confused with Barclay's *Daily Study Bible*. It's a critical introduction to what Biblical studies has to say about these books – and it's one of the best introductions to New Testament scholarship ever written. *The Gospels and Acts* is in two volumes: volume 1 covers Matthew, Mark and Luke; volume 2 covers John and Acts.

The Mind of St Paul is a short and accessible introduction to Paul's life and thought. This is for anyone who wants to understand one of the key figures of early Christianity, and what Paul meant when he wrote his letters to the earliest Christian communities. Published 2010.

We're intending to publish more of William Barclay's work in 2010. Please keep an eye on our website for details.

Published by the Vivekananda Centre London Ltd and available to order from St Mark's Press:

Hinduism for Schools
Seeta Lakhani

'A valuable and comprehensive guide… It is beautifully illustrated with photographs and a good range of Hindu art and because of its authentic origins should be an essential asset for all teachers of religious education. Here is a publication that reflects a Hindu experience of life in 21st century Britain.

   'A Hindu perspective of a pluralist society results in an explicit treatment of the issues of inter-faith dialogue. *Hinduism for Schools* deals with current ethical issues and so teachers will have access to Hindu perspectives on marriage, life and death, drug abuse and the media. As well as a thorough chapter on Hindu practice in daily life, this valuable reference work for teachers and secondary students offers excellent chapters on philosophy of religion and religion and science.'

Mark Brimicombe
Former member of The Association of Religious Education Inspectors, Advisers and Consultants

For more information on Hinduism, please visit the website of the Hindu Academy: www.hinduacademy.org

www.stmarkspress.com   email info@stmarkspress.com